Succeeding as an MFL Teacher

Succeeding as an MFL Teacher

**SILVIA BASTOW
AND
JENNIFER
WOZNIAK-RUSH**

BLOOMSBURY EDUCATION
LONDON OXFORD NEW YORK NEW DELHI SYDNEY

BLOOMSBURY EDUCATION
Bloomsbury Publishing Plc
50 Bedford Square, London WC1B 3DP, UK
Bloomsbury Publishing Ireland Limited
29 Earlsfort Terrace, Dublin 2, D02 AY28, Ireland

BLOOMSBURY, BLOOMSBURY EDUCATION and the
Diana logo are trademarks of Bloomsbury Publishing Plc

First published in Great Britain 2026 by Bloomsbury Publishing Plc
This edition published in Great Britain 2026 by Bloomsbury Publishing Plc

Text copyright © Silvia Bastow and Jennifer Wozniak-Rush, 2026
Images © Shutterstock, 2026

Silvia Bastow and Jennifer Wozniak-Rush have asserted their rights under
the Copyright, Designs and Patents Act, 1988, to be identified as Authors
of this work.

All rights reserved. No part of this publication may be: i) reproduced or
transmitted in any form, electronic or mechanical, including photocopying,
recording or by means of any information storage or retrieval system
without prior permission in writing from the publishers; or ii) used
or reproduced in any way for the training, development or operation
of artificial intelligence (AI) technologies, including generative AI
technologies. The rights holders expressly reserve this publication from
the text and data mining exception as per Article 4(3) of the Digital Single
Market Directive (EU) 2019/790

A catalogue record for this book is available from the British Library

ISBN: PB: 978-1-80199-756-0; ePub: 978-1-80199-757-7

2 4 6 8 10 9 7 5 3 1 (paperback)

Cover design by James Fraser
Typeset by Lumina Datamatics Ltd

Printed and bound in Great Britain by TJ Books, Padstow, Cornwall

To find out more about our authors and books visit www.bloomsbury.com
and sign up for our newsletters
For product safety related questions contact productsafety@bloomsbury.com

Dedications

To my husband, David – thank you for always being by my side, for cheering me on whenever imposter syndrome crept in, for keeping me going with endless cups of coffee and for cooking countless meals while I was busy writing. Your patience, encouragement and willingness to be my very first reader mean a lot. I am grateful for your love and support.

Silvia

To my husband, Chris, whose patience, love, and encouragement made every step of this journey possible. Thank you for believing in me when I doubted myself, when the writing felt heavy and the days felt long.

Jennifer

Finally, to all our fellow MFL teachers, this book is for you. It's a small thank you for your creativity, perseverance and the countless ways you inspire learners to see beyond borders and embrace other cultures. We hope these pages capture a little of the joy, the struggles and the belief we all share that teaching languages really does change lives.

Silvia & Jennifer

Contents

Acknowledgements ix
Foreword xi

Introduction 1

1 Applying the science of learning and second language acquisition in the MFL classroom 3

2 Understanding the curriculum and creating a coherent sequence of lessons 29

3 Retrieval practice, modelling, guided and independent practice 63

4 Adaptive teaching: Responding to the needs of all students 89

5 Supporting all learners, including those with SEND 113

6 Empowering the higher attainers in language learning 133

7 Effective assessment and feedback in all four language skills 159

8 Enrichment inside and outside the language classroom 197

9 Personal professional development 229

10 Developing your language teaching team: Strategies for growth and collaboration 249

11 Leading your language department: Strategies for effective leadership 265

References 287
Glossary 295
Index 297

Acknowledgements

We would like to extend our heartfelt thanks to everyone who contributed to *Succeeding as an MFL Teacher*.

To the authors of the case studies: Steve Smith (Chapter 1), Verity Howorth and Hannah Pinkham (Chapter 2), Esmeralda Salgado (Chapter 3), Tracy Williams (Chapter 4), Vincent Everett (Chapter 5), Wendy Adeniji (Chapter 6), Elena Díaz (Chapter 7), Suzi Bewell (Chapter 8), Crista Hazell (Chapter 9) and Adam Lamb (Chapter 10), thank you for generously sharing your time, reflections and invaluable advice. Your insights have added depth and authenticity to this book, making it a richer resource for aspiring and experienced MFL teachers alike. A big thank you to Steven Fawkes for his thoughtful foreword, which set the perfect tone for this book.

We are also grateful to Sharon Barnes, Dannielle Warren, Wendy Adeniji, Martine Pillette, Esther Mercier, Liz Stillman and Rachel Hawkes for contributing specific resources that have enhanced the practical value of this book.

A special thank you goes to those who allowed us to include images that have added further dimension to the content: Tom Sherrington, Oliver Caviglioli and Dylan Wiliam (Chapter 7), Juliet Park and Graphics Factory (Chapter 6).

Our deepest gratitude goes to our editors, Joanna Ramsay and Deborah Lee-Swaden, for their invaluable guidance and unwavering support throughout this journey. Joanna and Deborah, your expertise and encouragement have truly brought out the best in this work.

We are also immensely grateful to our publisher, Bloomsbury, for giving us the opportunity to bring this project to life. Your trust and belief in our vision have made this book a reality.

ACKNOWLEDGEMENTS

And, of course, an extra big thank you to our families for always being there for us. Whether it was looking after everything while we were busy writing, making endless cups of coffee or just cheering us on when the imposter syndrome took over, your support means the world to us.

Writing this book has been a demanding but incredibly rewarding journey and we couldn't have done it without all of you. It has been a privilege to pour our experiences, thoughts and ideas into this work, and we hope that it serves as a valuable resource for all those striving to succeed as MFL teachers.

Thank you!

Silvia & Jennifer

Foreword

Being a teacher is not for everyone; it requires great skills of communicating and being active listeners in the classroom; broad – and precise – knowledge; awareness of the curriculum and examination requirements; professional skills such as marking and giving feedback; and excellent time management skills in order to complete all of the tasks that arise in our educational systems!

Teaching a language is especially demanding. It clearly needs knowledge of the language(s): vocabulary, grammar, sound system, culture and maybe script; more importantly it requires awareness of the classroom, of everybody in it, and of the interactions that are going on. As language teachers we develop a sense of what learners enjoy, what they find difficult, how they are progressing in their acquisition of language and what they need to do next. In particular we consider how to engage, and keep learners motivated to carry on, in spite of the challenges of retention and problem-solving inherent in language learning. Our hope as a community of language learning/teaching professionals is to develop learners' self-efficacy (recalling, manipulating and actually using language to do what they want to do) so that it remains alive well beyond their years of study. We aspire to giving our future citizens confidence as adults to meet other people, engage in appropriate interaction, travel and work in other places.

As our colleagues in Ofsted remind us (e.g. in their Curriculum Review 2021) there is no single way of teaching a language; teachers are pragmatists who will find things that work in their context, for their students and for their teaching style. We work closely with our learners every day, and are wary of any suggestion that 'one size fits all'; we recognise a wide variety of motivations and skills in our classrooms. Catering for our learners, especially under the pressure of time, is both demanding and rewarding for the teacher, just as learning a language can be life-enhancing for the learner.

The authors of this book, Jennifer and Silvia, along with their array of contributors, are highly aware of these realities of the Languages classroom – we are pressed for time! They organise their themes succinctly and know the importance of finding balance:

- For the learner in terms of finding a cognitive load which is challenging and interesting, not spoon-feeding and not over-demanding.
- For the teacher, in terms of workload and job satisfaction.

The book reflects the experience and thoroughness which Jennifer and Silvia are well-known for in the languages community, supported and extended by the contributions of many others whose names will be familiar. These combine to give the book the feeling of a great conference, with a range of voices and relevant ideas, organised around the central theme in a structured sequence, and epitomising the willingness to share that language teachers enjoy.

As well as relishing new ideas, teachers look for things they recognise in their reading. Close to my heart are these moments – when the emphasis is on engaging the learners, in all their diversity:

What matters most is that the curriculum supports learning, and not that it looks polished on paper.

or on going beyond the exam specification:

Enrichment isn't just 'nice to have'. It plays a big role in boosting motivation, widening students' horizons and helping them to see language learning as something exciting, relevant and real.

or on collaboration:

Good behaviour doesn't come from a single policy or poster. It comes from a team culture.

When things come together in a lesson (or sequence of lessons) that really goes well and has a positive impact on learners, the sense of satisfaction for teachers can be immense. In our time-poor environment this book gathers together concise and contemporary advice to help language teachers succeed in, **and enjoy**, their important work.

Steven Fawkes
Co-President of the Association for
Language Learning 2025-26

Introduction

Welcome to *Succeeding as an MFL Teacher*! We are so glad that you have picked up this book; it has been specially created to help you to make the most of your language teaching journey. Whether you are just starting out or already have years of experience under your belt, this book is here to be your trusted companion at every stage of your career.

We have filled it with practical advice, useful strategies and fresh ideas that you can easily try out in your classroom. No complicated jargon – just clear, straightforward tips that you can put into action right away. Whether you are an early career teacher (ECT) finding your footing or stepping into a leadership role and guiding your own team, we've got you covered.

This book is packed with answers to the real-life questions that modern foreign languages (MFL) teachers face every day. From planning lessons to managing assessments and even handling those tricky moments with less-than-enthusiastic Year 10s on Friday afternoon, we have made sure that every chapter offers something valuable. We hope that it becomes a resource you will turn to again and again.

Writing this book was a real labour of love. Every page reflects our passion for teaching languages, plus years of experience and plenty of hard-earned lessons. We have pulled together research-informed strategies like retrieval practice, direct instruction and metacognition and made them practical, so that you can use them right away. Imagine reading a tip and thinking, 'This will work perfectly with my Year 9s tomorrow!' That is exactly what we're aiming for.

We will also explore techniques like adaptive teaching and effective questioning to help you to tailor your lessons to your students' needs. Plus, we will share ideas for encouraging cultural appreciation and making language learning truly engaging. From lesson planning to assessment strategies, we want to help you to create impactful lessons for every key stage, all without having to overhaul your entire system or jump through hoops for senior leadership approval.

What makes this book unique is that it is grounded in real classroom experiences. The tips and strategies here are not just theoretical; they have been tested and proved by teachers who have been through it all, from inspiring moments to the toughest challenges.

We are thrilled to share this journey with you. Our goal is to inspire and support you in helping your students to grow their language skills and cultural understanding. *Succeeding as an MFL Teacher* is here to be your guide, cheerleader and go-to resource.

Let's get started on this exciting adventure together!

You can scan the QR code or visit bloomsbury.pub/succeeding-as-MFL to see extra resources and larger versions of the figures in this book, which have been written by teachers for classroom use.

1

Applying the science of learning and second language acquisition in the MFL classroom

Introduction

Understanding how people learn and how second languages are acquired is key for language teachers who want to enhance their teaching practice. This chapter looks at how these ideas and principles can be used in teaching to create a more effective and engaging learning environment. By using strategies based on research in science of learning and second language acquisition (SLA), you can help your students to learn and remember languages better.

The science of learning

Great language teaching relies on understanding important learning principles like memory, focus and motivation. These mental processes are central to how students take in, understand and remember new information. By learning about these principles, you can adapt your teaching approaches to support students to succeed in language learning.

Memory: The key to learning

Memory is the brain's ability to store and recall information, which is essential for learning a language. Students need to remember words, grammar and language patterns and how to use them. Memory can be divided into three main types:

1. **Sensory memory:** This is the first step, where information comes in through the senses, like sight, hearing, smell, taste or touch. It only lasts a few seconds unless something grabs your attention.

2. **Working memory:** This is where information is briefly held while being processed. It can only handle a small amount of information at a time, usually four to nine items, depending on the learner.

3. **Long-term memory:** This is where information is stored for a long time. For language learners, transferring information from working memory to long-term memory is key to remembering it.

To help your students to improve their memory for language learning, you can use strategies like the following:

- **Spaced repetition:** Review information at longer and longer intervals to help it to stick in long-term memory.

- **Mnemonics:** Use tools like acronyms (see examples) or pictures to make information easier to remember.

- **Contextual learning:** Teach new language in meaningful situations so that students can better remember and use it.

Example 1: Mnemonics to aid recall

French:
MRS VAN DER TRAMP is an aide-mémoire for remembering which verbs use *être* as their auxiliary verb in the past perfect tense.

CROISSANT can be used to support writing: Connectives, Reasons, Opinions, Infinitive phrases/Intensifiers, Star phrases, Subordinate clauses, Adjectives/Adverbs, Negatives, Tenses.

BANGS helps with remembering adjectives that precede the noun: Beauty, Age, Number, Greatness, Size.

German:
The mixed (two-way) prepositions can be memorised by reciting them to the tune of 'Twinkle, Twinkle, Little Star': *an, auf, hinter, neben, in, unter, über, vor, zwischen.*

For remembering verb endings in the present tense, use: Every STrict Teacher ENjoys Telling off ENdlessly.

Spanish:
DOCTOR PLACE can be applied to the use of the verbs *ser* (Date, Occupation, Characteristic, Time, Origin, Relation) and *estar* (Position, Location, Action, Condition, Emotion).

Generic (can be applied to any language):
PPOF (from Ben Currier, Assistant Principal, Inclusion lead and SENDCO in an all-through school and previous Head of International Languages) can be used to remind students what to use in their paragraph: Past, Present, Opinion, Future.

Attention: The path to learning

Attention is a process where students focus on certain information while ignoring distractions. It is crucial for language learning because it decides what your students process and remember. Attention can be influenced by:

1. **Interest and relevance:** Your students will focus better on material that is interesting and relevant to their lives.
2. **Engagement:** Interactive and engaging activities will hold your students' attention better than passive learning approaches.
3. **Minimising distractions:** A clear, distraction-free classroom will help your students to stay focused. Even classroom displays can be a source of distraction if overdone.

You can improve students' attention by using engaging materials, varying your teaching approaches and creating a distraction-free learning space. Activities like purposeful games, role-plays and multimedia tools can make lessons more exciting, while keeping the focus on learning. However, remember that while it's great for students to enjoy these activities, their main goal is for students to progress in learning.

Motivation: Driving force behind learning

Motivation is what drives your students to start and keep going with their learning. It is a big factor in language learning success. Motivated students are more likely to stay engaged, practise often and overcome challenges. There are two types of motivation:

1. **Intrinsic motivation:** This comes from the student's personal interest or enjoyment in learning.
2. **Extrinsic motivation:** This is driven by external factors, like grades, rewards or recognition.

To build motivation, you can:

1. Help your students to set clear and achievable goals for learning the language.
2. Provide your students with positive feedback and celebrate their achievements.
3. Create a classroom culture that values effort, persistence and mutual support.

By using strategies based on the knowledge of how people learn, you can make lessons more effective, engaging and enjoyable, helping your students to learn and remember the new language better.

Principles of SLA

SLA research looks at how people learn languages other than their first one. While researchers don't agree on one single SLA theory, many have created their own ideas and principles to guide language teaching: professor emeritus of ESL (English as a second language), H. Douglas Brown (2000), linguist and research professor, Rod Ellis (2005) and emeritus professor of applied linguistics, Paul Nation (2008) all suggest different principles and frameworks to guide language teaching. This section focuses on five key principles shared across these ideas, to guide effective language teaching.

1. Focus on meaningful input

One of the core ideas in SLA is that learners need input that they can mostly understand but which also challenges them slightly. This is called 'comprehensible input' (CI), often described as i+1 by emeritus professor, linguist and educational researcher Stephen Krashen (2020). To make this work, students should be exposed to materials that are just a bit harder than their current level, with help from context, pictures and support like scaffolding to make it accessible and easier to understand.

To implement this, you can:

- Select reading and listening materials that stretch your learners' abilities without causing frustration – 98% CI.
- Utilise context clues, images and other visual aids to support students' understanding. For example, you could use www.thenounproject.com for images to use with the new vocabulary that you introduce.

Example: Visual aids using dual coding

FIGURE 1.1: *Example of dual coding when introducing vocabulary*

Employ scaffolding strategies, such as pre-teaching vocabulary and using guiding questions, to help students navigate more complex texts and dialogues.

Example: Negotiating meaning

Teacher: *Die Kinder spielen im Park. Der Junge im Hintergrund, der gerade ein Buch liest, interessiert sich sehr für das Buch.* [The children are playing in the park. The boy in the background, who is reading a book, is very interested in the book.]

Student: *Entschuldigung, ich verstehe 'interessiert' nicht.* [Excuse me, I don't understand 'interested'.]

Teacher: *Ah ja, er findet das Buch interessant! Du verstehst das Wort 'interessant', ja?* [Oh, yes, he finds the book interesting! You understand the word 'interesting', yes?]

Student: *Ah, ja, ich verstehe es jetzt. Also, 'interessiert' ist das Verb!* [Oh, yes, I understand it now. So, 'interested' is the verb!]

Giving your students plenty of chances to hear or read language that makes sense to them helps them to naturally learn new words and grammar in an enjoyable way.

2. Focus on meaningful output

In addition, using the language through speaking and writing (output) is just as important as understanding it (input). Engaging in meaningful output activities helps your students to process language at a deeper level, reinforcing their learning and improving their communication skills. You can support this by:

- Giving your students opportunities to engage in presentations, write essays or have conversations in the target language.
- Planning activities like storytelling, role-plays or casual chats that encourage students to speak or write spontaneously.

- Offering constructive feedback that focuses on both their ideas and their language use so that they can improve over time.

Example: Interaction language

In every lesson, I ask my students how they are and why. Starting the lesson by making students speak allows them to think and use the target language and put them in the zone for the lesson. Here is an example of the greetings routine that I use with my Year 7 students:

FIGURE 1.2: *Example of a greetings routine for Year 7*

Another example of interaction language is when I ask my class what they think we are going to do in the lesson today. There is some vocabulary on the board, but students also use the language that they know. For instance, when it comes to Year 8, students know 50 –*ar* verbs in Spanish and they manipulate the language with the vocabulary that they have learned.

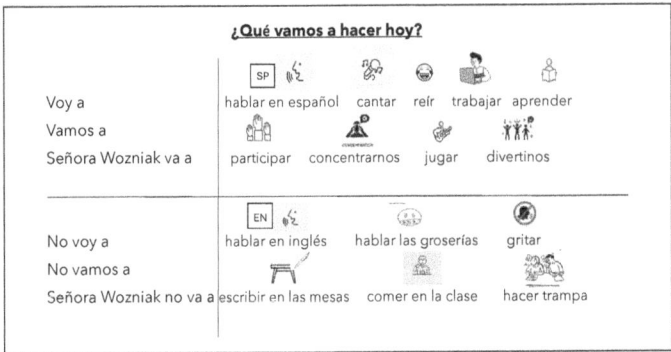

FIGURE 1.3: *Example of a routine to set the objective*

Interaction language can also be used to reinforce the language that has been learned within a topic. For example, when my students have learned a range of adjectives to describe their personality, the vocabulary can be used after a pair-work activity where students tell you how their partner was. It is a way in which to reinforce what has been previously taught and keep reusing it.

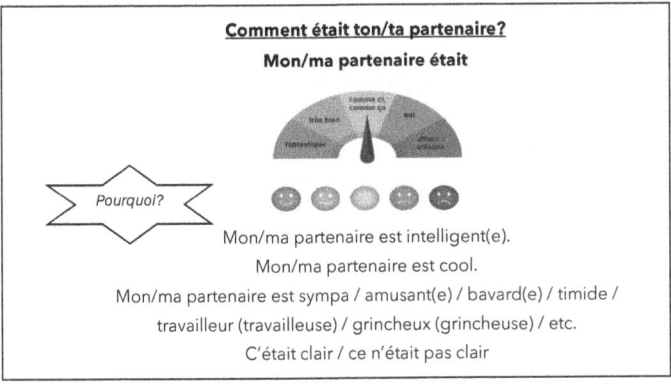

FIGURE 1.4: *Example of a 'describe your partner' routine*

Routines can be very motivating and helpful for a class, especially in mixed-ability settings, as they encourage participation and help students to internalise language patterns. They are key to building language skills and developing spontaneous speaking. Routines also allow students to express themselves and ask for new words to say what they want at a given moment. Meaningful output activities ensure that students not only understand the language but can also use it effectively in different situations.

3. Focus on form

While communication is mainly about meaning, focusing on how language is structured – the form – is just as important. This includes attention to phonological (pronunciation), lexical (vocabulary), grammatical, discourse, pragmatic and sociolinguistic (how language is used in different social situations) aspects of language. Knowing how these parts work in real communication helps students to use them correctly.

To include a focus on form in your teaching, you can:

- Highlight and practise specific language features during activities that focus on meaning.
- Use explicit teaching strategies to explain grammar rules, vocabulary and pronunciation.
- Incorporate activities that help your students to notice and fix mistakes, like error correction exercises or targeted practice drills.

Example: Noticing

In this example, students are given five words or short sentences, each containing a mistake, and they must identify the error in each one. This is a great way in which to focus on common areas where students struggle. For example:

1. **Adjectival agreement:** The adjective does not match the noun.

2. **Auxiliary verb:** With the verb *aller*, we must use *être* as the auxiliary and not *avoir*.

3. **Adjectival agreement:** This would be a similar issue to that in number 1.

4. **Near future tense:** The second verb should be in the infinitive form (*jouer* instead of *joué*).

5. **Spelling:** It contains a common spelling error.

Each mistake in this example addresses a key misconception in French. Activities like this help students to focus on grammar, encouraging them to think critically and improve their understanding.

Trouvez les erreurs!

1. Elles sont sain.
2. J'ai allé.
3. Une cravate vert.
4. Je vais joué.
5. malheuresement

A: Je pense que numéro 1 est ....
B: Je suis d'accord ✓/ Je ne suis pas d'accord X
B: Je pense que numéro 2 est ....
A: Je suis d'accord ✓/ Je ne suis pas d'accord X

FIGURE 1.5: *Example of 'find the mistake'*

Balancing form and meaning helps your learners to develop a more comprehensive understanding of the language.

4. Focus on fluency

Fluency in a second language means being able to speak, listen, read and write quickly and easily. To become fluent, students need lots of practice to turn what they have learned into automatic skills. Fluency also frees up their minds to focus on higher-level thinking processes, like solving problems or inferencing. However, building fluency takes time and consistent practice. To help your students to develop fluency, you can:

- Create activities with real communication purposes that encourage natural language use.
- Use timed tasks like speed reading, quick-fire questions and conversational drills, to 'train' students to process language faster.
- Provide regular, varied practice that mirrors real-life situations, to build students' confidence and skill.

Example: Speed dating

For this activity, I have my students form two rows so that each student has a partner to talk to. I ask a question or give a topic, and the students discuss it with their partner within a set time limit. When I give a signal (like a countdown in the target language), the activity stops and the students in one row move one space down to meet a new partner. Then, I ask either the same question or a new one and the students discuss it with their new partner. I use the signal to mark the start and end of each round. This activity focuses on fluency, helping students to use the language more naturally and confidently.

5. Focus on needs

According to Ryan and Deci's (2000) self-determination theory (SDT), students learn better when their basic needs for autonomy, competence and connection (relatedness) are met (p.68–76). This kind of motivation, called self-determined motivation, is linked to better language learning outcomes. To meet these needs, you can:

- **Support autonomy:** Let your students make choices about their learning activities to give them more control.
- **Build competence:** Create tasks that challenge your students at the right level and allow them to succeed.
- **Encourage connection (relatedness):** Build a positive and supportive classroom where your students can work together and feel valued.

By addressing these psychological needs, you can create a more motivating and effective environment for learning. Using SLA principles in your teaching can greatly improve how your students learn and remember the language. Balancing input, output, language structure, fluency and students' needs creates a more dynamic and supportive learning environment.

Practical examples

Integrating SLA principles into your lessons can make your teaching more engaging and effective. This section offers practical strategies that you can use, such as providing meaningful input, encouraging students to produce language (meaningful output), supporting language practice and creating a supportive and collaborative environment. The examples presented are intended to guide you with flexible, practical strategies for enhancing language learning and teaching.

Incorporating meaningful input

Here are some ways in which to include meaningful input in your lessons:

- **Authentic materials:** Incorporate newspapers, podcasts, videos and other authentic materials that reflect real-life language use. For example, you can use a news article to discuss current events or a podcast episode to analyse spoken language (see the list of useful websites on the companion website for examples and where to find these).

- **Dual coding:** Support comprehension with images, charts and diagrams. For instance, when introducing new vocabulary, you could pair words with relevant pictures to enhance understanding.

FIGURE 1.6: *Example of dual coding*

- **Context:** Provide context for new language items by embedding them in stories or scenarios. For example, you could teach new vocabulary within the framework of a short story (like the example of a narrative in the case study in Chapter 2) or a real-life situation.

- **Scaffolding:** Break down complex texts or dialogues into manageable chunks and guide your students through them step-by-step. Use pre-reading or pre-listening activities to prepare your students for the main content.

Example: Spot the missing words in the text

In this activity, I ask my students to listen carefully, find the missing words and spot any extra words to add to the text. They need to pay close attention because they won't know how many extra words are in the recording, so staying focused is key to getting a high score. For the first two tries, I play the recording at a normal, manageable speed. On the third try, I speed it up to make it more challenging, which helps to keep students engaged and motivated.

Providing opportunities for output

Helping your students to practise using language is crucial for building their skills. Here are some simple ways in which to do this:

- **Interactive activities:** Have your students talk to each other in pairs or groups in role-plays, conversations or discussions. For example, for the topic on 'employment and careers', I have my students act out a job interview in the target language (TL).
- **Writing tasks:** Assign different kinds of writing – essays, diary entries, storyboards or blogs.
- **Presentations:** Let your students give presentations on topics that they like. You can provide support

(scaffolding) if needed. This not only practises language but also builds confidence. For example, I get my students to present about a cultural aspect of a country where the language is spoken.

- **Role-plays:** Use both scripted and unscripted dialogues to practise conversational skills. For instance, I create scenarios for my students to act out, such as ordering food at a restaurant or asking for directions.

Encouraging language practice

Here are other ways in which you can encourage your students to use language effectively:

- **Fluency activities:** Try timed activities like speed reading, quick-fire Q&As or translations to promote quick language use. For example, I conduct a timed reading session where students summarise a text within a set time limit. The summary criteria can be adapted to students' proficiency level – one or two sentences, a short paragraph, etc.

- **Task-based learning:** Create activities that mimic real-life language use, such as planning a trip or solving a problem. After we process the key structures and vocabulary needed, I task my students to work in groups to plan an itinerary for a weekend trip, discussing and negotiating the details.

- **Regular practice:** Encourage consistent practice through daily language exercises, such as short writing prompts or conversation starters. For example, I begin each lesson with a language interaction using register routines.

- **Feedback and reflection:** Offer constructive feedback and encourage self-reflection. For instance, after a speaking activity, I offer my students specific advice on areas like pronunciation and grammar and have students think about how they did and where they can improve.

Creating a supportive learning environment

Creating a positive and supportive classroom atmosphere is essential to effective language learning. Here are some ideas for how to foster it:

- **Encourage collaboration:** Use group projects and teamwork so that your students support each other.
- **Build relationships:** Get to know your students – check in with them regularly and talk about their progress. Show interest in your students' lives, progress and challenges.
- **Celebrate successes:** Acknowledge and celebrate your students' achievements, no matter how small through verbal praise, certificates or a classroom bulletin board displaying their work.

Flexible guiding principles

These strategies are designed to be flexible and adaptable to different teaching contexts and learner needs:

- **Adapt techniques:** Adjust activities based on the proficiency level and interests of your students. For example, I adjust the complexity of tasks for novice versus advanced and expert learners.

- **Encourage autonomy:** Support your students in taking ownership of their learning. For instance, I give students the choice of topics for projects or allow them to select reading materials that interest them.
- **Integrate technology:** Use digital tools to enhance learning. For example, I suggest to my students what language learning apps and videos to use for extra practice and exposure to the language.

Technology and language learning

Technology has transformed how we teach and learn languages, offering exciting tools that go beyond traditional teaching methods and approaches. This section delves into how you, the teacher, can effectively use technology to boost your students' engagement and autonomy, ranging from online language learning platforms to immersive virtual environments. Here is how you can use technology to make learning more personal and active and help your students to take charge of their progress.

Online language learning platforms

Online language learning platforms provide structured courses and resources that complement classroom teaching or support independent study. Key features and benefits include:

- **Interactive exercises:** Platforms like BBC Bitesize, Duolingo, Babbel, Language Gym, Linguascope and Languagenut have interactive activities that cover listening, speaking, reading and writing skills. These exercises offer instant feedback, which helps your students to correct mistakes quickly and strengthen their learning.

- **Adaptive learning:** Many platforms use adaptive technologies to tailor content based on a student's progress. For example, if your student struggles with a specific grammar point, the platform gives extra practice in that area.
- **Gamification:** Apps like Duolingo use points, badges and streaks to make learning fun and encourage daily practice.
- **Access to native speakers:** Some platforms, like italki and Verbling, connect students with native speakers for one-on-one tutoring sessions, offering authentic conversational practice.

Immersive virtual environments

Virtual reality (VR) and augmented reality (AR) can bring language learning to life:

- **Virtual reality:** Apps like Mondly VR and ENGAGE put students in realistic scenarios where they can practise speaking and listening. For example, your students can virtually visit a marketplace in a target language country and interact with vendors.
- **Augmented reality:** Tools like Google Translate's camera feature show real-time translations when students point their device at an object. AR flashcards and interactive storybooks can also make learning new words and phrases fun and visual.

- **Artificial Intelligence:** AI is now widely accessible and offers enormous potential for enhancing the teaching and learning of Modern Foreign Languages (MFL). It can support vocabulary learning through adaptive learning, provide personalised grammar explanations using chat-based tools like ChatGPT or Claude, and enable real-time translation and pronunciation feedback via tools such as DeepL, Microsoft Translator, or Speechling. AI-driven voice assistants and chatbots like Mizou can also simulate authentic conversation practice, allowing learners to engage in meaningful target-language interactions beyond the classroom.

Digital tools for language practice

Numerous digital tools can be incorporated into language learning to boost learning and enhance engagement:

- **Vocabulary learning apps:** Apps like Memrise, Anki and Quizlet offer customisable flashcards and spaced repetition systems to help your students to remember vocabulary and grammar rules.

- **Speech recognition:** Tools like Google's speech-to-text feature and apps like Speechling help your students to practise pronunciation and get instant feedback on their spoken language.

- **Language exchange platforms:** Websites and apps like HelloTalk and Speaky connect language learners around the world for language exchange, allowing your students to interact with native speakers in real conversations.

* A word of caution: some of these platforms and apps may be more suitable for older learners, so test them first to ensure that they are age-appropriate.

Integrating technology in your teaching

To effectively integrate technology in your teaching:

- **Choose the right tools:** Pick digital tools that match your students' age, skill level and learning objectives or goals. Test them yourself to ensure that they are helpful and appropriate. I evaluate the effectiveness of different technologies through trial and feedback.

- **Mix traditional and digital methods:** Combine traditional classroom activities with technology to create a balanced and dynamic learning environment. For example, I use digital flashcards for vocabulary practice alongside in-class speaking practice.

- **Guide your students:** Teach your students how to use these tools effectively and help them if they get stuck. I encourage responsible and effective use of technology for learning.

- **Teach digital literacy:** Show your students how to find trustworthy resources online and avoid unreliable information.

By using technology wisely, you can make learning more engaging, interactive, personalised and autonomous. The integration of digital tools can complement traditional teaching and open up exciting opportunities for practice, helping your students to build confidence and independence.

REFLECTIVE QUESTIONS

- How does the science of learning inform your current teaching practices and what new strategies do you implement based on this knowledge?
- How do the principles of SLA align with your teaching approach and what adjustments do you make to enhance language learning for your students?
- What role do input, output and interaction play in your planning and how can you create more opportunities for these elements in your lessons?
- What are some practical ways in which you integrate the principles of SLA into your classroom and how have these methods impacted the learning outcomes of your students?
- How has the integration of technology changed your approach to language teaching and what tools have you found most effective?
- In what ways do you use technology to personalise language learning experiences and support students with varying proficiency levels?

CASE STUDY

Bridging the gap: Applying cognitive science and SLA principles in the MFL classroom

Contributor: Steve Smith, retired MFL head of department, educator, blogger and author

What was the issue?

As a young teacher, I encountered a very common issue. It can be framed by the statement that you often hear: 'I've taught and practised this so many times, but the students still can't get it right.'

After teaching the perfect tense in French and practising its use through exercises such as question-answer drills, transformation drills, gap-fills and easy translation, I found that only a minority of students were able to subsequently reuse the structure accurately in speech and writing. Although most students would initially do exercises accurately and be able to explain rules such as 'use an auxiliary and a past participle' or 'the past participle is formed by… ', when it came to writing a paragraph of their own using the same verbs, it would all go wrong and they would resort to translating directly from English, making up forms that they had not previously used. For example, instead of writing *J'ai joué* (I played), they would write *J'ai joue* or *Je joué*. The same mistakes would occur in later work and in exam conditions.

How did we resolve it?

A key thing that I learned was that for students to correctly apply new learning, it is much easier if the conditions of the retrieval are the same or very similar to the conditions under which the item was first learned. In the cognitive science literature, this is called 'transfer-appropriate processing', or the TAP effect. For example, if I tested the students using the same type of exercises that I had used initially, they would cope much more easily with the retrieval task. I learned, therefore, that classic end-of-unit tests should largely replicate the way in which the structure was originally practised. If I taught using gap-fill, I should test using gap-fill.

Only a minority of higher-attaining students would be able to apply their previous learning to quite different contexts – for example, using a different format, such as translation, or using less familiar vocabulary. These students benefitted from the greater challenge of applying their knowledge to new contexts.

However, there was a second, broader issue involved, to do with findings from SLA research. Researchers tell us that it is actually quite hard to convert *declarative* knowledge of grammatical rules ('knowing that') into *procedural* knowledge ('knowing how'). In other words, a student may be able to explain a rule, such as how to form the perfect tense, but cannot turn this knowledge into actual use in speech or writing. The process of acquiring grammatical structures for spontaneous use takes time and involves more than just applying a rule. Researchers tell us that it is more about just picking up the rule through repeated exposure and usage over time – so-called *implicit* learning. Knowing this made me aware that I just had to be patient when it came to using new structures spontaneously and accurately, and that sometimes grammar just cannot be 'taught'. My classroom practice became mainly focused on using language to *communicate* rather than teaching rules.

What was the impact?

As far as the TAP effect is concerned, since I took care to use and design activities and tests that resembled the previous teaching tasks, especially with lower-achieving groups, students achieved *higher test scores* and improved their *feeling of competence* in the subject – a key driver of motivation. I would never test students in a format that they had never seen.

As regards the second issue of converting grammatical knowledge into actual skill, I learned that some students never master the process, since there is just not enough time, so I had to be *realistic* and use a more limited range of constructions. This led me to focus less on teaching and practising grammatical structures with GCSE classes, and more on completing *achievable tasks* within a limited range of language and on a suitable range of high-priority grammar points, depending on the proficiency of the class.

Chapter summary

In this chapter, we have explored some ideas that we should consider when planning for effective language learning.

- Understanding how we learn will support planning that builds memory, attention and motivation, leading to better language retention and engagement.

- Language input and output should be meaningful, challenging but accessible, and embedded in real-life or relevant contexts to deepen understanding.

- Explicit focus on language form such as grammar, vocabulary and pronunciation should be integrated alongside fluency-building tasks.

- Effective teaching addresses learner needs by promoting autonomy, competence and positive relationships to support motivation and progress.

- Practical strategies, including scaffolding, role-plays, fluency drills and use of technology, help to create supportive and engaging learning environments.

Further reading

- *Working memory: The multiple-component model* by Baddeley and Logie (1999) is a key read for understanding how different components of working memory function and interact – essential for considering cognitive load in your lesson planning.

- *The four strands: Innovation in language learning and teaching* by Paul Nation (2007) is an important read, introducing Nation's four strands model and offering a practical and research-based way in which to balance effective language learning activities.

- *Principles and Practice in Second Language Acquisition* by Stephen Krashen (1982) outlines his influential theories of second language acquisition, including the input hypothesis, making it essential reading for any language teacher.

- *Memory: What Every Language Teacher Should Know* by Steve Smith and Gianfranco Conti (2021) is a practical and very accessible guide linking memory research to classroom practice, packed with strategies to help learners to retain and retrieve language more effectively.

- *Improving Foreign Language Teaching, Towards a research-based curriculum and pedagogy* by E. Macaro., S. Graham and R.Woore (2015) presents a research-based framework outlining eight principles for effective language learning, offering practical guidance, activities and assessment strategies to enhance teaching and learner progress in secondary classrooms.

2

Understanding the curriculum and creating a coherent sequence of lessons

Introduction

This chapter dives deep into the intricacies of the MFL curriculum, leveraging insights from the MFL programme of study (DfE, 2013) and the findings of the MFL Ofsted research review (2021). The aim is to provide you with a comprehensive framework for understanding the curriculum and crafting a coherent sequence of lessons that are engaging, educational and culturally rich.

Curriculum fundamentals

Understanding what students have learned at the primary level ensures a smoother transition and continuity in language education. Effective curriculum design must consider the linguistic journey from Key Stage 2 through to Key Stage 4, ensuring that it builds progressively on students' prior knowledge and skills. It is key to look at the MFL programme of study from Key Stage 2 and to assess what students know and to what extent at the beginning of each Key Stage.

Decisions around whether to adopt a two- or three-year Key Stage 3 model and whether languages are compulsory at Key Stage 4 can also significantly impact curriculum design. Most secondary schools have a three-year Key Stage 3 model to ensure more depth. Decisions regarding languages being made compulsory at Key Stage 4 are up to each school, but for most schools, it remains an optional subject.

The design of a high-quality MFL curriculum hinges on a deep understanding of its core elements and goals. The curriculum should surpass the breadth of the National Curriculum, with a sharp focus on the intricate components that form the foundation of language learning. You must identify the smaller building blocks, like verb conjugation, that scaffold the learning of more complex ideas. A meticulously planned curriculum not only meets the requirements set by the National Curriculum but also addresses the unique challenges and decline in language proficiency among students. At its core, the MFL curriculum aims to foster linguistic competence and intercultural awareness. This involves mastery of the four primary skills – listening, speaking, reading and writing – while embedding cultural insights to help students to understand the context of the language. According to the Department for Education's National Curriculum (DfE, 2013), language learning should provide students with:

- **practical communication skills:** enabling learners to express ideas, understand others and engage in conversations

- **cultural awareness:** introducing the traditions, customs and ways of life of countries where the language is spoken

- **analytical and problem-solving skills:** promoting linguistic and cognitive development through the study of grammar and syntax.

The Ofsted research review (2021) further emphasises that progression in MFL is about 'knowing more and remembering more'. This means carefully planning the curriculum to build robust knowledge of phonology, grammar and vocabulary, while ensuring opportunities for retrieval and application.

It is key to also refer to the GCSE content published by the DfE, as the document details the learning outcomes and content coverage required for GCSE specifications so this should be used to ensure that your Key Stage 4 curriculum is in line with the requirements for the GCSE.

Intent, implementation and impact

Intent

The curriculum's primary intent should be to cultivate effective communicators in foreign languages, aligning with the overarching aims of the National Curriculum. This includes fostering a solid foundation in phonics, vocabulary and grammar – the three pillars of language progression. Language brings these elements together in four modalities: listening, speaking, reading and writing.

Each aspect serves to bolster the students' abilities to navigate the language and its applications. It should outline ambitious goals for students, such as fluency in the language and a profound understanding of the associated culture. Teachers should ask themselves:

- Why are these topics and skills being taught now?
- How does this fit into the students' broader educational journey?

Less is more, so when designing your curriculum, you need to think about the number of topics taught, especially because within the topics you need to incorporate the phonics that you will be teaching, the grammar to be taught and the grammar to be revisited, but also the culture and authentic material that you would like to include. Simply covering numerous topics is not enough. The danger of teaching too many topics is that you do not have enough time to go into depth and to practise all the different skills within each topic.

Overview KS3 French Curriculum – Year 7

	CONTEXT	GRAMMAR	VOCABULARY	PHONICS	CULTURE
Bonjour, c'est moi W – Ça va conversation	• Saying how I feel and why • Alphabet • Asking and saying how old I am • Asking and giving my birthday • Describing my personality • Describing my appearance	• The verb être and avoir - using I and you • question words • Possessive adjectives (mon / ma / ton / ta) • Adjectival agreement • Negative 'ne…pas / jamais'	• Basic greeting and introduction phrases • Numbers 1-31 • Months and days • Personality adjectives (je suis and je ne suis pas / jamais) • Appearance – size / hair / eyes	SPFC a i eu o u ou silent final e é	• Cultural quiz • La Bise • Discuss formal and informal 'you' • Why languages are important poster • Where can languages take you video • Christmas in France
Voici ma famille W – rainbow writing family	• Asking and saying who is in my family • Saying what my family is like • Saying what pets I have	• avoir (1st and 2nd person singular when describing my appearance) • Être (1st, 2nd and 3rd person singular in present tense and 3rd person plural) • Adjectival agreements (according to gender of noun and plurals) • Possessive pronouns • Simple opinions • Negative structure	• Recap personality traits • Recap appearance • Family members plus il y a • Numbers 1-100 • Animals • Colours • Family members + s'appelle • plus / moins… que	é o eu en / an on in è ai oi	• Facts about the Eiffel Tower • Describing a French-speaking celebrity • Valentine's poem • Poisson d'avril • Where can languages take you? • Why learn languages?
Miam miam! W – restaurant conversation	• Saying and understanding others talk about what they eat for all meals • Saying what food and drink I like and why • To order food in a restaurant • To describe mealtimes and understand prices • To say what you would like to buy	• Question words • Use of manger, boire and prendre • Infinitives with je voudrais • Adjectival agreement • Negatives (ne…pas / jamais / rien) • opinions • Partitive article (du / de la / des) • C'est + masculine	• Food and drinks high frequency vocab • Different kinds of meals • Adjectives to describe food • Frequency adverbs • Opinions and justification • Time phrases • Restaurant vocabulary • Shopping, money, prices	eu / oeu gn ge th (t) ain on j r er	• Typical food in French-speaking countries • French menu • French recipes (crêpes) • Where can languages take you? • Why learn languages?
Boucle et Bill W – describe a character	• Film study – recap appearance, personality, family and pets	• Present tense of être and avoir full paradigm • Opinions and reasons	• Retrieval: Family / pets / appearance / personality	• Recap of phonics	• French film study

FIGURE 2.1: *Example of a Year 7 overview curriculum, scan the QR code for the full-size version*

As you can see, only three big topics are being taught, but the aim is that, within each one, time is given to ensure that phonics and grammar are delivered in depth through the four different skills, including reading aloud and dictation. Time is also dedicated to discussing the importance of learning another language, while culture plays the 'fourth pillar'.

On this overview, a film study is also carried out at the end of the year, to bring even more culture and also to reinforce everything that has been covered throughout the year. Here are some suggestions of film studies that can be conducted at Key Stage 3:

French:

- **Year 7:** *Boule et Bill* to recap appearance, personality, family and pets
- **Year 8:** *Le Petit Nicolas* to recap appearance, personality, daily activities, where they live and description of bedroom
- **Year 9:** *Les Choristes* to recap personality, description, music and future tense.

Spanish:

- **Year 7:** *Encanto* to recap appearance, personality, family and pets
- **Year 8:** *Zipi y Zape – El Club de la Canica* to recap appearance, personality, school and rules
- **Year 9:** *Coco* to recap appearance, personality, festival, past tense and future tense.

German:

- **Year 7:** *Ostwind* to recap appearance, personality, pets and family
- **Year 8:** *Rock it!* to recap music, hobbies, time and school
- **Year 9:** *Baloon* to introduce imperfect tense and cultural context (Cold War).

Implementation

Effective curriculum implementation revolves around structuring content to facilitate sequential learning. This involves logical planning of how and when each language component is introduced and taught, ensuring that it builds upon previously established knowledge. For instance, the explicit teaching of phonics should come before advanced vocabulary in order to solidify pronunciation and comprehension.

How are you going to translate curriculum goals into classroom practice? Key considerations include:

The role of phonics

Phonics is the sounds that the letters make – it's the way in which words are pronounced and links are made to how they are written. When teaching phonics, you need to think of the meaning-bearing sounds (phonemes) of the language: how the phonemes are written and how the written form is pronounced (phoneme–grapheme correspondences). It is essential to remember that clear and reliable pronunciation and the links between sounds and spelling are integral parts of second language learning.

Starting with phonetic drills helps students to recognise sound-spelling patterns, but phonics must be revisited throughout the curriculum. It's about stopping your lesson when some words are not being pronounced properly – going back to the specific phoneme is key – and ensuring that plenty of practice is given to your students so that, over time, they do not continue to make the same mistake.

Questions to ask yourself:

- Do your curriculum plans show clear logic behind progression in phonics, including around when to teach differences between English sound–spelling correspondences and those of the target language?

- Have you planned enough practice and review of phonemes and how these link to graphemes throughout your curriculum?
- Do your curriculum plans show how small differences in sound can unlock meaning for students?

Vocabulary

By vocabulary, we mean the words that students need to know and need to learn, but also the words that students need in order to be able to communicate with purpose and which relate to them and their experiences. For example, do not limit the number of pets that you introduce to the examples given by the exam board, as students want to talk and describe their own pet, so ensure that you include them. The same would apply for any topic; another example will be with the adjectives taught to describe their personality and the personalities of their friends and family – students might want to use certain words, so do not limit your curriculum to the word list being provided.

Questions to ask yourself:

- Do you prioritise high-frequency words and verbs?
- Have you considered carefully which topic-based vocabulary (other than high-frequency words) you teach?
- Can students use these words across different contexts?
- At what point are items of vocabulary learned?
- How and when do you introduce more advanced systematic aspects of vocabulary knowledge (e.g. synonyms, antonyms, shades of meaning and how they change with context)?

Systematic grammar instruction

By grammar, we mean the rules for combining words to make universally understood meaning – how words change to convey meaning. Grammar should be broken into manageable chunks and introduced progressively. It is important that there is a logic behind grammatical progression in curriculum plans, from simpler to more complex concepts and structures. For instance, introduce only a few subject pronouns and simple verbs in Year 7, then introduce more in Year 8 and so on. The same works for the tenses. It is not recommended to introduce all forms of the past tense at once or within one single topic; instead introduce them gradually and build on it over time and throughout a range of topics. If you introduce fewer topics, you will have more time to revisit tenses and build on them. A continuum of grammar teaching will be to move from implicit understanding, where students are exposed to the grammar in a meaningful context, to explicit knowledge, where you ensure that an explicit but succinct description of the grammatical feature is taught and that students are being given plenty of opportunities to practise the grammar point through listening and reading, as well as through practice in productive use of the features being taught through writing and speaking. Grammar teaching should be integrated with vocabulary learning, ensuring that students can apply grammatical rules to the vocabulary that they learn. This should include using grammar to understand and produce meaning in both written and oral forms.

Questions to ask yourself:

- Have you considered the nature and rate of grammatical progression, the complexity of grammatical concepts and structures and which aspects of a grammatical structure are introduced and when?

- Have you considered productive use of grammar in free writing and speech in a range of contexts?
- Is your curriculum providing ample opportunity to revisit the same grammar in different contexts, for different tasks and with a range of vocabulary?

Interleaving and spacing

Revisiting phonics, grammar and vocabulary at regular intervals ensures knowledge retention. For example, if you think of adjectival agreement, where might it be taught and revisited consistently and cumulatively between Year 7 and Year 11? Example answers might be in Year 7, when students describe pets using colours or when describing the personality of their family; in Year 8, when describing places in town; in Year 9, when describing teachers or subjects that they learn at school; and at Key Stage 4, when looking at marriage and partnerships.

Questions to ask yourself:

- Does your curriculum show when the three pillars are being revisited over time?
- Can you explain how and why it is revisited at certain points? What's the rationale behind it?

Impact

The impact is assessed through the progression model, which gauges students' ability to know more, remember more and do more. Success is measured by how well students can apply what they have learned in order to communicate effectively in the target language. This requires regular assessments to ensure that the intended knowledge is not only delivered but also retained and utilised by the students. This includes assessing whether students have achieved fluency, cultural understanding and confidence in applying their knowledge.

Lesson sequencing

Sequencing in the MFL curriculum is critical for ensuring that subsequent learning builds logically on what has previously been established. It is essential to plan the curriculum so that each new learning phase aligns with the last, ensuring that students can connect new knowledge with familiar concepts and that they can build on their knowledge and skills over time. This methodical approach prevents cognitive overload and aids in the natural accumulation of language skills, from basic phonetics and vocabulary to complex grammatical structures.

For example, what does using opinions and justifying them look like in Year 7 all the way through to Year 11? How do you build on it?

You might start by introducing *j'aime* in Year 7 and then, in Year 8, students can use *ce que j'aime* to then move to *ce que j'aime le plus*. As soon as students know it with one structure, you can make links and challenge them to say 'what I hate the most' or 'what I prefer the most', etc. in French.

When planning lessons within a topic, the most important thing is to know what you want students to be able to achieve at the end of that topic; it is then a case of planning backwards with that end goal in mind. It's not thinking one lesson at a time; it's having a clear sequence of learning, so that you know how each lesson fits with the others. This backwards-planning approach ensures that each lesson builds upon the previous one, leading systematically towards the end goal. It provides a structured learning path, making it easier for students to accumulate knowledge progressively and apply what they have learned in a meaningful and cumulative way. This methodical sequence also allows you to identify any gaps in understanding or skills as students progress, making adjustments as necessary to meet the unit objectives effectively.

Students also need to be clear about what they are learning and why they are learning it. For example, share the roadmap with them so that they know what they will be learning within the topic.

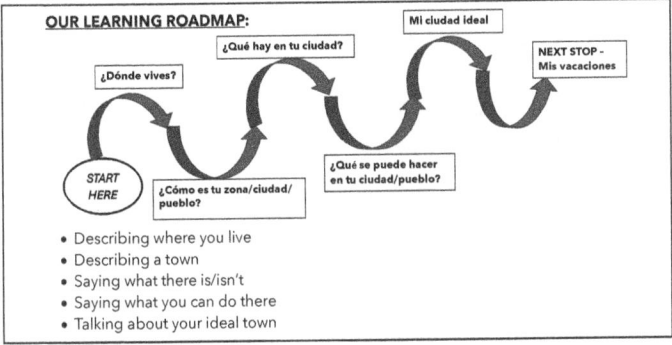

FIGURE 2.2: *Example of a road map for the topic of 'town'*

Then, for each step, share the learning intentions with your students. For example, when learning about where you live, you will learn about:

- the vocabulary for some countries
- how to conjugate the verb *vivir* (to live) in Spanish – you already know how to say 'I live' and 'you live', so we will learn the other subject pronouns
- using the verb *vivir* with the countries that we have learned
- facts about some cities in Spanish-speaking countries

- the compass points, so that you can say exactly where your town is located

- the difference between *estar* and *ser.*

When designing a sequence of lessons, you must consider a variety of critical components that contribute to a successful learning experience. These components range from understanding the overarching goals of the unit to the nitty-gritty of logistical execution.

Ingredients to think about when planning include:

- the big ideas of the unit and your learning goals for all students

- your students: what they are like and what they need

- the specific lessons needed to carry a unit to a successful conclusion

- the length of your lesson

- the logistical details of materials, equipment, movement and individual, pair or group work

- securing students' attention

- thinking about your objective

- thinking about prior learning

- what you want your students to achieve by the end of your lesson

- how you will do that and which activities you will plan

- making students practise

- providing guidance

- thinking about the timing

UNDERSTANDING THE CURRICULUM

- considering when you are going to give feedback

- thinking about checking understanding/assessment – how you will find out what students already know and what they have learned.

In addition, it is essential to also carefully plan the amount of practice to give to your students. For example, when introducing new vocabulary, time is needed for repetition in order to drill the new words, but then students must be given plenty of opportunities to practise it. For this, there are a range of pair-work activities that can be done. For example:

- Student A does the action and student B says the word in the target language.

- Student A mumbles one of the words and student B has to guess which one it is.

- Student A thinks of one of the words and student B must guess which one it is.

- Students A and B can take turns saying the words one at a time for a certain amount of time.

Following that stage, get rid of the language and only use the pictures to play some repetition games. For example, you play against the class: point to a picture and say the word in the target language. If what you say is correct, students repeat it, but if what you say is not, then students must be quiet. If one of the students says the word, then the point goes to you. The first to five points wins. By getting rid of the vocabulary and only having the pictures for that stage, it allows students to think about the meaning of the words; otherwise, it is only a reading activity.

Integrating skills and content

If we want students to actually use the language and not just memorise rules, we have to connect what we teach to real communication. That means building lessons that don't just focus on one skill in isolation. Whether it's a grammar point or a new topic, we need to give students chances to hear it, say it, read it and write it. All four language skills – listening, speaking, reading and writing – should be worked into the lesson in a way that feels natural and purposeful.

- **Listening and speaking:** Early instruction should focus on phonetics and phonology to help students to recognise and produce the sounds of the language. This foundation supports their ability to understand spoken language and engage in speaking with correct pronunciation and accent.

- **Reading and writing:** As students progress, the curriculum should emphasise the connection between spoken and written language, helping them to see how phonetic sounds correlate with written words. Reading reinforces vocabulary and grammatical structures, while writing allows students to apply their knowledge in creating coherent text.

Here are some examples of activities for each modality:

Reading

1. **Information hunt:** Students are in teams of four and are given at least three texts with information on them; these texts can be as complicated and as long as you wish. There are also questions relating to the texts

cut up into strips (one question per strip) and these are located somewhere in the classroom. Each team has a set of questions; it is easy if you print them on coloured paper, so that students can distinguish where their team's questions are. Start the challenge by shouting out the number of the person who must run (walk swiftly!) to the questions, pick up one question to take back to their team to find the answer and then bring it to you to check, before going to collect the second question. The first team to complete their questions is the winner. Change the 'runner' frequently throughout the game so that everyone has to give answers. It is a great way to tackle reading comprehension. You can differentiate through the details that you require in your answers, and if you group the students by a mix of ability then the more able coach the less able. I find that it works best if you mix the questions, so that each team answers them at different times.

2. **Reconstruction:** After reading a text, students are given several key sentences from the text, scrambled. Their task is to reconstruct the story in the correct order.

3. **Narrow reading:** This is an idea from one of Dr Gianfranco Conti's posts on reading instruction on his Language Gym website (www.language-gym.com). It requires students to read three to six short paragraphs on the same topic, with each paragraph containing similar chunks and structures that have been previously taught, thus enabling students to have significant exposure to chunks and syntax without being too repetitive. Students then have to answer 'who' questions from the different texts.

4. To explore students' comprehension of the text that you provide, you could ask students:

- multiple-choice questions
- true/false/not-in-text questions
- 'who' questions
- cloze exercises
- to find synonyms
- to order the pictures.

Reading aloud

1. **In a style of...** : Display a text on the board, making sure that you have checked understanding and that you have read it with the class. Then, in pairs, students take turns reading the text aloud in the style of…

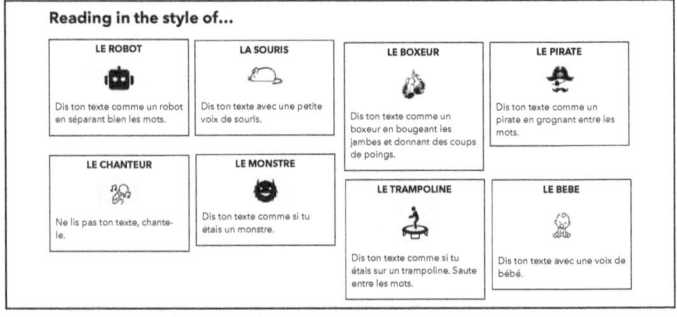

FIGURE 2.3: *Example of reading aloud cards 'in the style of...'*

During this time, circulate the room and listen for any problems with pronunciation. If there are any, stop the class and address it.

2. **À la bombe:** Students play in pairs. They take turns and read either one, two or three words from the sentence on the board. The student reading the last word from the sentence loses.

UNDERSTANDING THE CURRICULUM

> **Attention à la bombe!** 💣
>
> 1. Je m'entends bien avec ma mère car elle est gentille et compréhensive. 💣
> 2. Malheureusement je me dispute avec mon frère cadet parce qu'il m'énerve. 💣
> 3. Si j'avais une petite sœur je voudrais qu'elle soit drôle et sportive car j'aime faire du sport donc nous pourrions en faire ensemble. 💣

FIGURE 2.4: *Example of a sentence reading game*

3. **BEEP:** Display ten sentences on the board. Students take turns reading these sentences out loud with their partner. The student who is not speaking when they hear a BEEP wins a point. If a student mispronounces anything and the other student corrects them, they also win a point!

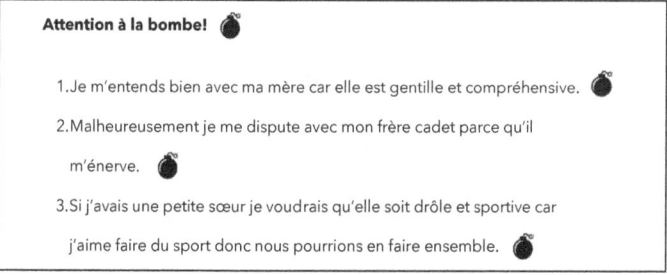

> Take turns reading these sentences out loud with your partner. If you are speaking when you hear a BEEP then you partner wins a point. If your partner mispronounces anything and you correct them you win a point!
> 1. *On habite au Portugal.*
> 2. J'habite avec mon chien.
> 3. *Ils habitent dans un village en Écosse.*
> 4. Elles habitent à la montagne en France.
> 5. *Je m'appelle Bob et j'ai onze ans.*
> 6. Je m'appelle Sarah et j'ai quinze ans.
> 7. *À mon avis c'est affreux.*
> 8. C'était ennuyeux et nul.
> 9. *Ça ne va pas parce que je suis fatigué(e)*
> 10.   Ça va très bien parce que c'est vendredi.

FIGURE 2.5: *Example of pronunciation and listening game (credit: Charlotte King)*

4. **Pronunciation relay:** Pick a short text with a few tricky words or phrases. Split students into pairs or small groups. One student reads a section out loud while the

others listen carefully and spot any mispronunciations. They give feedback to help their partner to get it right. After this, the student reads the same section again to practise and improve. While they are working, circulate the room, listen and note any common mistakes. At the end, bring everyone together and go over these mistakes as a group. Use 'listen and repeat' with the whole class to practise and get better.

Dialogue example: Ordering at a café – Year 7

A: Guten Tag! Kann ich dir helfen?
B: Ja, ich hätte gern einen Kaffee und ein Stück Apfelkuchen, bitte.
A: Möchtest du Kaffee mit Milch und Zucker?
B: Ja, mit Milch, aber ohne Zucker, bitte.
A: Kommt sofort! Möchtest du sonst noch etwas?
B: Nein, danke. Wie viel kostet das?
A: Das macht 6 Euro, bitte.

Listening

1. **Find the error:** Give students a transcript but change some of the words beforehand. Play the listening recording and students must find the errors on the transcript. Then play it again and ask students whether they can correct the mistakes.

2. **Gap fill:** Give the transcript to students but ensure that you have put some blanks in there. Students listen and fill in the blanks. After this, they can answer questions about the listening.

3. **Find the correct answer:** Play a recording or a video from YouTube and give students a table with different

UNDERSTANDING THE CURRICULUM

options. Students must listen and pick the correct answer out of the two possible options.

4. Please search for 'Le zoo de Beauval abrite 500 nouveaux-nés' on Youtube for a helpful video and use the example below from Martine Pillette.

	A	B
1	44 kilos	34 kilos
2	avril	juillet
3	la dernière naissance	la nouvelle naissance
4	un bébé jaguar	un bébé tigre
5	animaux menacés	animaux sauvages
6	parcs animaliers	parcs zoologiques
7	conservatoires scientifiques	conservatoires génétiques
8	la biodiversité	l'écodiversité
9	le mâle dominant	le mâle trop vieux
10	cinq repas par jour	sept repas par jour

FIGURE 2.6: *Example of a listening activity*

5. **Put it in order:** Provide students with a list of pictures (more than what is needed) and they must arrange the pictures according to what they hear.

FIGURE 2.7: *Example of a listening activity*

Phonics

1. **Act it out:** Play a song or any listening tracks and students have to perform a certain action every time they hear a certain sound (e.g. clap when they hear the 'a' sound, stamp for 'i'). Do not give them too many actions/sounds, as it becomes unmanageable.

2. **Respond:** Students must respond only if the word that you say contains the sound that you have selected. You can use any words you like, since the focus is not on comprehension. If using cognates, show each one after students have responded in order to consolidate mastery of the sound–spelling link.

   Example: *Ecoutez. Il y a le son /è/, oui ou non?*

   (Sample: *neige, reine, seize, peinture, fenêtre, dent, intéressant, cependant, naître, mètre, temps, mère, derrière...*)

3. **Record yourself:** Ask students to record themselves saying a list of words to practise the phonics taught so far. Students can use the Vocaroo website (www.vocaroo.com) to do this.

Example:
troi**s*
dou**ze*
moderne***
*****é****l****è****ve*
*****en****fant*
garç**on*
gauch**e*
donner***
matin***
vrai***

4. **Find the syllable:** Students must identify specific syllables in the words that you say. You can use any words you like, since the focus is not on comprehension.

Example from Martine Pillette: *Écoutez chaque mot et cherchez la bonne syllabe dans la liste.*

(**You show:** *pé – pa – poi – pu – pan – po – peu – pou*
You say: *caporal – capuche – peuplier – épouser – appétit – potiron – poivre – capable – purée – pétale – épave – patron – poison – poulet – apeuré – ampoule – amputé...*)

Speaking

1 **Process it:** Display a sentence on the board. Students have to:

- ask you a question about it
- add a detail to it
- give a positive opinion about it
- give a negative opinion about it
- put the sentence in the future tense
- put the sentence in the past tense.

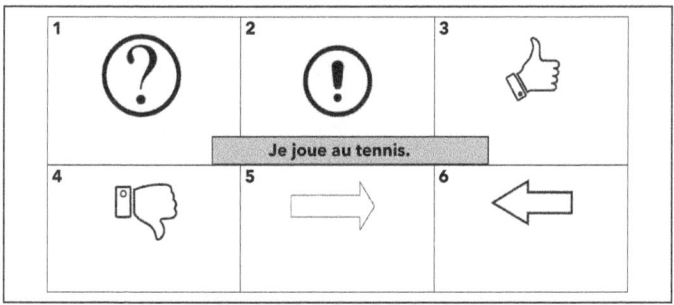

FIGURE 2.8: *Example courtesy of Rachel Hawkes*

2. **Q & A:** Using role-plays, speed dating or puppets, ask students to ask and answer questions in the target language (they can be as simple or as complex as you want).

3. **Keep talking:** This activity, from Rachel Hawkes, is very useful at Key Stage 4. Students click on the question mark to roll the dice. A student from each group then has to talk for one minute (you can start with 20 seconds and build the time as students gain confidence) on that theme; the others listen and make notes in English of what has been said. In this way, all are engaged simultaneously.

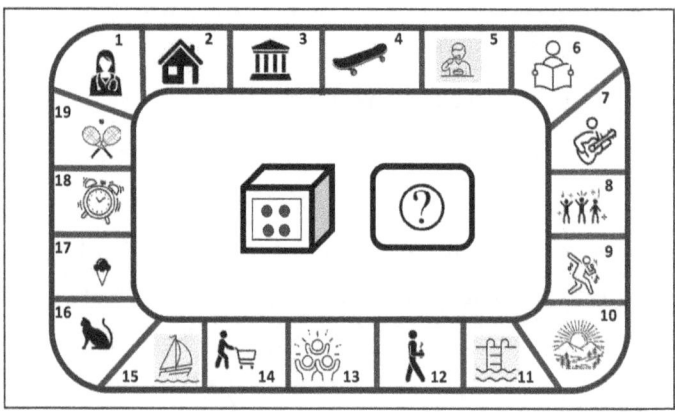

FIGURE 2.9: *Example courtesy of Rachel Hawkes*

4. **Other:** Encourage all students to speak by creating as many pair-work activities as possible.

5. **Examples include:** ping pong, mumble, telepathy, lip reading, talking auction, actions.

Writing

1. **Stand up:** Split your class into two teams. On each team, every student gets a number and a whiteboard. You ask a question, give thinking and writing time so that all students write an answer, and then you shout out a number. Both students stand up and the correct answers get points. You then ask to see all the boards.

2. **Find the wrong one:** Students write three or four sentences and one of them needs to be false. To ensure accuracy, you can ask the class to write the sentences at the end of your lesson, collect them, check them and give them back at the beginning of the next lesson. Students go around the classroom, read their sentences to other students and they try to find the wrong one.

3. **Bubble translation:** In this example from Esther Mercier, students use the bubbles to translate the text.

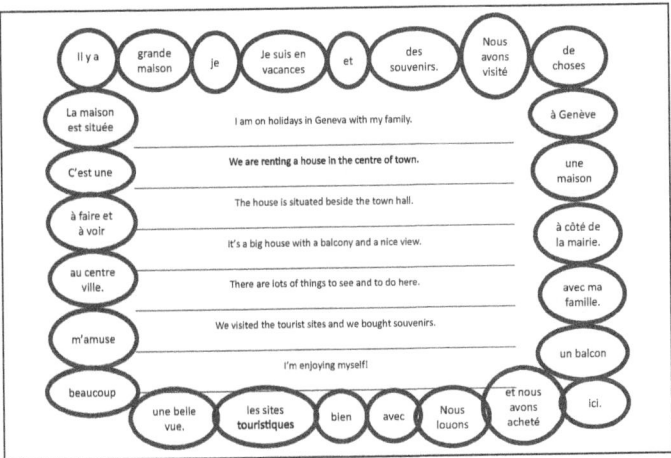

FIGURE 2.10: *Example of bubble translation, courtesy of Esther Mercier*

4. **Social media post:** Ask your students to write a short Instagram caption or tweet in the target language, describing their day, an event or a celebration. Encourage them to include fun and relevant hashtags to make the activity creative and engaging. Afterwards, ask them to exchange posts with a classmate and respond to each other's posts. Alternatively, you can ask your students to translate their partner's post or provide feedback on its accuracy.

- Example1: *Heute habe ich Fußball mit meinen Freunden gespielt. Es hat Spaß gemacht!* ⚽😊 #Sport #Freunde #Spaß

- Example 2: *Gestern habe ich an einem Schulausflug ins Museum teilgenommen. Die Ausstellung über die antike Geschichte war unglaublich faszinierend! Ich habe so viel gelernt.* 🏛📚 #Bildung #Geschichte #Kultur

Dictation

1. **Running dictation:** Place texts around the classroom. Students work in pairs: one is the 'scribe' who stays at the desk with paper and pen, and the other is the 'runner' who goes to the text, memorises a part, runs back and dictates it to the scribe. Alternatively, you can do a running dictation with groups of three or four students in each group.

2. **Buzzed dictation:** In this activity, from Esmeralda Salgado, you dictate sentences or a paragraph and every so often stop and say 'beep' or use a buzzer. Students write what you have dictated and when they hear a 'beep' or the buzzer, students need to write a

UNDERSTANDING THE CURRICULUM

word that makes sense in the given context, to replace the missing word.

3. **Delayed dictation:** In this idea from Dr Gianfranco Conti, you dictate a sentence and students must listen but are not allowed to write what they have heard. During this time, students need to try to memorise by mentally repeating it to themselves in their heads. Say 'now' (in the target language) after ten seconds and students write the sentence.

4. **Selective dictation:** Provide a text with certain words missing. Read the text aloud and students fill in the blanks with the words that they hear.

Authentic materials

Learning a language isn't just about getting the grammar right or ticking off vocabulary lists. At some point, students need to see how the language works outside the classroom. That's where authentic materials come in. The Ofsted research review (2021) underscores the importance of authentic materials in fostering both linguistic skills and cultural understanding.

Examples:

- **Articles and news:** Explore resources like '*1jour1actu*' (current events in French), 'Kindernetz' (suitable for intermediate learners) or Spanish-language podcasts.

- **Literature and poetry:** Introduce students to texts like *Un hombre sin cabeza* by Armando José Sequera, *Dans Paris* by Paul Eluard or *Emil und die Detektive* by Erich Kästner for creative reading and interpretation.

- **Cultural media:** Use songs like 'J'ai demandé à la lune' to practise the *passé composé* in French. Explore fairytales such as *Rotkäppchen* (Little Red Riding Hood) to study word order in subordinate clauses, direct and indirect objects and the preterit tense. Additionally, watch films like *Les Choristes* or *Coco* to reinforce other concepts in context.

- **Virtual tours:** A virtual tour of the Louvre Museum in French, Neuschwanstein Castle in German or La Sagrada Familia in Spanish can serve as a springboard for descriptive writing. Students could create advertisements to encourage others to visit these sites, integrating vocabulary, grammar and cultural insights.

A robust MFL curriculum facilitates a seamless weaving of these modalities, supporting the three pillars of phonics, vocabulary and grammar. Just keep coming back to these key pillars, but teach them through things that matter to the students. A song, a story, a news article – they'll remember that much more than a worksheet. Language lessons should feel like they have a point beyond the exam. If students come away thinking 'I could actually use this', then the job is done.

Review and evaluation

You can't always assume that just because you've taught something, students have fully understood it. That's why it's so important to check in regularly – not with formal tests every time, but through small, everyday checks that give you a sense of where they're at. Sometimes students appear to grasp a topic in the moment, only to forget it the next week. So, it's about spotting the gaps before they widen. Here are a few simple ways in which to do this:

- **Short recap activities:** These can be as straightforward as a few questions on the board when students walk in, or a five-minute quiz to jog their memory.

- **Peer-to-peer feedback:** Let students look at each other's work, particularly when it comes to speaking and writing. They often notice different things, and it helps them to reflect on their own work too.

- **Classroom reflection:** It's worth asking questions like:
  - 'What did you struggle with today?'
  - 'Was there something that helped the grammar to make sense?'

These conversations don't need to be long or formal. A quick chat or a few notes in students' books can give you a good feel for where they're confident and where they need more support. And often, if one student is finding something tricky, others are too.

When you sit down with colleagues to go through student books or recent assessments, you get a much clearer picture of how things are going across the board. It's not about checking the marking; it's about asking, 'Are we actually giving students the right level of challenge?' and 'Is this bit of the curriculum landing the way that we thought it would?'

Moderation helps with consistency, but it also opens the door to useful discussions. You might spot things that others miss or pick up a new approach that works better. It's also a good way in which to catch blind spots, like areas where all students seem to struggle or parts of the curriculum that feel rushed. Looking at real examples of student work side by side can lead to honest, practical conversations that help everyone to sharpen their practice.

Designing a language curriculum that makes sense to students and not just on paper isn't easy. You've got to think carefully about the sequencing of the curriculum, how different skills build on each other and where to weave in culture and real-world context. It's not just about ticking boxes; it's about helping students to see the bigger picture and feel like they're making real progress. It's also worth remembering that no plan survives completely intact once it hits the classroom. What works in theory might fall flat in practice. That's why it's important to revisit your curriculum regularly. Keep asking: Is this working? Do the lessons connect well? Are students getting enough time to practise before moving on? Be ready to tweak and adjust. Talk to students. Talk to colleagues. What matters most is that the curriculum supports learning, and not that it looks polished on paper.

REFLECTIVE QUESTIONS

- How does your curriculum design address the goal of 'knowing more and remembering more' (Ofsted, 2021) as part of the progression in MFL learning?
- In your curriculum planning, how do you balance the teaching of phonics, grammar and vocabulary to ensure comprehensive language development?
- Reflect on the sequencing of lessons in your MFL curriculum. How do you ensure that each lesson builds on the previous one and contributes to the overarching goals of the unit?
- What strategies do you employ to integrate cultural awareness within the MFL curriculum to enhance students' understanding of the language context?
- Reflect on the systematic grammar instruction in your curriculum. How do you ensure that grammar teaching is not only about rule acquisition but also about meaningful application in varied contexts?
- The integration of listening, speaking, reading and writing skills is fundamental to language learning. Can you identify any gaps in how these skills are currently taught and practised in your curriculum? How might you address these gaps?

CASE STUDY

Case study: Innovative strategies for inclusive language learning at Reach Academy
Name of school: Reach Academy Feltham
Contributors: Verity Howorth, Director of Training at The Reach Foundation; Hannah Pinkham, Trust Assistant Principal for Research & Development in Languages at Dixons Academies Trust.

What was the issue?

Reach Academy in Feltham is a diverse school with a strong commitment to ensuring that all students succeed in language learning. Our student body reflects a wide range of academic abilities and we pride ourselves on nearly 100 per cent entry rates. We noticed that our students struggled with understanding and applying grammatical concepts in French and Spanish. Traditional grammar teaching methods and textbook-heavy approaches overwhelmed many students, particularly those at the lower end of the academic spectrum. Given our inclusive approach, it was essential to develop a language teaching strategy that catered to everyone, from high achievers to those who find language learning challenging.

How did we resolve the issue?

To address these challenges, we restructured our teaching approach to make learning more concrete and reduce cognitive load. Our main strategy involved front-loading vocabulary and delaying complex grammar instruction until students had a solid foundation.

Strategy 1: Teaching grammar as vocabulary

In the early years, we taught grammatical structures as vocabulary items. Essential concepts like adjective agreement and noun gender were introduced early, but verb paradigms were postponed until Year 9, i.e. students learned phrases such as 'I am' and 'You are' without diving into the full verb conjugation tables. This approach built a strong vocabulary foundation and made students more comfortable with basic grammatical concepts.

Strategy 2: Using narratives and characters

We created a narrative involving three characters from different Hispanic countries: Pedro from Madrid, Marta from Colombia and Joaquin from Bolivia. This allowed cultural elements to be naturally integrated into lessons. Each term, students listened to texts read aloud, initially without seeing the written version. They identified familiar words and phrases, which boosted their confidence. Consequently, students were more engaged and could relate language learning to real-world contexts. Their listening and comprehension skills improved significantly.

Strategy 3: Parallel texts

We used parallel texts with Spanish on one side, literal English in the middle and idiomatic English on the right. This approach helped students to understand and internalise new language structures: students compared the Spanish text with the English translations, aiding their understanding of sentence structure and vocabulary, which improved reading comprehension and better retention of vocabulary and grammar. Activities that we used included:

- reading aloud and tracking the text with a finger
- chanting and educational games

- focused pronunciation exercises
- storytelling with gestures.

What about assessments?

When designing assessments, we focused on what students have been taught, ensuring no surprises and fostering a sense of achievement.

- **Writing:** Starting in Year 6 or 7, students reproduced learned texts. They used it as a basis and were encouraged to expand on it. *Example:* 'Write about Pedro's day using the text that we studied, adding more details if you can.'
- **Reading:** We used familiar texts with comprehension questions to reinforce content and test understanding. *Example:* 'Read the text about Marta's family and answer: What does Marta's brother do? Where does her family live?'
- **Listening:** We used dictation exercises to test listening comprehension and spelling accuracy. *Example:* 'Listen to the story about Joaquin's trip and write down the sentences as you hear them.'
- **Speaking:** We used practice questions from texts to assess speaking skills. *Example:* 'Describe your favourite activity using phrases from the text about Marta's hobbies.'

What was the impact?

Our approach led to significant improvements in student outcomes, including better summative assessment results. Test scores improved markedly, especially among lower-attaining students, who showed increased confidence and competency. By Year 9, students were

> well-prepared for advanced texts and explicit grammar instruction. In Years 10 and 11, the adapted parallel text approach provided excellent preparation for GCSE writing tasks, leading to strong exam performance.
>
> The success of the Reach Academy in Feltham serves as an inspiring example for other colleagues and departments in language teaching. By focusing on vocabulary acquisition before introducing complex grammatical structures, they addressed a common issue in language education: students' struggle to retain and apply grammatical concepts effectively. This strategy not only made learning more concrete and more effective in their context but also reduced cognitive load, essential for better comprehension and retention.

Chapter summary

In this chapter, we've looked at how to plan and deliver a well-structured MFL curriculum that helps students to build their language knowledge over time.

- A strong MFL curriculum starts with understanding what students already know, particularly from primary school, so that phonics, vocabulary and grammar can be introduced in a logical, connected way.

- These key elements need to be carefully developed across listening, speaking, reading and writing, with regular chances to revisit and practise them.

- We explored how thinking carefully about curriculum intent, implementation and impact can shape not just what we teach but also when and why we teach it.

- Sequencing learning thoughtfully and returning to key ideas regularly helps students to make sense of the content and remember it for the long term.

- We shared a range of practical strategies, such as phonics routines, vocabulary games, grammar teaching and using authentic resources, all of which bring the curriculum to life in real classrooms.

- Throughout, we highlighted the importance of planning with clear outcomes in mind and creating regular opportunities for students to reflect, practise and grow in confidence.

- Ultimately, a well-planned MFL curriculum does more than meet expectations. It shows students that language learning is achievable, relevant and worth the effort.

Further reading

- *Huh: Curriculum Conversations Between Subject and Senior Leaders* by Mary Myatt and John Tomsett (2021) offers a thought-provoking exploration of curriculum leadership, with practical insights into how subject and senior leaders can work together to build a meaningful, subject-rich curriculum.

- The DfE's languages programme of study for Key Stages 2 and 3 (2013) sets out the statutory requirements for MFL at Key Stages 2 and 3, offering a clear framework to guide curriculum planning and progression across the key stages.

- Ofsted's 'Research review series: Languages' (2021) presents evidence-informed guidance on high-quality language education, with a focus on curriculum coherence, progression in phonics, vocabulary and grammar, and the role of cultural knowledge.

- The DfE's GCSE subject content for modern foreign languages (2022) outlines the expectations for the MFL GCSEs from 2026, making it essential reading for teachers designing a Key Stage 4 curriculum that aligns with the new reforms.

3

Retrieval practice, modelling, guided and independent practice

Introduction

Learning a new language isn't always easy. It takes careful planning and smart teaching techniques to make the process effective. In this chapter we will explore practical strategies, informed by research, to help your students succeed. These include retrieval practice, modelling, guided practice and independent practice. Each one can make a big difference in keeping your students engaged, helping them to remember what they have learned and improving their skills in the target language. Our goal is to give you simple, actionable tips to create a better learning environment for your students.

Retrieval practice

Retrieval practice is a powerful way in which to help students to remember what they have learned. Instead of just rereading or reviewing, it involves actively recalling information from memory. The concept of retrieval practice is based on the work of cognitive psychologists like Robert Bjork (1988), who argues that it helps not only in strengthening memory but also in identifying gaps in knowledge. When students struggle to recall certain information, it shows areas that need more attention.

Why does retrieval practice work? Every time students try to recall something, it strengthens their understanding and helps them to remember it for longer. This is especially helpful in language learning, where students must remember large amounts of vocabulary and grammar over several years. Ebbinghaus (1885) argues that retrieval practice helps to fight the 'forgetting curve' (pp. 62–78), which is the tendency to forget things over time unless we actively use or regularly recall them. By regularly including retrieval activities in your lessons, you can help your students to retain what they have learned and build on it over time.

Language learning is different from many other subjects because it is cumulative. Students need to constantly revisit and reuse earlier vocabulary and grammar, which means that they are naturally practising retrieval all the time. That is why this strategy is so effective for MFL lessons, as it fits right into how languages are learned.

Here are some easy practical examples of ways in which to add retrieval practice to your lessons.

Quizzes

You can use regular low-stakes quizzes as an effective way in which to implement retrieval practice. These quizzes should cover previously taught material to encourage students to recall and apply their knowledge. These low-stakes quizzes should not just be end-of-unit assessments but instead integrated into daily or weekly routines.

RETRIEVAL PRACTICE, MODELLING, GUIDED

Multiple-choice questions

1. English is more interesting than Chemistry.
    - A. El inglés es menos interesante que la química.
    - B. El inglés es menos interesantes que la química.
    - C. El inglés es más interesante como la química.
    - D. El inglés es mas interesante que la química.
    - E. El inglés es más interesante que la química.

4. Maths is as important as Science.
    - A. Los matemáticas es peor importante que las ciencias.
    - B. Las matemáticas es tan importantes como las ciencias.
    - C. Las matemáticas son tan importantes como las ciencias.
    - D. Los matemáticas son tan importante que las ciencias.
    - E. Las matemáticas son tan importantes que las ciencias.

FIGURE 3.1: *Example: Multiple-choice questions*

1	du wirst
2	Ich habe Tennis gespielt.
3	fell
4	She fell over (down) in the swimming pool.
5	I don't like
6	Er wird viel Geld verdienen.
7	danced
8	sie wird
9	She will study drama.
10	I saw many / lots of countries.

FIGURE 3.2: *Example: Retrieval roulette, an excel spreadsheet with a formula that generates quizzes randomly, adapted from Adam Boxer*

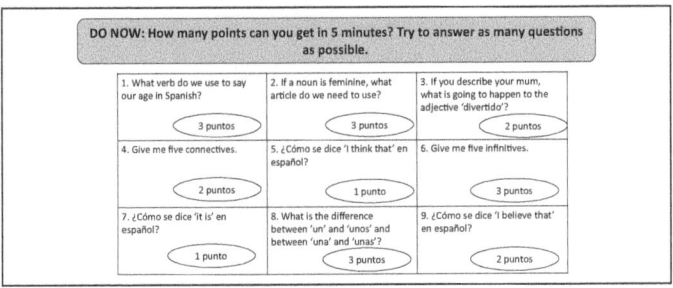

FIGURE 3.3: *Example: Retrieval grid, adapted from Kate Jones*

Flashcards

In class or as an independent study at home, you can advise your students to use digital or physical flashcards, which are excellent tools for retrieval practice. Tools like Flippity, Plickers and Quizlet can make spaced repetition easier by automatically showing flashcards at the best times to help students to remember them for longer.

Free recall

At the end of a lesson, you can ask your students to write summaries or reflections or do a brain dump on what they have learned. This not only reinforces their memory but also improves their ability to organise and express their thoughts in the target language.

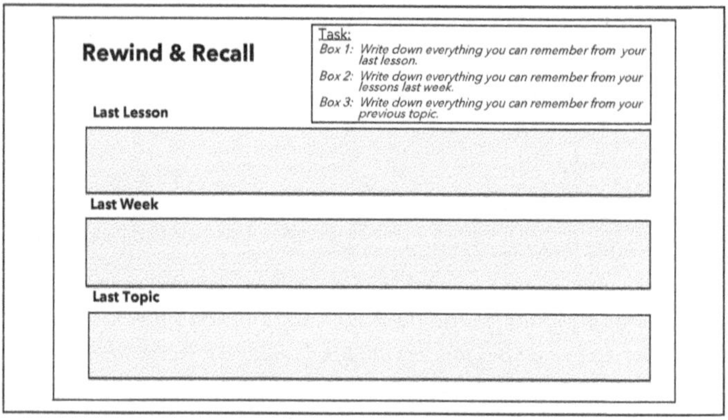

Rewind & Recall Last Lesson	Task: Box 1: Write down everything you can remember from your last lesson. Box 2: Write down everything you can remember from your lessons last week. Box 3: Write down everything you can remember from your previous topic.

Last Week

Last Topic

FIGURE 3.4: *Example: Rewind and recall*

Fast translations or questions

I often use this activity, either with mini whiteboards or verbally. I ask my students to translate words or phrases into English or the TL. Translating into the TL is more challenging and pushes their skills further. Sometimes, students work in pairs, taking turns in answering questions in the TL. Alternatively, I use the 'think-pair-share' technique to give them extra scaffolding and support.

Retrieval Run		Task: Try to answer as many questions as you can in full sentences. First person to reach the finish line will be the winner!		
Start	Wie ist dein Zimmer?	Was isst du zu Hause?	Was hast du gestern Abend gemacht?	Wo möchtest du am liebsten wohnen?
Warum?	Was ist dein Lieblingsessen?	Bist du sportlich?	Liest du gern? Warum?	Was wirst du heute Abend hören?
Was willst du heute Abend nicht hören?	Warum?	Was für Musik hast du am Wochenende gehört?	Wie findest du die Sekundarschule?	Was hast du getrunken?
Was für ein Instrument hast du gespielt?	Wohin bist du gefahren?	Wie muss dein idealer Freund/ideale Freundin sein?	Was wirst du am Montag machen?	**Ziel**

FIGURE 3.5: *Example: Retrieval Run as per the task*

Modelling

Just because you have taught something, it doesn't mean that your students have fully learned it. This is especially true in language learning, where knowledge builds over time. Many of us – me included – have said something like: 'I taught them the past perfect tense! Why can't they use it? I introduced it in Year 8, we practised it thoroughly with worksheets, different examples and personal pronouns. They even did well on the test right afterwards!'

But despite all that effort, your students may still struggle to use this knowledge in later years, like Year 9, 10 or 11. It can be frustrating and most MFL teachers can relate to this feeling.

The issue here is the difference between *performance* and *learning*. Students might do well right after being taught because the information is fresh in their short-term memory. However, it hasn't yet been stored in their long-term memory, which is key for truly mastering and retaining a concept over time. Rosenshine (2012, p. 15) argues in his fourth principle of instruction ('provide models') that providing models and worked examples helps students to learn more effectively. This is especially important in language teaching, where modelling plays a huge role.

When you model something in the classroom, you show your students how to use the language by providing clear examples for them to follow. For example, you might demonstrate how to pronounce a word, build a sentence or carry out a conversation. This gives students a clear picture of what is expected, guiding their understanding and helping them to apply the language themselves.

Modelling is crucial because it gives your students a concrete way in which to see how language works. It helps them to internalise pronunciation, intonation, grammar rules, vocabulary and the subtleties of communication, making it easier for them to use the language correctly and confidently in different situations.

Here are some practical examples for using modelling in your teaching.

Live modelling

Live modelling is one of the most effective strategies in your 'teacher toolkit'. It is a way in which to guide students step-by-step through a task, showing them exactly how to approach it. This approach not only helps them to understand the task but also develops their thinking skills. It is the first step in scaffolding, where you talk students through your thought process while solving a problem or completing a task, giving them a clear example to follow.

As the teacher, you guide and challenge your students as they learn. Live modelling works well for writing tasks; a visualiser is a great tool for this. When modelling, students shouldn't write anything; instead, they watch closely as you work through the task. Keeping them engaged is key, so ask questions and encourage them to share ideas. Model each stage clearly, from analysing the question and breaking down key grammar and vocabulary to writing the final response together as a class.

Thinking aloud

Thinking aloud builds on live modelling by making your thought process even clearer. This technique helps students to develop independence by showing them how to plan, monitor and evaluate their own work. You are essentially walking them (your novice learners) through how an expert would think. Here is how you can guide their thinking at different stages:

- **Planning stage:** (Before the task) Have I seen this kind of task before? What's my first step? What strategies can I use to tackle it?
- **Monitoring stage:** (During the task) Am I on the right track? How can I tell? Do I need to change anything?
- **Evaluation stage:** (After the task) What worked well? What have I learned and can I use it again next time?

Worked examples

Worked examples are incredibly helpful in language teaching. They show your students exactly how to complete a task, step-by-step. This is especially useful for breaking down tricky concepts like grammar, sentence structure or vocabulary use into smaller, easier-to-understand chunks.

Worked examples give your students a clear roadmap to follow. They boost confidence because your students can see how to apply what they have learned, making challenging tasks feel more manageable. Plus, they reduce cognitive overload by letting students focus on one skill at a time before trying it on their own.

There are a number of models that you can use, such as:

- **Deconstruction models:** Breaking down a complete example into parts.

- **Comparison models:** Showing good vs. bad examples to highlight what works and what students are aiming for.

- **Co-construction models:** Working through an example together with your students. I always do this under a visualiser. Don't worry, you don't need anything fancy – a basic camera works just fine!

- **Models of excellence:** Providing high-quality examples for inspiration.

Each of these approaches can help your students to better understand and apply new language skills.

Example: Deconstruction models

Examples of connectives:	**Text analysis**	Examples of 'other' people:
Examples of adjectives:	Am Wochenende spiele ich oft Fußball, weil es Spaß macht und gesund ist. Mein Bruder mag Fußball nicht so gern, er spielt lieber Videospiele, weil er sie spannend findet. Ich finde Videospiele langweilig, weil man dabei nicht aktiv ist. Früher habe ich oft mit meinen Freunden draußen Fangen gespielt, aber jetzt treffen wir uns meistens, um Karten zu spielen. Letzten Freitag habe ich mit meiner Familie einen Filmabend gemacht. Wir haben einen Abenteuerfilm gesehen, den ich richtig toll fand, aber meine Mutter meinte, er war zu lang. Nächste Woche möchte ich ins Schwimmbad gehen. Meine Cousine hat auch Lust mitzukommen, und wir werden danach ein Eis essen. Das wird sicher ein schöner Tag sein!	**Examples of present tense verbs:**
Examples of opinion phrases:		**Examples of past tense verbs (perfect/imperfect):**
Examples of time / frequency phrases:		**Examples of future/conditional:**

FIGURE 3.6: *Example of a deconstruction model text*

Also see the Morgan MFL blog (https://morganmfl.weebly.com/blog/gcse-writing-preparation) for more templates.

Example: Comparison models

Example of Grade 5 French writing:
Où es-tu allé en vacances l'année dernière? (Where did you go on holiday last year?)

L'année dernière, je suis allé en France dans un petit village au bord de la mer avec ma famille et mes amis. J'ai beaucoup aimé jouer avec mon petit frère et visiter le village. C'était cool. Le soir, j'ai souvent mangé des crêpes et j'ai regardé des spectacles dans la rue. C'était très amusant et relaxant!

(Last year, I went to France in a small village by the sea with my family and my friends. I liked playing a lot with my younger brother and visiting the village. It was cool. In the evening, I often ate crepes and watched street performances. It was very fun and relaxing!)

Example of Grade 8 French writing:
Où es-tu allé en vacances l'année dernière? (Where did you go on holiday last year?)

L'année dernière, je suis resté trois semaines au Canada avec ma famille. Nous avons décidé d'y aller pour découvrir le pays et la culture. Nous avons commencé notre aventure à Québec, où nous avons visité les quartiers animés de la ville. J'ai aussi beaucoup parlé français. Je pense que c'était génial. Ensuite, nous avons voyagé vers les Chutes du Niagara; à mon avis, c'était à couper le souffle. J'ai adoré et je voudrais y retourner dans le futur.

(Last year, I stayed in Canada for three weeks with my family. We decided to go there to discover the country and the culture. We started our adventure in Québec, where we explored the lively neighbourhoods of the city. I also spoke a lot of French. I think it was great. Then, we travelled to Niagara Falls; in my opinion, it was breathtaking. I loved it and I would like to go back in the future.)

Example: Excellence in Spanish

Creo que la tecnología trae muchas ventajas y paso mucho tiempo usándola. Mi móvil es muy útil: me despierta por la mañana, lo uso para charlar con mis amigos y para sacar fotos, y siempre miro mis mensajes antes de acostarme. Es muy fácil hacer la compra por Internet y suelo comprar todos mis regalos allí. Usamos mucho la tecnología en el colegio y tengo un portátil que me ayuda con mis estudios y es divertido jugar a videojuegos. Todavía no sé exactamente lo que voy a hacer en el futuro para ganar dinero. Mi profesor dice que debería considerar una carrera en educación, o posiblemente como abogado, pero esos empleos me parecen bastante aburridos. En el colegio, se me dan bien las ciencias y las matemáticas, y por eso he pensado en ser ingeniero, posiblemente en el ejército, porque habrá oportunidades para viajar y me pagarán bastante bien. Es una decisión muy difícil.

(I believe that technology brings many advantages, and I spend a lot of time using it. My mobile phone is very useful: it wakes me up in the morning, I use it to chat with my friends and to take photos, and I always check my messages before going to bed. It's very easy to shop online and I usually buy all my gifts there. We use a lot of technology at school, and I have a laptop that helps me with my studies and it's fun to play video games. I still don't know exactly what I'm going to do in the future to earn money. My teacher says I should consider a career in education, or possibly as a lawyer, but those jobs seem quite boring to me. At school, I am good at science and mathematics, and that's why I have thought about becoming an engineer, possibly in the army, because there will be opportunities to travel, and they will pay me quite well. It's a very difficult decision.)

Guided practice

Guided practice is all about giving your students a chance to try out new language skills with your help. It is the step between you showing them how to do it (modelling) and them doing it on their own. This stage lets your students practise in a safe, supportive environment, where you can guide them and offer support and scaffolding, as well as provide quick feedback.

By using guided practice, your students can gain confidence and improve their skills before moving onto more independent tasks. Activities like structured dialogues, role-plays, group tasks and language games work well here. Your role is to stay involved by circulating around the room, helping your students when they need it and correcting any mistakes.

Guided practice is also key to helping your students to avoid forming bad habits and ensures that they get the support that they need as they learn.

Here are some practical examples of guided practice that you can use in your lessons.

Choral repetition

Choral repetition is a simple but effective activity where your students repeat words, phrases or sentences together as a group. The issue can be that teachers sometimes don't spend enough time on it and move on too quickly. Here is how it works:

1. You say a word or sentence clearly.
2. The whole class repeats it back together.

This activity helps your students to improve their pronunciation, intonation and speaking confidence. Practising as a group takes the pressure off individuals and creates a supportive atmosphere. You can also give immediate feedback to make sure that everyone is saying the words correctly. Repeating out loud like this also strengthens memory and improves overall language skills.

Oral scaffolds and guided conversations

In this activity, you guide your students through structured speaking practice using oral scaffolds and guided dialogues. I often have my students work in pairs or small groups and provide them with scaffolded support to follow. These scaffolds could include prompts, sentence starters or key vocabulary related to the topic. These activities help your students to practise speaking with proper grammar, vocabulary and sentence structure. Students can rehearse what they have learned, work on their fluency and improve their pronunciation and intonation. By practising with peers and using your guidance, your students will feel more confident using the language. It is a great way in which to build their conversational skills while still having you there to help when needed.

Sentence starters

Using sentence starters is a great way to help your students to organise their thoughts and express themselves more easily. By giving them the beginning of a sentence, you provide a helpful framework that makes it less daunting to write or speak.

This approach not only helps your students to improve their writing and speaking skills but also boosts their confidence. You can create sentence starters based on your lesson objectives and adapt them to fit your students' needs, ensuring that everyone has a strong starting point to build on. To gradually remove the support, you can replace the words with just first letters or pictures to increase challenge and independence.

Example: Sentence starters in Spanish when talking about your personality

- *Pienso que soy...*
- *Sin embargo, no soy...*
- *Por otro lado, mis profesores piensan que...*
- *En el futuro...*

Cloze gap-fills

A gap-fill exercise is a useful way to help your students focus on context and meaning while practising vocabulary and grammar. You give them a text with strategically removed words and your students use contextual clues and their knowledge of the language to infer and fill in the correct words. This can also be used as a listening activity. Its aim is not only to boost students' comprehension skills but also to reinforce vocabulary and grammatical structures in a meaningful way. Your students will develop a deeper understanding of how words behave within a text, promoting better reading and writing skills. To make this accessible, you can provide a word bank with options for your students to choose from.

Drills

Drills are all about repetition to help your students to reinforce key language forms, such as verb conjugations or grammar rules. By consistently repeating these forms, your students can improve their accuracy and fluency. You can lead them in saying or writing these forms repeatedly to ensure that they stick and they can use them confidently in various contexts. This activity works well for practising tricky grammar explicitly, and they can be adapted to stretch and challenge your higher-attaining students with more complex structures.

Dictation

Dictation is a classic activity where you read a text or sentences aloud and your students write them down as accurately as possible. It is great for improving listening skills, spelling and grammar. Afterwards, you can review the text together with your students to correct mistakes and discuss any challenges. This activity is especially useful for preparing your students for tests and exams like the GCSE, which emphasises accuracy in listening and writing.

Example: Dictation

You will now hear four short sentences. Listen carefully and, using your knowledge of French sounds, write down in French exactly what you hear for each sentence. You will hear each sentence three times: the first time as a full sentence, the second time in short sections and the third time again as a full sentence. Use your knowledge of French sounds and grammar to make sure that what you have written makes sense. Check carefully that your spelling is accurate.

- Sentence 1: *J'aime beaucoup... aller au cinéma.*
- Sentence 2: *Mon copain... est amusant.*
- Sentence 3: *Le samedi... on mange... du poulet.*
- Sentence 4: *Nous avons visité... une belle... ville.*

Example: Dictogloss

This technique was developed by applied linguist, researcher and writer Ruth Wajnryb (1990, pp. 5–6). Here is how it works:

1. The teacher reads a text aloud. Students listen carefully and *do not take notes*.
2. After listening, students write down as many words as they can remember.
3. Pens are down. The teacher reads the text again and students listen carefully.
4. Students pair up and use their notes to reconstruct the text together.
5. Pens are down. The teacher reads the text for a third time and students listen carefully.
6. Students work with their partner again to improve or complete their reconstructed text.
7. The teacher hands out a jumbled-up version of the text. Students use this and their notes to check and finalise their reconstruction.
8. Students write a reflection about the activity: What did they find hard? Why?

Independent practice

Once students move past guided practice, independent practice becomes essential for helping them to become more self-reliant and take control of their own language learning. At this stage, your students are encouraged to take responsibility for their progress and improve their language skills on their own. During independent practice, your students work on activities independently, without your direct support. This step is important because it helps them to strengthen and solidify what they have learned. It also gives them the chance to use their skills in different situations and at their own pace, which makes their learning more meaningful.

Independent practice plays a key role in building student autonomy. By working on self-directed tasks, your students learn to take charge of their learning, set goals and find resources on their own. This not only enhances their language skills but also prepares them for their future studies.

Here are some practical examples of independent practice for your teaching.

4, 3, 2 technique

This technique was developed by emeritus professor of applied linguistics, Paul Nation (1989). The activity involves your students preparing a short talk on a given topic, but they can't write anything down. They start with talking for two minutes, then three minutes and finally four minutes. Depending on the class or age group, you can adjust the timing (e.g. one or two minutes) or simplify the task by reducing the number of topics or providing sentence starters for extra support.

4, 3, 2 technique		
❑ *You work in a pair. You have 5-10 minutes to prepare a 4-minute talk on the topics in the table. You may (not) write anything down.* ❑ *You should now deliver your talk to your partner who makes notes on a whiteboard on what they hear. Use your stop watch to time the 4-minute talk. Then swap roles and time your partner as they deliver theirs.* ❑ *You should now switch partners. Deliver your talk to your new partner but this time see if you can do it in 3 minutes.* ❑ *Switch again. This time you're down to 2 minutes for each of your talks!*		
You • talk about yourself: your name, age, where you live • talk about your appearance/personality	**Your family** • talk about your family • talk about their appearance/personality • say whether you get on with relatives	**Your free time** • talk about your hobbies: what you like/dislike doing in your free time and how often • talk about sports you like/dislike doing – why?
your school • talk about your subjects: likes / dislikes • talk about your teachers • talk about your school building	**your holidays** • talk about where you normally go on holiday • talk about where you went last year • talk about what you did	**where you live** • talk about where you live: a house or a flat and where it is • talk about where you would like to live in the future

FIGURE 3.7: *Example of the 4, 3, 2 technique*

Translations

There are various activities suitable for independent translations, such 'Quiz Quiz Trade' (one of Kagan's cooperative learning structures). For this activity, ask your students to write a sentence on a sticky note and then walk around the classroom to find a partner. If they can successfully translate each other's sentences, they swap notes. Students should keep track of their swaps and the one with the highest number of swaps wins.

Q and A

This activity involves your students working in pairs asking and answering questions. You could make this activity more engaging by turning it into a dice game or a board game activity.

Example: Q and A

Split the class into two teams. Ask the students to stand in two lines, facing each other. One line could wear funny glasses and the other line could wear Hawaiian necklaces – both items can be purchased cheaply in bulk online. Display a set of questions on the board relevant to the topic being taught. For example, for Year 7 Spanish, you might use:

¿Cómo estás?
¿Cómo te llamas?
¿Cuántos años tienes?
¿Cuándo es tu cumpleaños?
¿Cómo es tu pelo?
¿De qué color son tus ojos?

One line will ask the questions and the other line will answer. After one minute, have the groups switch roles so that everyone has the chance to both ask and respond. At the same time, rotate students within each line: the first student in one line moves to the back, ensuring that in each round students interact with a new partner. If there is an odd number of students, one can take on the role of a 'language police officer', who walks around ensuring that no English is spoken. Rotate this role every minute as well, so that everyone gets a turn to participate in the conversation. This activity is adaptable for any year group; simply modify the questions according to the vocabulary or grammar being covered.

Exam-style questions

Practising exam-style questions with your students helps to reduce their anxiety and boosts their confidence by providing a clear understanding of what to expect. By regularly exposing your students to exam-style questions, you also improve their time-management and problem-solving skills, which will lead to better exam outcomes.

RETRIEVAL PRACTICE, MODELLING, GUIDED

	SHORT WRITING TASK – INDEPENDENT PRACTICE
1 •	
2 •	
3 •	
4 •	

Task: Writing Strips! Write an extended paragraph using the bullet points to guide you. Once finished, double check for your work for accuracy.

FIGURE 3.8: *Example: Writing task, teachers can add their own bullet points depending on the topic*

Giving your students a chance to practise language on their own is essential for building their confidence and fluency. It helps them to use what they have learned in real-life situations and encourages creativity and critical thinking. You can keep track of their progress by trying different approaches. For example, you can circulate around the classroom to offer help, have regular check-ins, use self-assessment checklists or include peer feedback to see how they are doing.

Have you....	Tick
answered all parts of the task?	
included some connectives? (eg. pero / entonces / también)	
included a range of intensifiers? (eg. bastante / un poco)	
included opinions?	
ensured that opinions are justified as much as possible?	
used a range of vocabulary to avoid repetition?	
checked adjectives endings for accuracy? (what happens if it's feminine? What happens if it's plural?)	
checked that you have a verb in all your sentences?	
checked your tenses? Use your knowledge organiser to help you.	
checked word order?	
included some negatives?	
included some complex structures or idioms?	

FIGURE 3.9: *Example: Self-assessment checklist*

Using strategies like retrieval practice, modelling, guided and independent practice can make a real difference in how well students learn a language. These approaches help to build stronger memory, boost confidence and give students the support that they need to move towards working more independently. When used regularly and clearly, they make language learning more effective, achievable and rewarding for everyone.

REFLECTIVE QUESTIONS

- How do you currently incorporate retrieval practice in your lessons and what impact have you observed on student retention and recall?
- In what ways can you improve or diversify retrieval practice activities in your classroom?
- How effectively do you use modelling to demonstrate language structures and usage to your students and how successful is it?
- What challenges have you encountered when modelling language use and how can you address these to improve student understanding?
- How do you structure guided practice activities to ensure that they effectively scaffold students' language learning?
- What strategies do you use to provide feedback during guided practice and how does this feedback support students' language development?
- In what ways do you encourage students to take ownership of their language learning through independent practice and what outcomes have you observed?

CASE STUDY

Case study: How an approach of modelling and retrieval practice contributed to a significant improvement in students' uptake at GCSE
Name of school: Princes Risborough School, Princes Risborough, Buckinghamshire
Contributor: Esmeralda Salgado, Lead Practitioner, Head of MFL, Digital and e-Learning Lead, advanced skills teacher and Pearson National Teaching Awards Silver winner.

What was the issue?

I teach in Princes Risborough School, a comprehensive school in Buckinghamshire surrounded by grammar schools. When I joined in September 2023, I found a well-established MFL department; however, the numbers of students enrolled in GCSE languages was significantly below average: only 13 students in Year 10 were studying Spanish and ten were studying French. Our main target was clear: to increase GCSE uptake more in line with the national average, taking into account the fact that most of our students were not typical academic students. Why weren't our students taking languages to GCSE, despite having trips, extra-curricular activities and clubs? A thorough review of the department revealed that the main issue was a very cramped curriculum, which was not investing enough time and resources into prior knowledge and was not entirely following a specific language journey based on Rosenshine's principles (2012): modelling, structured guided production and independent practice.

Consequently, our students were not sufficiently confident and independent in their knowledge of the language and the application of grammatical structures, which, as a consequence, was contributing to a negative perception of the language, hence the low numbers at GCSE.

How did we resolve the issue?

If we wanted to increase uptake, we had to make two fundamental changes: reducing our curriculum at Key Stage 3, under the premise of 'less is more', and modifying our pedagogical approach to teaching and learning, based on Rosenshine's principles (2012). We made sure that only one topic per term was taught in Years 7, 8 and 9, with a clear progression to Key Stage 4, and we introduced vocabulary that was already part of the new GCSE syllabus. Similarly, we pre-established the vocabulary and structures that students needed to master by the end of a given topic via sentence builders, and we made sure that when planning our lessons we always followed the learning journey of modelling, guided practice and independent learning. This was underpinned by meaningful feedback, constant retrieval practice and interleaving of topics, so that structures could be embedded easily in our students' long-term memories – hence being able to use the language!

We created our 'pedagogical approach document' as part of our departmental handbook, where our philosophy was thoroughly explained with specific examples of activities for all teachers to use at each stage of the teaching and learning journey. At the model stage, choral repetition of small chunks became the norm, followed by a wide range of dictation and listening/reading activities for learning, aiming to retrieve vocabulary via meaningful input. Independent listening practice at Key Stage 3 was introduced every two weeks, not only to maximise listening skills – often the most difficult skill in the GCSE exam – but also as a means with which to retrieve and revisit vocabulary and topics every two weeks, via listening. All lessons started with a 'five a day task', which was our way to retrieve last week, month or even year's vocabulary and structures and apply this knowledge to the current taught topics. During our guided practice stage, again the retrieval of vocabulary and structures was the core, via the use of scaffolded translations from English into the target language through a wide range of interactive and meaningful games and activities, and many through the use of digital tools. Once in the independent stage of learning, we remodelled texts to showcase for students what was expected of them; we would share the thinking process when tackling a speaking or written task; we started carrying out specific games and activities to encourage students to start using the language within specific time constraints and be more creative with it. Again, retrieval was key here; without it, students could not automatise vocabulary and structures.

What was the impact?

The impact of these changes was clear: interest in language learning increased. Students' results in internal assessments improved; students' vocabulary had been better embedded into their long-term memory, thanks to interleaving and the constant retrieval in lessons, meaning that they could put it into use more freely. They started experiencing success and became more motivated. This meant that when GCSE options week came along, students' perceptions of their learning

> language journey was more positive. They felt confident, so they were more likely to pick up a language as one of their choices. We went from ten students studying French in Year 10 to 22 and from 13 in Spanish to 48. The impact was overwhelming, thanks to our committed approach as a department to reducing the curriculum and placing modelling, retrieval and guided practice at the core of our lessons.

Chapter summary

In this chapter we have explored practical, research-informed strategies to support effective language learning.

- Retrieval practice strengthens long-term memory and combats the forgetting, making it especially effective for building and retaining vocabulary and grammar.

- Modelling language use through clear examples supports learners in internalising structures, pronunciation and communication strategies.

- Guided practice offers structured opportunities for learners to try out language with support, promoting confidence and preventing misconceptions.

- Independent practice encourages learner autonomy and helps students to consolidate skills through set tasks in varied contexts.

- Combining these strategies regularly creates a supportive learning environment that builds memory, confidence and independence in language learners.

Further reading

- *Powerful Teaching: Unleash the Science of Learning* by Pooja Agarwal and Patrice Bain (2019) translates cognitive science into classroom-ready strategies, with a strong emphasis on retrieval practice and metacognition.

- *Retrieval Practice: Research and Resources for Every Classroom* by Kate Jones (2019) is a concise and practical guide that brings the research on retrieval practice to life with ready-to-use classroom examples across subjects.

- *Making Every MFL Lesson Count: Six Principles to Support Modern Foreign Language Teaching* by James Maxwell (2019) is a highly recommended book that adapts key pedagogical principles specifically for MFL, linking theory with everyday teaching practice.

- *Secondary Languages in Action* by N Servini, D. Shanks, L. Hameed and J. Violette (2025) offers summary of research and thinking on diffrent approaches to MFL teaching focusing on classroom application.

4

Adaptive teaching: Responding to the needs of all students

Introduction

Adaptive teaching is a learner-centred approach that tailors lessons to fit learners' unique needs, prior attainment and interests. By recognising that no two learners are the same, this approach emphasises flexibility in teaching methods, resources and lesson pace. Through regular formative assessment, teachers can identify students' individual strengths and areas for development, allowing them to adjust their approach as needed. Adaptive teaching fosters inclusivity, ensuring that ALL students can access the curriculum and succeed. It promotes engagement, resilience and autonomy, creating a supportive environment where every student can thrive.

What is adaptive teaching?

In an adaptive teaching approach, learners share the same objectives and tasks. However, the level of challenge is adjusted to their needs. This can mean increasing or decreasing the difficulty based on the learner's progress. Real-time adaptations are made based on immediate feedback gathered during the lesson. This approach involves:

- recognising the diverse needs and abilities of learners
- responding to these needs with tailored support and challenges
- promoting language learning and engagement by providing the right level of challenge for each learner.

Effective MFL teaching requires modifying strategies to ensure that all students can access the curriculum and progress, as well as responding to students' needs in the moment. It focuses on the unique strengths and needs of each learner. Adaptive teaching does not mean creating different curricula for various types of students. Instead, it enables teachers to address a wide range of learning needs without lowering expectations or increasing their workload. Essentially, adaptive teaching describes many practices already used in the classroom.

The term 'adaptive teaching' has now been used for several years and is incorporated into both the DfE's teachers' standards (2021a) and early career framework (ECF) (2019). The ECF guidance emphasises several key points for teachers, such as:

- Teachers need to recognise and address the unique needs of students through targeted support.
- Teachers need to consider how students' prior learning influences their current learning.
- Teachers need to maintain high expectations for all students.
- Teachers need to assess impact and engagement using strategies such as assessment for learning or book looks.

The ECF points out the availability of well-designed resources that are already out there; therefore, teachers don't need to create new resources. It also recommends flexible grouping of students, both within classes and across year groups, to optimise the learning environment for each student, including those with special educational needs in mainstream schools (DfE, 2019, pp. 8–25).

What is not adaptive teaching?

Different worksheets

Adaptive teaching is often misunderstood as simply providing different materials to students, which is a misconception. Adaptive teaching is not differentiation. Over the past few years, 'differentiation' has become less favoured within the teaching profession, due to its numerous negative connotations. Adaptive teaching is not about distributing different worksheets based on predetermined learning goals, such as 'all, most, some', or using fixed groupings in classrooms. Rather than setting static, one-size-fits-all tasks, adaptive teaching requires a more nuanced and responsive approach. It involves observing students' individual responses and adjusting instruction in real time to suit their evolving needs. Adaptive teaching is a dynamic and interactive process, vastly different from the more rigid, preparatory methods often mistaken for genuine adaptivity in teaching.

Technology only

While technology can be a powerful tool in facilitating adaptive teaching, providing personalised learning experiences through adaptive software or apps, it is not a prerequisite for adaptive teaching. The essence of adaptive teaching lies not with technology but with us, as teachers. It's about gauging learning progress and making decisions in the moment that respond to students' needs. Your insightful observations and interactions with students are the key – skills that you most likely already have and are using frequently.

Oversimplification

In addition, adaptive teaching does not mean simplifying course content to the point where academic standards are compromised. Rather, it involves scaling and modifying instruction to make learning accessible, while still challenging students. Another misconception is that adaptive teaching is only for students who struggle. In reality, adaptive teaching benefits all learners, including those who are more advanced.

Challenges linked to adaptive teaching

You might worry that adapting your teaching to cover various needs could slow down the progress of the curriculum. However, continuing to teach without ensuring that students have grasped key concepts means that they may fall behind and struggle to catch up. By adapting your teaching to spend more time on challenging concepts, students might actually grasp subsequent points more quickly, ultimately aiding their progress.

Frequent and effective assessment plays an important role in adaptive teaching. Having a range of strategies, such as checking for understanding, circulating the classroom or using low-stakes quizzes, can help with ongoing formative assessment and support students' learning.

Some students may already have a strong grasp of the material, leading you to question the benefits of adaptive teaching for them. However, even for these students, adaptive teaching offers valuable consolidation and practice. Regular practice and rehearsal are essential for transferring information to long-term memory, so additional practice will only enhance students' retention. At the same time, adaptive teaching allows you to challenge these students further, stretching their thinking with more complex tasks, deeper questioning or opportunities to apply their knowledge in new and creative ways.

What does adaptive teaching look like in practice?

Here are some practical tips that we can apply to support our adaptive teaching approach throughout every stage of a lesson.

Questions to ask yourself before the lesson

- Who are my students? Use the seating plan, students' passports and EHCPs (education, health and care plans).
- Are there any students with SEND (special educational needs and disabilities) or EAL (English as an additional language)? What are their needs?
- What is my students' prior knowledge? What do they know already and how do I know?
- What does their assessment data and classwork tell me about them? Do I have a 'full picture' of the class and what they need to learn?

- What are their barriers to learning?
- What are the common misconceptions about the topic or the concept?
- Do my students with SEND or EAL require extra materials or technology, such as a laptop to write?
- How am I going to address these barriers? Am I going to use resources such as texts, PowerPoint presentations or scaffolded worksheets?

Tom Sherrington (Sherrington and Caviglioli, 2020) advocates for understanding the 'zone of proximal development' for each student, a concept originally developed by psychologist Lev Vygotsky (1978). This theory suggests that teachers should target their teaching just beyond what a student can do independently, as this is where optimal learning takes place. In the context of MFL, this could involve recognising when a student is ready to move from using the 'I' form of the verb to another subject pronoun. For example, after a student has successfully used '*J'étudie* + school subject' (I study + school subject) with confidence, you might ask, '*Comment dit-on "she studies"?*' (How do you say 'she studies'?), prompting the use of the third person singular, or moving to the negative '*Je n'étudie pas*', etc.

Strategies that you might use during the lesson

- employing formative assessment and classroom circulation
- using diagnostic or hinge questions
- using mini whiteboards or low-stakes quizzes

- using checking for understanding during the lesson to inform immediate adaptations
- making spontaneous adjustments, responding to the students' needs then and there = responsive teaching
- using modelling
- using analogies relevant to students' experiences
- adjusting scaffolding (increasing or decreasing) or removing it as needed
- providing additional examples and non-examples
- encouraging peer support.

Dylan Wiliam highlights the importance of formative assessment as a crucial tool for adaptive teaching (2018, p. 56). He argues that making constant, agile adjustments based on formative assessment feedback can significantly enhance student learning. In our MFL classroom, this might involve using exit tickets to assess understanding after a lesson on verb conjugations, enabling you to identify who needs additional instruction and who is ready to move forward.

When I notice that I need to adapt my teaching, I do this immediately. What will benefit one student will more than likely benefit all of them, even if it is just reinforcing what they already know.

Considerations for after the lesson

- Reflect on YOUR observations from the lesson: did you cover what you hoped to cover?
- Did all students achieve the expected level of understanding and knowledge and how do you know?

- Which students will require additional support in the next lesson?
- Which students exceeded your expectations?
- Use this information to guide your future planning.

Both early career and experienced teachers can find it challenging to integrate adaptive teaching strategies into their daily planning and teaching, despite many of these strategies likely being already used, so the following section gives some practical ideas for how adaptive teaching can be integrated into lessons.

Practical examples for the MFL classroom

Example 1: Checking for understanding and application of grammar

Complete the sentences below by conjugating the *-er* verb in brackets into the correct form based on the subject given. Do not use your notes!

J' (aimer) _____ la musique française.
Il (travailler) _____ dans un restaurant.
Ils (regarder) _____ un film ce soir.
Tu (jouer) _____ au tennis après l'école.
Nous (étudier) _____ pour l'examen.

Bonus question:
Choose any verb from the above and write a negative sentence using '*ne... pas*'.

You can quickly assess individual students' grasp of how to conjugate *-er* verbs in the present tense by their ability to fill in the blanks correctly. Incorrect answers or patterns of mistakes can help to identify students who might need additional practice or explanation on specific aspects of verb conjugation. Students who answer correctly and confidently, especially those who can successfully form a negative sentence in the bonus question, demonstrate a readiness to move on to more complex grammatical structures. This example of an exit ticket allows you to collect immediate data on student learning, helping to inform the next steps in instruction, whether that be reinforcement for those who struggled or advanced tasks for those who excelled.

Example 2: Diagnostic questioning

Using diagnostic questioning is very powerful, especially, when students respond using mini whiteboards. This interactive strategy offers teachers immediate visual feedback on each student's current understanding and mastery of the material. As students write their answers on the mini whiteboards, you can quickly scan the responses, identifying who has grasped the concept and who may need further instruction. This instant feedback mechanism is crucial for adaptive teaching, as it allows you to modify the lesson's direction in real time, based on students' needs.

For instance, if a lesson focuses on conjugating *-er* verbs in French and a student incorrectly writes the conjugation on their whiteboard, you can immediately see this mistake. This enables you to provide specific feedback to that student or to decide whether a broader re-explanation is needed for the whole class. This approach ensures that teaching is responsive and truly adapted to the learning pace and needs of all students in the classroom, minimising the risk of students falling behind or becoming disengaged due to unaddressed misunderstandings. By employing diagnostic questioning with mini whiteboards, you embody the principles of adaptive learning, constantly tuning your instructional strategies to optimise student learning outcomes.

Another common example will be if the class is working on adjectival agreement in Spanish and you observe that several students are struggling with the position of adjectives; you can adjust the lesson by revisiting and explaining the rule, and then offering more practice opportunities using the mini whiteboards. There is no need to move on until students have practised sufficiently and improved. As a result, you might spend more time on it than you had expected, but you need to ensure a good success rate before moving on. It is also important to revisit this concept again later and in a different context, to ensure that students can recall and apply it successfully in various situations and through all four language modalities.

Tips for effective use of mini whiteboards:

Before using mini whiteboards, I strongly recommend establishing rules about how they should be used. This ensures that the whiteboards are tools of learning and not distraction. It is essential to remind students that they need to show their answers after a countdown; otherwise, some students will put their board up straight away and others will just copy. It also allows you to scan the room and determine whether you need to give students a bit more time so that everyone can have an answer on their board.

I remind my students that their work should be legible so that both the teacher and peers can understand what is written. Additionally, my students know that the purpose of using mini whiteboards is not always to get the 'right' answer but to encourage thinking and participation, so that I can adapt my teaching according to their answers and understanding.

As we continue to sail on the digital tide, it is essential not to lose sight of the foundational tools that have served us well for decades. Mini whiteboards are a testament to the idea that effective teaching tools do not always have to be high-tech, and they remain an embodiment of effective teaching and learning. These simple tools can be wielded to foster an interactive, engaging and dynamic learning environment, where there is active student engagement, teachers can give immediate feedback and mistakes are seen as a part of the learning journey.

Example 3: Multiple-choice questions, probing and process questions

Using questions that allow us to check for understanding, that prompt students to deepen their understanding by making connections between new learning and what they already know or that allow students to think is imperative. Multiple-choice questions (MCQs), as low-stakes testing, are particularly effective for diagnosis; they indicate what students might need to work on next and can give a specific diagnosis of conceptual understanding, helping teachers to identify what students know and what requires revisiting. Moreover, they are valuable for assessing students' understanding and application of grammatical concepts.

Below is an example of checking for understanding questioning in German. The main goal of this example is to demonstrate an effective way of using diagnostic questioning to gauge and enhance students' understanding of grammatical concepts in German, specifically focusing on tense, participle form and auxiliary verb usage. The technique showcased here involves a sequential questioning strategy, where each student is asked to build upon the previous student's answer, deepening their collective understanding of the grammar being reviewed.

Teacher: In which tense is the sentence on the board... Karim?

Karim: It's in the past perfect tense.

Teacher: Excellent, Karim! How did you determine that... Ellie?

Ellie: Because it has a past participle at the end of the sentence.

Teacher: Well done, Ellie. Can you tell me whether the past participle is regular or irregular... Eddie?

Eddie: It's regular because it starts with 'ge' and ends with 't'.

Teacher: Fantastic, Eddie! Why did you use the auxiliary verb *haben* instead of *sein*... Wiktoria?

Wiktoria: Because it's not a verb of movement.

Teacher: *Ausgezeichnet*! Now, you all have 15 seconds with your partner to change the sentence from the 'I' form to the 'we' form.

Looking at the example, you can see that the teacher uses a sequence of probing questions that progressively build on each student's response, thereby reinforcing and expanding the class's understanding of the grammar. Each question is tailored to review a different aspect of the sentence's grammar, such as tense identification, participle form and auxiliary verb usage. By addressing different students directly by name, the teacher ensures that multiple individuals are actively participating, fostering a more inclusive and engaging classroom environment. This technique also helps to keep students attentive, as they might be called upon next.

After discussing the theoretical aspects of the grammar, the teacher quickly shifts to a practical application task, asking students to work with a partner to convert the sentence from the first-person singular to the first-person plural form. This transition from theory to practice helps to cement the students' understanding through application.

The intent here is not just to show that the teacher should pause before adding a name, but rather to showcase a dynamic and interactive approach to checking for understanding. This approach efficiently confirms students' comprehension of multiple language elements in a single, fluid session, making it clear how these elements interconnect within the language structure.

Example 4: Constructive feedback

Acting on oral answers during the lesson involves responding to students' comments, addressing misconceptions and providing prompt, constructive feedback, all of which are essential aspects of adaptive teaching.

For example, in a role-play practice, students practise ordering food in a restaurant. A student says: '*Yo quiero lo pizza.*' You would respond with a clarifying question: '*¿Quieres decir que quieres la pizza?*' (Do you mean to say that you want the pizza?) This not only corrects the grammatical mistake (using *lo* instead of *la*) but also models the correct sentence structure. To reinforce the correct usage, you might then ask, '*¿Y si es pasta, cómo lo dirías?*' (And if it's pasta, how would you say it?) This encourages the student to apply the correct structure in a new context. You could also encourage peer feedback by asking another student to listen and provide feedback: '*¿Estás de acuerdo con cómo Sullivan ha pedido la pizza, Emily?*' (Do you agree with how Sullivan ordered the pizza, Emily?) This not only engages more students but also fosters a collaborative learning atmosphere, where students learn to give and receive feedback.

Another example could be when asking students to form sentences using *-er* verbs in the present tense in French. A student says: '*Elle regarder la télé.*' You gently correct the verb conjugation error by saying: '*Attention, "regarder" c'est* *l'infinitif. Comment conjugue-t-on "regarder" avec "elle"?'* (Pay attention, you used the infinitive form. How do we conjugate '*regarder*' for 'she'?) This prompts the student to self-correct to '*Elle regarde*'. After the student corrects the verb form, you can provide positive reinforcement: '*Très bien, maintenant c'est correct! Elle regarde.*' (Very good, now it's correct! She watches.) This not only acknowledges the correction but also reinforces the correct usage. To further embed the learning and ensure comprehension, you might then expand the question to include more subjects: '*Comment dit-on* "we watch"?' (How do you say 'we watch'?) This checks the student's understanding of other conjugations and deepens their grasp of the verb forms.

In both examples, feedback is not just about correction. It involves guiding students towards the right answers, encouraging them to think critically and independently and reinforcing correct language use through varied, contextual applications. This responsive approach not only corrects misunderstandings but also builds confidence and encourages deeper engagement with the language, central tenets of adaptive teaching in MFL.

Example 5: Visualisers

Visualisers are useful for sharing a learner's work with the entire class, either to highlight an especially effective method or to address a common misconception. For instance, when practising a grammar point with your class using the mini whiteboards, you could use a visualiser to display a few answers from students, asking the class whether they are correct or not and, if not, asking them what the problem is and how to fix it. It could also be used to display a student's written work that includes common errors. This allows for a live correction session, where the class can collectively identify mistakes and discuss improvements, turning individual learning moments into collective educational opportunities. Such interactive sessions not only clarify concepts for the student whose work is being discussed but also reinforce learning for others who might have similar misconceptions.

I also frequently use my visualiser to provide whole-class feedback on students' independent writing tasks. For example, in my Year 7 German class, after marking their work, I noticed that several students struggled with the correct verb order, particularly with verb inversion according to the 'verb as the second idea' rule in German. This observation sparked a lively class discussion on the complexities of German word order and prompted me to adapt my lesson to address this gap in my students' knowledge.

Example 6: Adapting vocabulary instruction – a responsive approach to enhancing spelling skills

This example underscores the student-centred nature of adaptive teaching. My actions were driven by the needs of the students, adjusting instructional approaches to better serve their learning preferences and requirements. A few years ago, I recall setting the first homework for my Year 7 French class, where I asked them to learn a list of set phrases. However, when I conducted a vocabulary test afterwards, it was a disaster! Although students knew the vocabulary, they struggled with spelling. Upon reflection, I realised that it was my oversight; I had not adequately explained the best approach to learning both vocabulary and spelling. Consequently, I had to do something about it, instructing the class to disregard the test and promising a retest the following week. I spent part of the lesson teaching my students how to effectively learn their vocabulary, using the 'guided vocabulary revision' technique shared by Dannielle Warren (see morganmfl.weebly.com for more ideas). This outcome prompted a critical reflection and adjustment in the teaching approach, which is a key aspect of adaptive teaching.

I realised that while the students could recall the vocabulary, their ability to spell the words was lacking. This awareness is crucial in adaptive teaching, as it involves identifying and addressing specific learning challenges that students face. Upon recognising the gap in students' knowledge, I promptly halted the planned vocabulary tests. This immediate response prevented further discouragement and confusion among the students, demonstrating flexibility in teaching plans to accommodate learner needs. By promising a retest and changing the approach to vocabulary learning, I ensured that the students did not lose confidence in their abilities and remained engaged in the learning process. This also reassured the students that their learning outcomes were important and that I was committed to helping them to succeed. This example of adaptive teaching illustrates how you can effectively respond to the immediate educational needs of students by altering teaching methods and materials based on direct feedback from classroom activities. It showcases the dynamic nature of teaching, where plans are not rigid but are flexible to accommodate and promote effective learning outcomes.

Example 7: Online collaborative tools

Students were tasked with writing a paragraph in the target language, which they would then upload to Google Docs. Peers and I provided real-time feedback and corrections directly on the document. This approach encouraged peer learning and made the revision process much more interactive and immediate. It helped students to understand common errors and correct them in a supportive environment, leading to improved writing skills. Additionally, it fostered a sense of community, as students engaged more actively with each other's work. For example, when giving feedback, start by highlighting what the student has done well, before pointing out areas of improvement. This not only boosts confidence but also makes students more receptive to suggestions. Instead of general comments like 'This is wrong', provide specific suggestions on how to improve.

This immediate insight allows you to adapt the ongoing lesson or future lessons to address these specific areas, ensuring that instruction is responsive to student needs.

Adaptive teaching is all about making sure that every student can access and succeed in their language learning. By being flexible with how you teach – whether that's through pace, support such as chunking or modelling, resources or activities – you can meet different needs and help everyone to make progress. It's not about doing something completely different for each student, but about knowing your class well and making smart, responsive choices.

REFLECTIVE QUESTIONS

- How effectively do you identify and respond to the diverse needs in your classroom?
- How do you ensure that your teaching is inclusive and responsive to the needs of all learners?
- How do you incorporate formative assessments into your teaching and how do you use this information to adapt your teaching?
- What challenges have you faced when trying to adapt lessons and how have you overcome them?
- Can you provide an example of a successful adaptation that you made? What about a less successful one? What did you learn from each?

CASE STUDY

Case study: Adaptive teaching in action: Improving learning through intentional monitoring
Name of school: Arthur Terry Learning Partnership, Birmingham
Contributor: Tracy Williams, Trust Lead for Languages, Languages SPL Arthur Terry SCITT

What was the issue?

By September 2022, schools were returning to normal post-COVID, allowing teachers to interact freely with students and provide live feedback. However, many teachers were reluctant to fully re-engage with these practices. During school visits across the Arthur Terry Learning Partnership (ATLP), a common concern emerged: how to encourage teachers to move around their classrooms, actively engaging with learners to provide high-quality feedback that drives progress.

Simultaneously, a shift towards centrally planned teaching resources was becoming more prevalent. While this approach reduced workload, it raised a critical question: was shared planning unintentionally leading teachers to deliver lessons passively, clicking through slide decks without fully considering what students needed to learn and retain? Without a deep understanding of the intended learning and likely misconceptions, how could teachers effectively check for understanding and adapt their teaching to maximise student outcomes?

These concerns highlighted a pressing issue: how could teachers be supported to engage in adaptive teaching, making real-time decisions to enhance learning?

How have we solved the issue?

To address this challenge, we explored Bambrick-Santoyo's concept of 'aggressive monitoring' and Doug Lemov's concept of 'active observation' (both cited in Lemov, 2021, pp. 92–102). Taking elements of both concepts and using the term 'intentional monitoring', we developed a framework to help teachers to plan for adaptive teaching: **AimTLP** (**A**ctivating **I**ntentional **M**onitoring **T**hrough **L**esson **P**reparation).

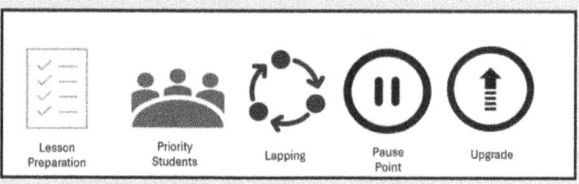

FIGURE 4.1: *Example of an adaptive teaching framework*

The AimTLP framework provides a set of structured questions to guide lesson preparation:

1. What key knowledge should students retain in their long-term memory?
2. Which key skills should students develop and be able to use?
3. Which prior knowledge must be activated to support new learning?
4. What misconceptions might arise?
5. What questions will you ask to check for understanding?
6. Which scaffolds will ensure accessibility for all learners?
7. How will students demonstrate their learning? What should their work look like?

Using these prompts, teachers could refine their lesson planning, ensuring clarity of learning objectives and equipping themselves to adapt instruction in the moment. Additionally, teachers were encouraged to identify six priority students per lesson, rotating over time to provide personalised feedback equitably. Another key strategy involved lapping, pause points and upgrades – a systematic way for teachers to move around the classroom with intent, assess work quality, pause the lesson to address misconceptions and provide opportunities for students to improve their work meaningfully. Through these strategies, teachers moved beyond delivering generic lesson plans to engaging deeply with the planned content and student needs, to drive better learning outcomes.

What was the impact?

Implementing the AimTLP framework transformed how teachers approached lesson planning and adaptive teaching. Initially, teachers found it time-consuming to answer the AimTLP prompts, but as they internalised the process, it became second nature. The framework shifted their focus from lesson activities to intended learning outcomes, enabling more strategic decision-making in the classroom.

Teachers reported increased confidence in their ability to monitor student progress, address misconceptions promptly and adjust teaching approaches in real time. Feedback from teachers highlighted the positive impact:

> *The AimTLP framework has helped refine my questioning and monitoring. It keeps me focused on the most impactful aspects of the lesson.'*
> (Languages associate teacher)

> *'It's a tool for thinking, not for writing.'* (Experienced language teacher)

> *'Using AimTLP helps me stay on track, ensuring I ask the right questions and provide meaningful upgrade opportunities for students.'* (Languages ECT)

Recognising its effectiveness, MFL heads of department across six ATLP secondary schools decided to integrate elements of AimTLP into collaborative planning for the new GCSE specification. This ensured that all teachers had a clear framework with which to adapt lessons effectively in real time.

Practical steps for adaptive teaching using AimTLP

1. Before planning a lesson, reflect on the AimTLP prompts. Does answering them clarify your lesson's objectives?
2. Be precise. Define knowledge outcomes clearly (e.g. rather than just 'the perfect tense', specify *je/j'* + *ai* + past participle).
3. Identify priority students in your seating plan and ensure that they receive meaningful feedback. Ensure that your priority students change from one lesson to another.
4. Lap with intent. Monitor student work strategically, pausing to clarify and praise excellence.
5. Use pause points effectively. Reteach or reinforce key concepts as needed.
6. Make corrections meaningful. Ensure that students engage deeply with feedback rather than simply copying answers.

The AimTLP framework has empowered teachers across the ATLP to plan with greater clarity, monitor with intent and adapt lessons effectively, ultimately leading to better results.

Chapter summary

In this chapter, we have explored what adaptive teaching means and how it supports inclusive and effective MFL teaching.

- Adaptive teaching involves adjusting challenge, support and pace to meet learners' needs, while keeping high expectations and shared learning goals.
- It relies on formative assessment, 'in the moment' decision-making and a deep understanding of students' prior knowledge, needs and barriers.
- Adaptive teaching is not about creating entirely different resources or simplifying content; it's about responsive, inclusive teaching for all learners.
- Flexible strategies such as scaffolding, modelling, diagnostic questions and classroom observations help to tailor support without increasing workload.
- Effective adaptive teaching in MFL means knowing your class well and making smart, timely adjustments to help all students to access, engage with and succeed in their language learning.

Further reading

- 'Moving from "differentiation" to "adaptive teaching"' by Jon Eaton (2022) explores the shift from traditional differentiation to adaptive teaching, offering practical insights into how teachers can respond flexibly to student needs while maintaining high expectations for all.
- *Responsive Teaching: Cognitive Science and Formative Assessment in Practice* by Harry Fletcher-Wood (2018)

blends cognitive science with classroom experience, offering practical strategies for adapting teaching based on formative assessment and student thinking.

- *Teach Like a Champion 3.0* by Doug Lemov (2021) is a widely used and practical teaching guide, presenting classroom techniques grounded in real practice to help students to succeed, with a strong focus on clarity, rigour and student engagement.

- *Teach to the Top* by Megan Mansworth (2021) challenges the notion of differentiation by encouraging teachers to raise expectations for all learners, offering strategies to support stretch and challenge in mixed-ability classrooms.

5

Supporting all learners, including those with SEND

Introduction

As a teacher, you have the privilege and responsibility of fostering an inclusive and supportive environment where every student can succeed. This is especially important for students with SEND and those who are struggling in language learning. By understanding their unique challenges and using targeted strategies, you can help them to overcome barriers, build confidence and make steady progress in learning a new language.

Understanding students with SEND and students who are struggling

Students with SEND and those who are struggling are often grouped together when discussing learning support, but their needs and challenges are different.

Students with SEND

These students may face physical, cognitive, emotional or sensory challenges that require specific interventions to support their learning. Their needs are often formally documented in plans like EHCPs. The goal is to give them fair access to the curriculum using tools like assistive technologies, adapted resources, adjustments such as larger font sizes or quiet workspaces. Examples include using text-to-speech software or providing lesson materials in advance. Other strategies include chunking of instruction and breaking new language into manageable steps.

Students who are struggling in languages

These students don't typically have diagnosed disabilities but may struggle academically for various reasons, such as limited prior learning, inconsistent schooling, socio-economic challenges or even lack of motivation. The main focus is on closing gaps in their knowledge and skills. This might involve extra teaching time, reteaching certain concepts, one-to-one support, tutoring or reinforcing foundational concepts in core subjects like literacy and numeracy, to help them to catch up to their peers and meet age-appropriate expectations.

Although both groups usually need significant support, the type of support can often vary. Students with SEND might need accommodations to address specific impairments like those mentioned above, while students with lower prior attainment in languages benefit from strategies that boost their understanding and retention of key concepts.

Challenges and support strategies

Both groups face challenges that can impact their ability to learn a new language.

For students with SEND

Physical barriers (e.g. hearing or visual impairments) or neurological challenges (e.g. anxiety, ADHD (attention deficit hyperactivity disorder), ASD (autism spectrum disorder) or dyslexia) can make language learning difficult. You can support students by:

- using assistive tools, like speech-to-text software such as Microsoft's immersive reader, a dictation tool or a laptop to write
- providing lesson materials and handouts in advance
- sharing lesson materials on coloured paper or encouraging students to use their overlays
- creating a stress-free environment with clear routines and supportive communication
- adapting seating plans to suit individual needs, seating them at the front or with a supportive peer
- chunking instructions into smaller steps
- checking in on them
- reducing cognitive load by not using 'busy slides'.

For students who are struggling in languages

Gaps in foundational skills like vocabulary, grammar knowledge or pronunciation can make advanced language topics harder. To support these students, you can:

- assess their current understanding and revisit basic concepts
- use visual aids and dual coding to reinforce learning
- provide regular practice and use formative assessments to track progress
- utilise effective learning homework
- use targeted intervention (break, lunch or after school).

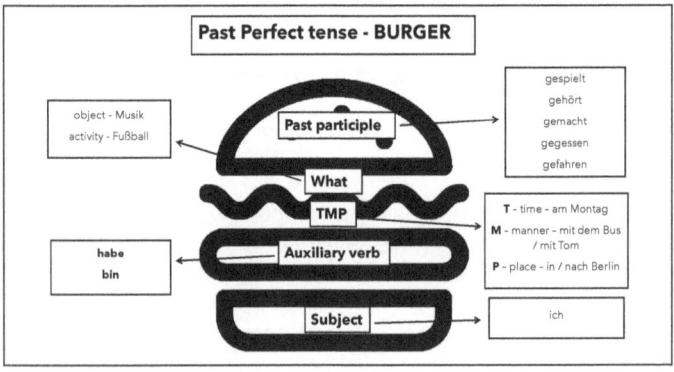

FIGURE 5.1: *Example: Grammar concept – past perfect tense in German (image credit: Freepik)*

Note: Initially, we would not include the whole verb paradigm

Students with lower prior attainment in language learning might have had little exposure to the target language outside the classroom. This might be due to factors like a lack of resources at home or few opportunities to participate in language-related activities. You can address this by creating a language-rich environment in your classroom. Use different types of materials, such as videos, music and interactive language apps, to give students more exposure to the language. Activities like role-plays or conversational practice can also help them to use the language in real-life situations, increasing their engagement and confidence.

Example: Role-play scenario: Visiting a French café

Objective:
To use French vocabulary related to ordering food and drinks in a café setting

Setting:
A small French café, complete with menus, tables, chairs and pretend food items

Materials needed:

- printable menus with pictures and French descriptions
- table and chair setups to simulate a café
- French music playing softly in the background to set the ambience.

Role-play:

Customer(s): [Enters the café and greets the waiter/waitress] *Bonjour!*
Waiter/waitress: [Responds] *Bonjour! Vous désirez?'* (Hello! What would you like?)
Customer(s): [Looks at the menu and orders, using phrases like...] *Je voudrais...* (I would like...)

Waiter/waitress: [Asks whether the customer would like something else] *Autre chose?* (Something else?)

Customer(s): [Looks at the menu and orders something else.]

Waiter/waitress: [Confirms the order, repeats it back and then says…] *Très bien, un moment s'il vous plaît.* (Very well, one moment please.) [Pretends to go and get the order, then returns to serve the food to the customer.]

NOTE: Do not forget your manners!

Customer(s): [After 'eating', asks for the bill] *L'addition, s'il vous plaît.*

Waiter/waitress: [Brings a pretend bill] *Voici l'addition. Merci de votre visite!* (Here is the bill. Thank you for your visit!)

Targeted intervention and support

Once you are familiar with the challenges faced by your students with SEND and those who are struggling, you can use targeted strategies to support their success in language learning. These strategies might include classroom changes, small group teaching, one-to-one support and scaffolding, as mentioned previously.

Classroom adaptations

Making adjustments in the classroom helps to create an inclusive environment for all your students. Simple changes, like reorganising seating, can make a big difference. For example, seating students with hearing impairments near the front helps them to hear and engage better. Visual aids like charts, pictures and graphic organisers can support your students with learning difficulties by adding a visual element to language concepts. Breaking down written instructions into smaller steps is helpful for your students with attention or language processing challenges. Regularly circulating around the room to check in on your students ensures that they stay on track and understand their tasks.

Smaller group teaching

Teaching in smaller groups allows you to focus on your students' specific needs, whether they are students with SEND, those with lower prior attainment or even higher-attaining learners. Smaller groups allow for more personalised instruction and interactive learning activities, which can help your students who struggle with traditional teaching approaches. For example, you can work on specific skills like vocabulary, pronunciation or grammar using games, sentence builders, flashcards and other engaging activities, while the rest of the class works independently on a task. I often use this approach even when I am teaching my mixed-tier GCSE classes, who might have different needs. Encouraging peer collaboration through pair work or group discussions not only improves learning but also builds social skills.

One-to-one support

One-to-one support, from you, a teaching assistant (TA) or a foreign language assistant (FLA), provides highly individualised help, especially for your students with significant challenges. This approach allows adaptive teaching that focuses on each student's strengths and weaknesses, with immediate feedback and reinforcement. Here, you can target areas like pronunciation, listening or writing skills, using multimodal techniques such as combining visuals, sounds and physical activities to improve learning and retention. Setting short, achievable goals helps to build confidence and keeps your students motivated.

Scaffolding

Scaffolding is a powerful strategy, where you provide temporary support to help your students to complete tasks that they wouldn't manage on their own. As they gain confidence and skills, you gradually reduce the support. For example, when teaching a new grammar concept, you might start by comparing it to their native language, using patterns and guided practice, and then slowly move to independent work.

A useful scaffolding tool could be, for example, a sentence builder or a structure strip, which is especially helpful for writing tasks in GCSEs or Key Stage 3. These strips outline what students need to write and include word counts and sentence starters. At first, the strips provide a lot of guidance, but it is important to gradually reduce the support as your students become more independent.

By using these targeted strategies, you can help your students to overcome barriers, build confidence and progress in their language learning journey.

SUPPORTING ALL LEARNERS 121

Write at least 90 words and you **must** include:
- what your hobbies are now
- why your hobbies are important to you
- what you did in your free time as a child
- an activity you and Lola can do together

20 words on what you like doing now	
Jetzt lese ich gern (reading)	
Jetzt sehe ich gern (watching)	
Jetzt fahre ich gern Rad (riding).	

20 words on why hobbies are important to you	
Ich finde Hobbys wichtig, weil sie… sind.	
Hobbys sind mir wichtig, weil ich siea… finde.	

20 words on what hobbies you did.	
Ich habe … gespielt (I played)	
Ich habe … gehört (I listened)	
Ich bin … gegangen (I went)	

20 words on future plans	
Wir werden … gehen.	
Wir werden … essen und trinken.	
Wir können … fahren.	

SUCCEEDING AS AN MFL TEACHER

Write at least 90 words and you **must** include:
- what your hobbies are now
- why your hobbies are important to you
- what you did in your free time as a child
- an activity you and Lola can do together

20 words on what you like doing now	
Jetz_ l_ _e i_h g_rn (reading)	
Je_ _t s_ _ _ i_ _ gern (watching)	
J_ _ _ _ fa_ _ _ ich g_ _ _ Rad. (riding)	
20 words on why hobbies are important to you	
Ich fi_de Hobbys wi_ _tig, w_il sie… si_d.	
Hob_ _s sind mir wic_ _ _g, we_ _ ich sie … fi_ _e.	
20 words on what hobbies you did.	
i_h h_ _e … g_sp_ _l_ (I played)	
I_ _ h_ _ _ … geh_ _ _ (I listened)	
Ich b_ _ … geg_ _ _ _ _ (I went)	
20 words on future plans	
W_r w_ _den … g_hen.	
Wir we_ _ _n … es_en und tr_ _ken.	
W_ _ kön_en …fa_r_n.	

SUPPORTING ALL LEARNERS

Write at least 90 words and you **must** include:
- what your hobbies are now
- why your hobbies are important to you
- what you did in your free time as a child
- an activity you and Lola can do together

20 words on what you like doing now reading watching riding	
20 words on why hobbies are important to you I find hobbies important because they are Hobbies are important to me because I find them	
20 words on what hobbies you did. I played I listened I went	
20 words on future plans We will go We will eat and drink We can ride Wir werden … essen und trinken. Wir können …fahren.	

FIGURE 5.2: *Example: Structure strips to support independent writing (idea courtesy of Wendy Adeniji)*

Building confidence and motivation

Creating a supportive learning environment is so important for building the confidence and motivation of your students with SEND and those who are struggling in language learning. By celebrating their efforts, offering positive reinforcement and promoting a culture of effort, and not only progress, you can also help these students to overcome challenges and aim for success.

Recognising and celebrating small achievements is a powerful way to boost confidence and motivation. For these students, language learning can be especially difficult, so it is important to acknowledge even the smallest progress. You can celebrate their successes with verbal praise, certificates, classroom rewards or even a quick email or phone call home. Praising a student for improving their pronunciation or correctly using a new word can encourage them to keep trying.

Additionally, sharing these achievements with parents or carers not only provides extra encouragement but also strengthens the support network for the student, helping them to feel more confident and valued.

Positive reinforcement is a great way in which to motivate students and encourage good behaviour. By giving clear and immediate feedback, you can show your students what they are doing well and where they can improve. It is important to praise effort and progress, not just results. For example, recognising a student's persistence in tackling a difficult language task, even with mistakes, can build their confidence and willingness to try. Using a range of reinforcement strategies like verbal praise, stickers, stamps or extra free time can keep students motivated and engaged.

Focusing on effort and growth, rather than just perfection, is especially important for supporting students with SEND and those who are struggling. This approach helps all students to see challenges as chances to learn and improve. You can foster this mindset by setting clear goals, offering regular feedback and showing a positive attitude towards learning. Encouraging your students to work together, such as pairing them with a peer with different strengths, can build teamwork, boost confidence and create a sense of safety and support.

Creating inclusive classrooms

An inclusive classroom is one where every student feels valued and supported. This starts with recognising and respecting the diverse backgrounds, abilities and experiences that your students bring to learning.

Using culturally responsive teaching is an important part of inclusivity. By including materials and perspectives that reflect your students' cultural backgrounds, you can make lessons more meaningful and engaging. Flexible grouping and collaborative activities can also help all your students to learn from one another, break down barriers and foster a sense of community. Creating an inclusive classroom also means making physical and technological adaptations. This could include arranging the room to ensure accessibility for students with mobility challenges or using tools like dictation software for students with disabilities like dyslexia.

Equally important is fostering a positive classroom environment, built on respect, empathy and openness. You can achieve this by setting clear routines and expectations, using inclusive language and celebrating the achievements of all students. Regular checks on progress and personalised feedback can help you to understand and meet individual needs, ensuring that no student is left behind.

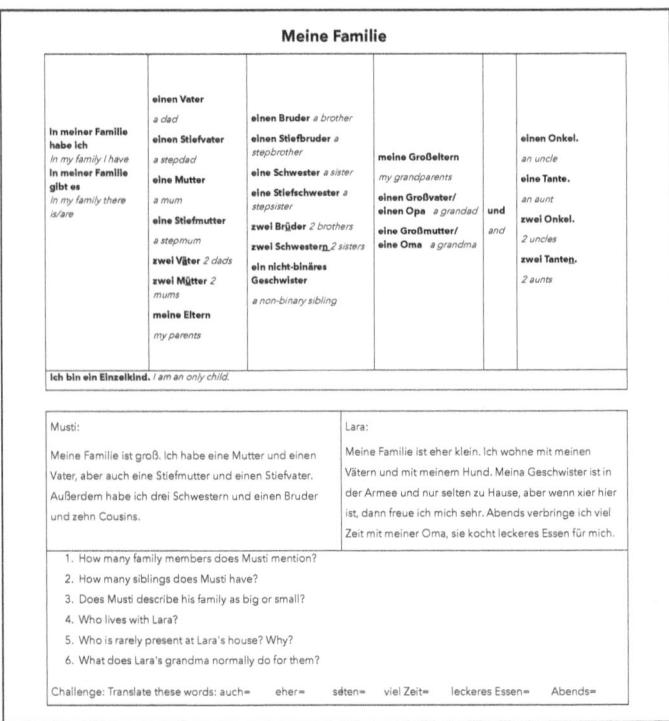

FIGURE 5.3: *Example: Inclusive language (with credit to Sharon Barnes)*

Supporting students with SEND and those who find language learning challenging means staying open to learning and working closely with others. Attending training, joining professional communities and working with colleagues, families and specialists like speech and language therapists can offer fresh ideas and valuable strategies. These partnerships help you to tailor support to meet individual needs more effectively.

An inclusive classroom is one where every student feels seen, heard and encouraged to succeed. By creating a space where all learners can thrive, regardless of their cultural background, ability or starting point, you enrich the experience for everyone. Helping students with additional needs requires a thoughtful, compassionate approach that builds confidence and removes barriers. With the right support and environment, every student in your classroom can make meaningful progress and enjoy their language-learning journey.

REFLECTIVE QUESTIONS

- How do you effectively identify and assess the unique needs and challenges faced by students with SEND and those who are struggling in your classroom?
- What classroom adaptations do you implement to ensure that students with physical and psychological barriers can fully participate in language learning activities?
- In what ways do you create a language-rich environment within your classroom to improve exposure to the target language for students with limited outside opportunities?
- How do you adapt your teaching to address the gaps in foundational language skills for students who are struggling and what specific strategies can you use to track and support their progress?
- What strategies do you use to build the confidence and motivation of students with SEND and those who are struggling and how can you celebrate their successes in meaningful ways?
- How do you collaborate with colleagues, specialists and families to create a cohesive support system for students with SEND and those who are struggling and what role does CPD (continuing professional development) play in enhancing your ability to support these learners?

CASE STUDY

Case study: Breaking down barriers: Enhancing language learning for students with lower prior attainment, including those with SEND, at Northgate High
Name of school: Northgate High School and Dereham Sixth Form College, Norfolk
Contributor: Vincent Everett, Head of Languages, author and speaker

What was the issue?

Traditionally, there may have been a belief among MFL teachers that students with lower prior attainment, including some with SEND, may not have benefitted from explicit grammar teaching. We assumed that the key was to motivate and interest them in language learning through communication and learning to say useful things, without worrying about the underlying grammar. It was suggested that once they had accumulated enough language, an awareness of grammatical patterns would eventually emerge at the students' own individual pace.

Recently, this view has been strongly challenged. It may be that this approach left students in a state of perpetual confusion over what words actually mean, starting with telling them that *Je m'appelle* means 'My name is'. These may be the learners who are least equipped with the cultural capital to figure the grammar out for themselves. They may, in fact, be crying out for things to be made clear and for little details to be explained properly, and not glossed over.

We set out to strengthen the clarity of explicit grammar teaching in our Year 7 booklets.

How did we resolve it?

Our lessons still had a communicative purpose – for example, teaching students to talk about what pets they have. But we were very clear with them that words like 'cat' or 'snake' would not be of major importance over the next few years of them learning French. What would be important in this case was the sound–spelling link, the concepts of gender, plurals and articles, and the verb 'to have', including negatives and contractions.

This meant giving explicit explanations in the booklets and in presentations on the grammar. Students did exercises where they had to transform sentences showing their understanding that if one word changed, then this would require a change in the form of other words in the sentence.

It meant teaching the vocabulary by explicitly asking students to apply their knowledge of phonics to new words, rather than repeating them after the teacher. And a great deal of time was spent on practising the pronunciation of the articles *un/une*.

We did not relinquish the communicative approach. Students were very strongly focused on asking and answering questions on pets and their names, eager to find out who had an owl called Archimedes. And we didn't exclusively tackle language through atomised grammatical rules. When it came to *je n'ai pas de*, we spent as long chanting it to a soundtrack of an accelerating steam train as we spent on examining how the apostrophe had eaten the letter 'e' in *je ai* and in *je ne ai pas de*.

What was the impact?

Firstly, I would say that there was no negative impact. Students did not lose their engagement with wanting to

> communicate – to use their French to interact, and with excellent pronunciation. A tweaked focus on grammar and form did not demotivate.
>
> In terms of success, it is still part of an ongoing learning process. In assessments, there were students who spelled *je n'ai pas de* as 'jernypadder', despite the focus on contractions and on phonics. But on the other hand, when in the following unit of work we learned '*le, la, les*', the students were able to successfully predict that *la étoile* would require the contracted form *l'*.
>
> Most interesting of all, in student voice surveys at the end of the first term, the vast majority of Year 7 students described their lessons as either 'good' or 'great'. And when asked to describe what they had learned, the majority selected 'I have learned some important things well' over 'I have learned a lot', which I think summed up what we were trying to do.

Chapter summary

In this chapter, we have explored how to support students with SEND and those struggling in language learning through inclusive teaching, targeted intervention and thoughtful planning.

- Students with SEND and those who are struggling have or might have different needs; therefore, support must be tailored, whether through adaptations, scaffolding or extra exposure to language.

- Practical strategies like classroom adaptations, small-group teaching and scaffolding can remove barriers and promote progress without reducing challenge.

SUPPORTING ALL LEARNERS

- Building confidence and motivation is key; celebrating effort, giving positive feedback and involving families all contribute to a supportive learning culture.

- Inclusive classrooms value diversity, make necessary adjustments and foster collaboration and cultural responsiveness in all aspects of teaching.

With the right mindset, professional development and collaboration, teachers can ensure that all learners, regardless of their need, can thrive in language learning.

Further reading

- The DfE's SEND code of practice (2015) is a statutory guide for schools and local authorities, offering a clear framework for identifying and supporting students with SEND.

- 'Five evidence-based strategies to support high-quality teaching for pupils with SEND' by Kirsten Mould (2020) is a concise summary of practical, evidence-informed strategies that every teacher can use to improve learning for students with SEND.

- *SEND Huh: Curriculum Conversations with SEND Leaders* by Mary Myatt and John Tomsett (2023) is a collection of practical and honest conversations offering real insight into how school leaders are adapting curriculum for inclusion.

6

Empowering the higher attainers in language learning

Introduction

Empowering higher attainers in language learning involves recognising their capabilities and providing them with opportunities to challenge themselves and excel. This chapter explores effective strategies for catering to these learners, drawing on insights from educational theorists like Mary Myatt, Tom Sherrington, James A. Maxwell and Megan Mansworth.

Ofsted's 'Research review series: Languages' (2021) addresses the importance of setting appropriate challenges in language learning to ensure student engagement and effective progression. It emphasises that a well-constructed curriculum should offer increasing levels of difficulty to match students' developing skills, thereby promoting deeper learning and retention. Effective challenges in language lessons help to maintain student motivation by aligning with their abilities and ensuring that they see tangible progress in their language competencies.

Understanding higher attainers

The National Association for Gifted Children (NAGC) has identified myths and facts about the most able students (2009). According to them, some of the myths are that these students don't need help, that they can help others by acting as role models, that the most able students tend to be the most well behaved in class and that all children are gifted in one way or another. However, some of the facts highlighted by the NAGC are that students with disabilities can also be high attainers, that the most able students do not always gain the highest grades and that they require challenging tasks (and this does not necessarily involve extra resources).

Higher attainers in language learning are students who exhibit advanced comprehension and communication skills relative to their age or grade level, a strong ability to make connections and an eagerness to explore subjects in depth. These learners often benefit from enriched learning environments that challenge their intellectual capacities. For instance, a higher attainer might be quick to understand grammatical concepts and able to use them in conversation, but they need opportunities to explore these concepts in varied and complex scenarios in order to stay engaged and progress. You can support these students by providing tasks that challenge their cognitive abilities and by encouraging them to apply their language skills in complex, real-world contexts.

Mary Myatt (2016) advocates for high challenge coupled with low threat environments, allowing students to explore complex ideas without fear of failure. This might mean engaging students in advanced literature studies, for example, or using more authentic materials. The following websites provide some opportunities to use languages in authentic contexts:

- 1 jour 1 actu: www.1jour1actu.com
- News in slow Spanish: www.newsinslowspanish.com

- Slow German: https://slowgerman.com
- Zdf: www.zdf.de/kinder/logo
- Kindernetz: www.kindernetz.de

A high attainer in the languages classroom typically exhibits several distinct characteristics that contribute to their success in language learning. They aren't just the ones who get full marks on a vocab test; they're the ones who really engage with the subject. They show a natural curiosity – not just about the language, but also about the culture, the people and how things are said differently. They'll ask random but thoughtful questions, like 'Why do they say it like that in Spanish but not in English?'. They usually pick things up quickly, especially vocab and pronunciation, and they seem to retain new structures without needing as much repetition.

You'll also notice that they make links between topics and grammar points. They might spot that a rule that they learned last term pops up again in a new context, or they'll find a way in which to use something that they've learned before without being prompted. They're not afraid to experiment either, trying out longer sentences, throwing in new phrases or even asking to use a word that they saw in a song or film.

They often go beyond the classroom too. Some will look up things on their own, watch foreign shows or try out Duolingo in their spare time. It's not about being perfect; it's that they're interested, switched on and not afraid to give things a try.

Underachievement among higher attainers

Despite their capabilities, higher attainers can sometimes underachieve, often due to a lack of sufficient challenge and engagement in the classroom. Without proper attention, these students might feel under-stimulated, leading to disengagement or disruptive behaviour.

One common issue is that high attainers may rush through their work, sacrificing depth and thoroughness for speed. Conversely, some may work excessively slowly, focusing too intently on minor details, which can impede their overall progress. These students can also be risk-averse, preferring to stick to known structures and vocabulary to ensure high marks, thus limiting their exposure to more complex language uses. This tendency to do the minimum required to secure top grades can lead to a superficial understanding, rather than a profound mastery of the language. Other high attainers sometimes overcomplicate their work, introducing unnecessary complexity that can detract from the clarity and effectiveness of their communication in the target language. Additionally, their quick grasp of language concepts can lead to boredom, which might manifest as disruptive behaviour in the classroom. Moreover, introverted high attainers may struggle with oral components of the language, preferring written work, where they feel more control and less exposure.

Addressing these challenges requires using a range of teaching strategies that engage students at the appropriate level of challenge, encouraging risk-taking in a supportive environment and fostering a balance between speed and accuracy, to maximise students' potential in MFL. Recognising the signs of underachievement is crucial for timely intervention.

Stretch and challenge

Tom Sherrington and Olivier Caviglioli (2020) talk about teaching to the top, identifying five relevant points (pp. 68–69). They refer to the following:

EMPOWERING THE HIGHER ATTAINERS 137

1. Pitch it up. Ensure that the curriculum is rich in challenge, including elements of difficulty to stretch all students. Adjust the level of challenge and difficulty responsively, depending on the degree of success that your students experience. Good curriculum planning should give a sense of the material that represents genuinely ambitious knowledge goals.

2. Use mixed-attainment classes rather than mixed-ability. Ability can be misunderstood and regarded (falsely) as a fixed characteristic. Identify the students who are the most confident and knowledgeable, based on objective assessments. Find out what they are capable of without presuming any limits. Set demanding tasks to test where they begin to experience significant difficulty.

3. Consider the heart of the concept: plan and teach so that the conceptual depth and sophistication of the material or degree of practical difficulty are always demanding for your highest attainers. This should be supported by the questions, tasks and problems that you set. These students should never feel that they are being held back or that the work is too easy.

4. Having planned the pathway for the top, consider appropriate forms of scaffolding to support the remaining students to reach the same standards, albeit with more help, guidance and time. Switch thinking from 'How can I make it easier for you?' to 'How can I help you to climb higher?'.

5. It's vital that high challenge is not viewed as a constant struggle. Everyone needs practice, including high attainers. Less confident students need more guided

practice; more confident students move rapidly to independent practice. Plan a range of practice tasks within your 'teach to the top' approach, adjusting in response to students' performance.

When aiming high to build confidence and resilience within our students, it's important to articulate and tell them that it will not be easy but that you believe that they can do it. You could say something like: 'I know this is going to be difficult but we are doing it because I believe in you and I know that you can achieve it. You are going to find it challenging, but if you think logically, lean on what you know, use your skills and demonstrate resilience, I'm sure you'll be able to succeed. I believe in you.'

Challenge is not an extension task and is not for the 'gifted and talented'. Low challenge is when students are engaged in tasks that are low-level; they may be 'working' but they are not thinking. They might be active, but their cognitive engagement is minimal and sometimes the thought process involved is trivial.

James A. Maxwell (2019, pp. 19-20) notes that struggle is beneficial when it challenges students in ways that support effective language learning over time. In MFL, appropriately pitched challenge helps students to develop procedural knowledge of grammar, vocabulary and discourse rules. You are looking for deep thinking; you want students to think hard and have plenty of opportunities for deliberate practice.

Maxwell goes on to say that if you want to increase the challenge in your lessons, you need to ask questions and devise activities that require students to apply their knowledge, analyse, synthesise and evaluate (Chapter 1, pp. 17–31).

- Do you accept one-word answers from your students, even when you know that they could answer by giving you a longer response?

- Do you let students say things in English, even if you have taught them how to say it in the target language?
- Do you always set high expectations for your students?
- How do you ensure that you are not being fooled into the false proxy that busy, engaged students equates to high-level challenge?
- How do you make it normal to do things that are difficult, challenging and academic in your classroom?

You can do this through both tasks *in* the language and tasks that involve thinking *about* the language. Do students have, at some point in your lessons, a time where their brain hurts – when it's harder?

What does stretch and challenge look like in practice?

It's essential to remember that what you do for the higher attainers will benefit all students in the classroom. It's not about doing something different; it's about teaching to the top and ensuring that you have scaffolds in place to support the weaker students. To effectively stretch and challenge students in lessons, you can adopt several practical strategies. First, you should set expectations for students to always extend their sentences, encouraging them to build complexity and depth in their communication. By providing opportunities for students to apply their linguistic knowledge and skills in various contexts, they foster a deeper understanding and greater skill proficiency. Demonstrating excellence in language use, perhaps through exemplary works or advanced language structures, can inspire students and set a high benchmark for quality. Incorporating real, authentic materials into lessons, such as articles, videos and literary works, can pique students' curiosity and provide relatable, tangible examples of language use in the real world. Lastly, mastering grammar is crucial; thorough and methodical teaching of grammatical rules not only reinforces a solid linguistic foundation but also empowers students to experiment confidently with language construction. Together, these approaches ensure that lessons are not only challenging but also enriching, helping students to achieve a higher level of linguistic competence.

You also have to ask yourself the question of the target language. There's always debate about the target language and whether it should be used or not. When it comes to your curriculum, it's imperative to focus on progression and a step-by-step development of students' knowledge (a logical scheme of work, in other words). The target language can, of course, support this when done well. But it can also confuse students when done badly. A focus on students' use of the target language is more beneficial as long as students understand and make progress, step-by-step in their understanding. The target language can help in aiming high for all students.

You can start by using routines and then bring more complexity as students gain confidence. For example, have a greeting routine – *Comment ça va?* – with students answering that question and then adding a reason for why they are feeling good, OK, not great, etc. Then make students use connectives with it. To challenge students further, you can then ask students to say what their partner just said, so that they have to change subject pronoun and say something like 'He said that he is not well because he is tired' (*il a dit qu'il ne va pas bien car il est fatigué*).

EMPOWERING THE HIGHER ATTAINERS

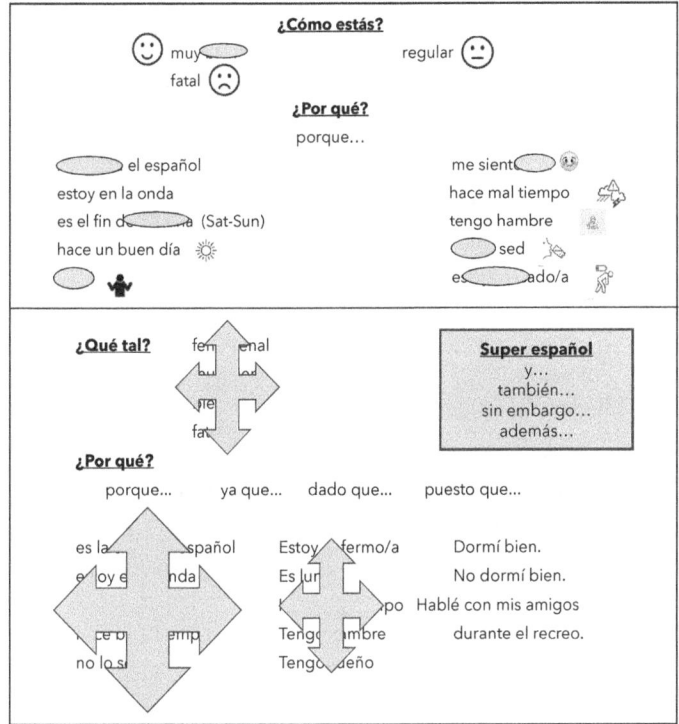

FIGURE 6.1: *Example: Progression in Spanish*

Other examples of challenging activities

Example 1: Puissance 5

An example of a challenging activity that could be used for speaking or writing practice is where students play '*Puissance 5*' and must use complex structures for it. The more that students use such structures, the more likely it is that they will become second nature for students and the better they will do in their exam if they are using them. Mixing the topics (as in the image below) also allows students to see that they can use the same complex structures with a range of different topics.

Puissance 5					
	Mon portable	L'écran	Les loisirs	La nourriture	La ville
After having done/eaten/finished...	👑	👑	👑	👑	👑
What I like the most is...	👑	👑	👑	👑	👑
To need...	👑	👑	👑	👑	👑
It's worrying...	👑	👑	👑	👑	👑
According to me	👑	👑	👑	👑	👑

FIGURE 6.2: *Example of 'Puissance 5' - template idea from Graphics Factory*

Example 2: Questions

Here are some questions to use when creating tasks, activities and assessments in the Bloom's taxonomy (1956) categories:

- **Remember:** Can the student *recall* or *remember* the information (e.g. vocabulary recall)?

- **Understand:** Can the student *explain* ideas or concepts (e.g. understand how to form the present tense)?

- **Apply:** Can the student *use the information* in a new way (e.g. use the rules for the present tense to conjugate verbs that they have never seen before)?

- **Analyse:** Can the student *distinguish* between the different parts (e.g. the differences when forming the perfect tense with *manger* and *rester*)?

- **Evaluate:** Can the student *justify* a stand or decision (e.g. what would happen if you wanted to switch two nouns around in the comparative)?
- **Create/design:** Can the student *create or design* a new product or point of view (e.g. design a lesson to teach a Year 8 student the perfect tense, thinking about the verbs they knew at this stage and how to go about it)?

Example 3: Authentic material

The image below provides an example of how you could use authentic material in a lesson.

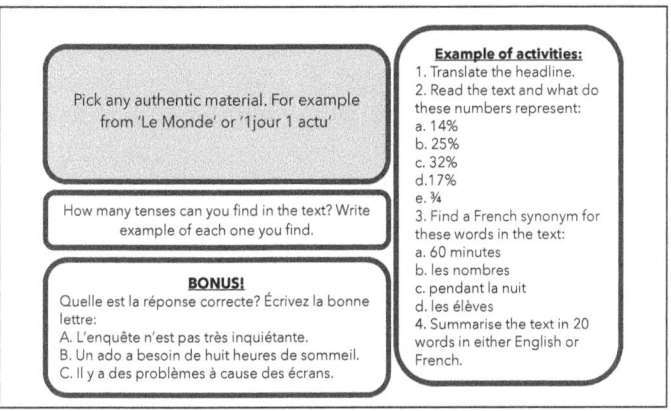

FIGURE 6.3: *Example of activities that can be used with an authentic text*

Example 4: Synopsis

Another activity involves using a synopsis before beginning the study of a film. For example, you can present the synopsis to the class and ask students to complete a range of tasks related to it. One option is to provide key words in the target language and ask students to find synonyms within the text. Alternatively, you can translate the synopsis aloud, deliberately including some errors; students must follow the original text and identify how many mistakes you make. You might also read a section aloud (or play an audio recording, if available) and insert intentional errors. Students should listen carefully and either raise their hands or make notes when they spot a mistake. This type of activity develops listening skills and deepens students' understanding of vocabulary and grammar.

Example 5: Mission cards

You could give students a secret mission card at the beginning of the lesson, and they must try to complete it during the lesson. If they do, they can get an extra point for their team or a merit. You can decide which secret mission card to give to which student, so it could be really personalised to them.

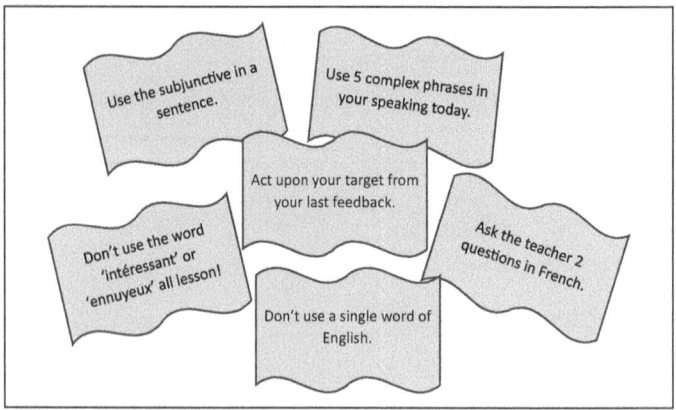

FIGURE 6.4: *Example of secret mission cards*

Example 6: Sentence extension

Another way to stretch students is by training them to always extend their sentences as much as possible, by starting with a simple sentence and seeing how far they can go, one step at a time. Articulate why each time the sentence is better, so that students understand what needs to be included to improve it (e.g. connective, intensifier, opinion, justification, etc.).

1. I love technology.
2. I love technology a lot.
3. I love technology a lot because it's very useful.
4. I love technology a lot because it's very useful but it's also fast.
5. I love technology a lot because it's very useful but it's also fast. On the other hand, I don't like forums because they are dangerous.
1. I like my mobile.
2. I like my mobile a lot.
3. I like my mobile a lot because it's fast.
4. I like my mobile a lot because it's really fast.
5. I like my mobile a lot because it's really fast. Furthermore, it's also very easy to use.
6. I like my mobile a lot because it's really fast. Furthermore, it's also very easy to use. However, I can't stand social media because it's ('they are') a threat.

FIGURE 6.5: *Example courtesy of Juliet Park*

Example 7: First letters

You could also give students the first letter of each word to form a sentence and students have to find which sentence it is. You could make your sentences longer each time to challenge students even more. For example:

- Jvtdlm: *Je vais télécharger de la musique.*
- Jvrlt: *Je vais regarder la télé.*
- Aarltjsaal: *Après avoir regardé la télé, je suis allé(e) au lit.*

- Ptjsaalpqjvrlt: *Plus tard, je suis allé(e) au lit parce que je voulais regarder la télé.*

- Aafmdjsaalpqjvd: *Après avoir fait mes devoirs, je suis allé(e) au lit parce que je voulais dormir.*

Example 8: Grammar challenges

Students can also be challenged with the grammar. There are plenty of activities that can be planned to stretch students and to make them practise conjugating in a range of ways, so that they end up conjugating with no problem. Martine Pillette proposes activities such as:

- **From one verb form to another:** You use *je* and students have to use the same verb but conjugate it with *nous* (e.g. *je vais/nous allons*).

- **From one tense to another:** You say a verb in the past tense and students have to give it to you in the present tense (e.g. *on a écouté/on écoute*).

- **From affirmative to negative:** You say the affirmative and they have to give you the negative (e.g. *je suis allé/ je ne suis pas allé*).

- **Grammar transference skills:** Students translate the following, then every week you use another verb but with the same structure. For example:

  a. I eat a lot.

  b. I am eating.

  c. I have eaten.

  d. I'll eat later.

- **e.** I have not eaten.
- **f.** I must eat more.
- **g.** I am going to eat.
- **h.** I want to eat more.
- **i.** I used to eat better.
- **j.** I had already eaten.
- **k.** I'd like to eat now.
- **l.** I could eat more.
- **m.** I should eat more.

Example 9: Torture Tenses

The 'Torture Tenses' idea from Liz Stillman works really well; it makes students conjugate key verbs in a certain amount of time and there's an incline of difficulty as students move from the 'I' form to the 'we' form, to the 'he/she' form and so on. The Torture Tenses can be used as a starter activity in one lesson every week. Only give five minutes for students to complete it – stop after five minutes, even if students have not finished. It only takes three minutes to mark. The students should know what level they are on each week and take the right level (coloured sheet) as they walk in. Initially, all the students start with 1A and if they get all the tenses correct in the time given, they progress to 1B and so on. If not, they have two more attempts at this level (or they could do more if you feel that they need the practice!). There are two marking booklets provided for each table and students mark their own work so that they can see what they got right and wrong. Students then enter their mark on a mark progress sheet stuck in the back of their exercise book.

TORTURE TENSES 1A - JE   Nom......................

YOU HAVE FIVE MINUTES ! Put the following infinitives into the first person singular form (**JE**) of the present tense, the perfect tense and the immediate future tense.

INFINITIVE	Present tense	Perfect tense	Future tense
regarder			
choisir			
manger			
attendre			
faire			
boire			
être			
aller			
avoir			
s'amuser			

/30

ANSWERS

TORTURE TENSES 1A - JE

INFINITIVE	Present tense	Perfect tense	Future tense
regarder	Je regarde	J'ai regardé	Je vais regarder
choisir	Je choisis	J'ai choisi	Je vais choisir
manger	Je mange	J'ai mangé	Je vais manger
attendre	J'attends	J'ai attendu	Je vais attendre
faire	Je fais	J'ai fait	Je vais faire
boire	Je bois	J'ai bu	Je vais boire
être	Je suis	J'ai été	Je vais être
aller	Je vais	Je suis allé(e)	Je vais aller
avoir	J'ai	J'ai eu	Je vais avoir
s'amuser	Je m'amuse	Je me suis amusé(e)	Je vais m'amuser

/30

REGARDER, CHOISIR, MANGER, ATTENDRE, FAIRE, BOIRE, ÊTRE, ALLER, AVOIR, S'AMUSER
1A   JE
1B   NOUS
1C   IL/ELLE/ON
1D   TU
1E   ILS/ELLES

REGARDER, CHOISIR, MANGER, ATTENDRE, FAIRE, BOIRE, ÊTRE, ALLER, AVOIR, S'AMUSER
NEGATIVES
2A   JE
2B   NOUS

POUVOIR, VOULOIR, DEVOIR, SAVOIR, DIRE, SE LAVER, VENIR, PRENDRE, METTRE, VOIR
3A   JE
3B   NOUS
3C   IL/ELLE/ON
3D   TU
3E   ILS/ELLES

FIGURE 6.6: *Example of Torture Tenses in French (idea courtesy of Liz Stillman)*

Independent learning

Getting students to become truly independent learners isn't easy. But for the more able learners, especially in languages, it can make a massive difference. Some students just seem to pick things up quicker; they remember vocab after one or two exposures, they spot grammar patterns without being told and they're curious about how language works. These are the students who really benefit from being given the space (and tools) to take control of their learning. But we can't just tell them to 'go off and be independent'. It doesn't work like that. You have to show them how to do it. At first, they need a bit of structure. You walk them through how to plan out a task, how to check their work and how to reflect on what they've done well or not so well. Then, slowly, you take the scaffolding away.

To cultivate an independent mindset among students, specific teaching approaches are essential:

- **Scaffolding techniques:** Begin by modelling an approach first – how to plan a paragraph or how to revise a topic – and then set a similar task for students to do solo.

- **Metacognitive skills:** Instruct students on how to analyse their learning strategies, including planning their approach to tasks, monitoring their ongoing progress and evaluating completed work to identify improvement areas.

- **Reflective practices:** Encourage students to regularly reflect on their learning experiences through discussions or self-assessments. This reflection helps them to enhance their future learning strategies.

Promoting independent learning is not without its challenges, which require thoughtful solutions:

- **Maintaining motivation:** Some students lose motivation when left alone too long. Implement regular check-ins and establish a peer mentoring system that fosters a supportive learning community.
- **Balancing guidance and autonomy:** Striking the right balance between providing necessary guidance and allowing freedom can be complex. Start with more structured guidance, gradually transitioning to increased independence as students demonstrate readiness.

Here are some examples of activities that you could try to foster independence:

- **Create and record podcasts:** Students pick a topic that they care about (music, travel, whatever), script it in the target language and record it. It's great for speaking and they feel like they're doing something 'real'.
- **Listen to authentic media:** Encourage your students to listen to audiobooks or radio stations in the target language, like Deutsche Welle for German or Radio France Internationale for French, etc.
- **Engage with literature:** Ask your students to read short stories or poetry in the target language. Start them with easy readers.
- **Annotate texts:** Give students a short text and ask them to highlight tricky words. Try translating it, breaking down the grammar and then summarising it in their own words.
- **Blog in the TL:** Ask students to write and keep a blog about anything that they want.

- **Creative writing:** Ask students to write diary entries, poems, fake emails or even short scripts. The point is that it's their voice and they're using the language to express something.

If you want your students to really grow in their language learning, they need to start taking some responsibility for it themselves. That means setting their own goals, picking out resources that work for them and keeping track of how they're doing. Things like listening to a podcast on the way to school, reading a book in the target language, keeping a blog or even chatting with a native speaker online can all make a huge difference. For high-attaining students especially, it gives them the space to stretch themselves, try harder content and figure out how they learn best. And with that comes confidence and real progress!

Motivation

Some students who are capable of excelling in languages do not always apply themselves fully. Some may do the bare minimum and therefore not achieve as much as they could. To motivate your students, it's essential to make language learning meaningful to them. When topics feel relevant to their lives and interests, they're more likely to engage and strive for success.

Another barrier can be fear, as some students worry about making mistakes in front of their classmates. To overcome this, it's important to foster a classroom culture where effort is celebrated and mistakes are viewed as a valuable part of the learning process. Encouraging risk-taking and praising persistence can help to build students' confidence and resilience.

Your own enthusiasm for languages and cultures can have a significant impact. Share your personal stories, whether they're about travel, cultural experiences or even language mishaps.

Students are also more likely to engage when they understand the practical benefits of language learning. Connect your lessons to real-world situations and highlight how knowing another language can open doors, both personally and professionally. From travel to careers in international business, government, education or intelligence services, the possibilities are wide-ranging. Helping students to see how languages can support their personal ambitions and career goals can be powerful.

Start embedding careers right from Year 7 and continue through to Year 11 and Year 13. Showcasing the relevance of language skills throughout students' educational journey helps to sustain motivation and builds a strong case for language learning as a valuable life skill.

There are many resources available to support this effort. For example:

- NST Group has lots of MFL resources that you could look at: www.nstgroup.co.uk/mfl-resources
- Halsbury Travel (2025) suggests five reasons why we should study languages.
- 'Where will languages take me?' (British Council, n.d.) is a collection of videos featuring real-life career stories from professionals in fields such as the RAF, GCHQ, government and education.
- Using guest speakers could also help. For example, David Binns from Sanako.com shares how languages have made him successful.
- Mingalaba (www.mingalaba.co.uk) uses the global appeal of football to teach and promote languages.

Incorporating these ideas consistently can inspire students to see language learning not just as a subject, but as a gateway to opportunity.

REFLECTIVE QUESTIONS

- Reflecting on the myths and realities presented about higher attainers, how can you ensure that you are not inadvertently supporting these myths in your teaching practices?
- What strategies do you employ to create a high challenge, low-threat environment in your language classes?
- Sherrington and Caviglioli (2020) suggest teaching to the top as an effective strategy. How do you use this approach in your lessons?
- What are some specific strategies that might effectively engage higher attainers in a language class?
- How does the use of authentic materials, like advanced literature or news websites in the target language, foster deeper learning? Can you share an example from your own teaching where such materials made a significant impact?

CASE STUDY

Case study: Listen, challenge, achieve: Stretching higher attainers in mixed-ability MFL classes
Contributor: Wendy Adeniji, school improvement and MFL consultant, leader, speaker and author

What was the issue?

A major problem for MFL teachers of mixed-ability classes is what to do to challenge higher-attaining (HA) students when completing listening activities. In the productive skills of speaking and writing, students can use more complex grammar structures and wider vocabulary, and in reading activities students can access more challenging texts and do more challenging things with them. However, during listening activities, led by the teacher, all students listen to the same item, so how can teachers make appropriate adaptations to ensure that HAs are sufficiently challenged?

The majority of Year 11 classes that I have taught most recently have included students with a range of prior attainment – in some instances with GCSE target grades ranging from 3 to 8. This is an issue many MFL teachers also grapple with. It is, of course, possible to split the class and complete a higher listening activity with students taking the higher paper and set students doing the foundation paper a different activity and then swap around.

How did we resolve it?

Sometimes, however, you need to use the same listening sound file with one class. Here are some activities that work well.

You can include a column of extra details if completing a table and ask HA students to fill it in as they go. You can also ask students to transcribe a particular sentence in the listening activity. This is a very effective way of developing their transcription skills and links well to the new dictation activity that is examined in the GCSEs in England.

You can also ask HA students to write their own extract afterwards, based on the recordings that they have heard. This is a challenging activity and before asking students to do this, it would be important to model it and to show exactly what you expect students to do. Another activity that I have found works very well is to take some words out of the transcript and either make it clear where the gaps are or do not provide the gaps, so that students have to listen even more carefully. Not providing the words that are omitted is particularly challenging, as students have no cues. Alternatively, you can provide extra words or mistakes in the transcript, which students must identify.

Technology can support students to have more individual listening activities. For example, I've used the Sanako Connect online platform as a virtual language lab, where I assign different activities to different students in the class, such as higher or foundation listening exercises. This technology allows students to slow down the sound files that they're listening to and also to play them as many times as they like, although the teacher can limit this if desired. Students can also listen to any text that is input, using AI-generated voices, and then repeat it and receive immediate feedback.

I also encourage students to watch foreign language programmes on Netflix and Channel 4 (*Walter Presents*) with the English subtitles, and to listen very carefully and read at the same time. This gives them lots of exposure to the language and they enjoy the storyline, but they also revise previously learned words, as well as learning new ones.

> **What was the impact?**
>
> The impact of thinking really carefully about how I deliver listening activities to stretch HA students is that these students have made accelerated progress in their listening skills. They have been able to achieve excellent grades in the higher GCSE listening exam, which is one of the most challenging exams that they take. In the classroom, HA students are no longer bored, having been given activities that are not sufficiently challenging. It means that, with a little extra thought and planning, higher prior attainers can flourish and make even better progress in the key skill of listening. It makes them feel more successful as language learners and gives them a strong sense of self-efficacy.

Chapter summary

This chapter looked at how we can better support higher attainers in language learning by making sure that they're stretched, challenged and given space to thrive.

- High-attaining students aren't always the ones who get full marks. They're often the ones who ask great questions, spot patterns and genuinely enjoy digging deeper into the language and culture.

- To keep them switched on, we need to offer them real challenge – things like complex texts, authentic resources and opportunities to think critically about how the language works.

- Challenge shouldn't be saved for a select few or tacked on as an extra. It needs to be built into the everyday classroom experience. That might mean raising the level of questioning, expecting fuller answers or asking students to apply what they know in unfamiliar contexts.

- Encouraging independence is just as important. Students benefit from learning how to plan, review and reflect on their work so that they can take control of their own progress. However, they need guidance at first. We can't assume that they'll just figure it out on their own.

- Motivation can dip if the work feels too easy or disconnected from real life. Making sure that students see the value of what they're learning – whether it's through future opportunities, cultural insights or practical language use – can help to keep them interested.

- If we set the bar high, support students to meet it and create a classroom culture where deep thinking is normal, our higher attainers will have what they need to flourish in MFL.

Further reading

- *Teaching WalkThrus 2: Five-Step Guides to Instructional Coaching* by Tom Sherrington and Oliver Caviglioli (2021) offers clear, visual walk-throughs of essential teaching techniques, including the 'teach to the top' approach.

- *Meeting the Needs of Your Most Able Pupils: MFL* by Gretchen Ingram (2008) provides subject-specific guidance for supporting more able learners in MFL, offering practical strategies and classroom approaches that ensure that these students remain engaged, stretched and supported.

- The National Association for Gifted Children's 'Myths about gifted students' (2009) challenges common misconceptions about high-attaining learners, offering clear, research-informed insights that help educators to better understand and support the needs of gifted students.

7

Effective assessment and feedback in all four language skills

Introduction

One of the skills that all teachers develop over time is that of assessment – both the summative (checking on learning at the end of a sequence) and the formative (to support planning and help students to see their progress). Ofsted inspectors are interested in assessment and also have an eye on the burdens that it might create for both teachers and learners. The task of effectively assessing and providing feedback in a language classroom is both a crucial and a complex endeavour.

Building an effective framework for MFL assessment

'Refocusing assessment' (SSAT, ASCL and NFER, 2017) is a resource put together by National Foundation for Educational Research to support schools in developing and reviewing their assessment practice. It identifies five key questions for all departments but here is the set for languages:

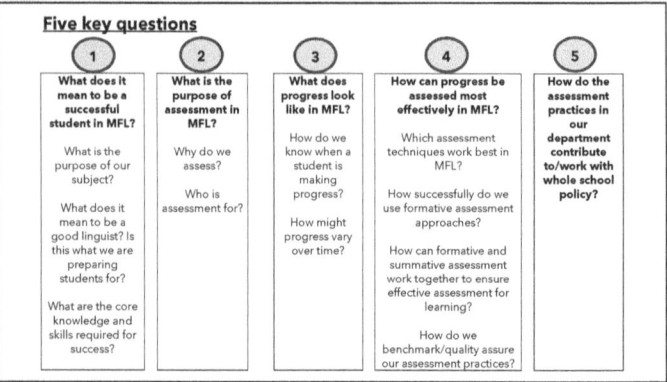

FIGURE 7.1: *SSAT, ASCL and NFER (2017). Refocusing Assessment [online]. Available: https://www.nfer.ac.uk/publications/refocusing-assessment*

Here's why the five key questions are important:

1. **Defining success:** By defining what success looks like for a student in MFL, you can align your teaching strategies, objectives and outcomes, ensuring that students are equipped with the necessary knowledge and skills.

2. **Purpose of assessment:** Understanding the purpose of assessment helps the department to ensure that evaluations are meaningful and beneficial to both students and teachers. It aids in tracking progress, identifying areas needing improvement and validating the effectiveness of the curriculum and teaching methods.

3. **Understanding progress:** Knowing what progress looks like in MFL enables you to recognise achievements and challenges in students' language acquisition over time. It also helps in customising instruction to meet diverse learning needs and pace.

4. **Effective assessment methods:** Discussing and determining the most effective assessment strategies can lead to more accurate and fair evaluations of student performance. It encourages the use of varied methods like formative and summative assessments to support and reflect actual learning.

5. **Alignment with school policy:** Ensuring that MFL assessment practices align with the broader school policies promotes coherence and supports school-wide educational goals. It also fosters a consistent approach to student assessment across different departments, enhancing the educational experience school-wide.

By examining these questions collectively, your MFL department can create a more integrated and effective approach to teaching and learning, promoting better educational outcomes for students and a more unified strategy across the department.

Your first step would be to think about your planning to create successful students. You will need to ask yourself what you want students to remember long after finishing the current unit, module, topic or even key stage. What is the most important, most useful knowledge for your students to retain in long-term memory? How will your students know what needs to be known? When will you present and then revisit things like grammar, tenses, key structures or vocabulary?

Start where students are and not where you as the teacher want students to be. Learning does not happen in the moment; learning is a change in the long-term memory.

Two of the major purposes of assessment are to check on students' understanding (in order to inform teaching) and to help students to embed and use knowledge fluently and develop understanding, rather than simply memorising disconnected details. So, questions that teachers or departments can ask themselves when reflecting on a unit of work include:

- What have students understood?
- Are there any possible misunderstandings?
- Are misconceptions addressed?
- What connections have they made with previous learning?

It may be that the department can share strategies for the informal, light-touch spotting of things that may slow or disturb the progression of the students, remembering that while assessment needs to be regular, consistent and purposeful, it should not interrupt the flow of learning and teaching.

Formative assessment

Formative assessment plays a pivotal role in the teaching of languages in England. The concept of formative assessment was significantly shaped by the research of Paul Black and Dylan Wiliam, particularly their seminal work *Inside the Black Box* (1998). In this study, Black and Wiliam define formative assessment as all those activities undertaken by teachers – and by their students in assessing themselves – that provide information to be used as feedback to modify the teaching and learning activities in which they are engaged (page 140 Vol. 80, No. 2). This feedback mechanism is crucial in MFL, where real-time responses to linguistic accuracy and fluency can greatly influence learner outcomes.

Principles of formative assessment in MFL

In the context of MFL, formative assessment incorporates several key principles:

- **Learner involvement:** Students are encouraged to participate actively in their learning process. They engage in self-assessment and peer assessment, reflecting on their language use and learning strategies.
- **Effective feedback:** Feedback in MFL needs to be specific, timely and constructive. It should focus on language use, pronunciation, grammar and cultural context, guiding learners towards targeted improvements.
- **Adaptive teaching:** Teachers use the insights gained from formative assessments to adjust their instructional strategies. This may involve altering lesson plans, teaching techniques or even class interactions to better suit the learners' needs.

Strategies for implementation

Effective formative assessment in MFL employs a variety of techniques:

Oral feedback

Immediate corrections and suggestions during oral exercises help students to refine their pronunciation and sentence structure. Responding to what students say, addressing any misconceptions and giving prompt constructive feedback are proved to be very effective.

Questioning

Use questions that allow you to check for understanding, that allow students to deepen their understanding by making connections between new learning and what they already know or that allow students to think. Multiple-choice questions as low-stakes testing are excellent for diagnosis; they indicate what students might need to work on next and can give a specific diagnosis of conceptual understanding.

Using hinge questions, such as the example below, can be very powerful as they help in diagnosing what the problem is. Is it pronouns? Is it sentence order? Or is it both? When designing hinge questions, it is key to start with the misconceptions in the language.

Which of the following is the correct translation for **'She sends the letter to us'**?

A. (Ella) nos envía la carta.
B. (Ella) la envía la carta.
C. (Ella) envía nos la carta.
D. (Ella) nos la envía carta.
E. (Ella) envía la carta nos.
F. (Ella) la carta nos envía.

FIGURE 7.2: *Example of multiple-choice question in Spanish*

A hinge question is based on the important concept in a lesson that is critical for students to understand before you move on in the lesson. The question can fall at the beginning (range-finding) or middle (mid-lesson correction) of the lesson. It should be diagnostic and not a discussion question. Every student must respond to the question within two minutes.

Multiple-choice questions (MCQs) can be effectively integrated with the 'heads down, thumbs up' activity. First, present a question and its possible answers to the class. Ask the students to silently consider which option they believe is correct. Then instruct them to place their heads down and extend a thumb for the answer that they chose when you prompt the options. This strategy ensures that students cannot see the choices that their peers are making. As a result, you gain insight into who understands the material and can identify any prevalent misconceptions that need to be addressed.

---

1. English is more interesting than Chemistry

  A. El inglés es menos interesante que la química.
  B. El inglés es menos interesantes que la química.
  C. El inglés es más interesante como la química.
  D. El inglés es mas interesante que la química.
  E. El inglés es más interesante que la química.

4. Maths is as important as Science

  A. Los matemáticas es peor importante que las ciencias.
  B. Las matemáticas es tan importantes como las ciencias.
  C. Las matemáticas son tan importantes como las ciencias.
  D. Los matemáticas son tan importante que las ciencias.
  E. Las matemáticas son tan importantes que las ciencias.

2. My ideal town would be in Spain.

  A. Mi ciudad ideal sería en España.
  B. Mi ciudad ideal estaría en Español.
  C. Mi ciudad ideal habría en España.
  D. Mi ciudad ideal sería en Español.
  E. Mi ciudad ideal estaría en España.

FIGURE 7.3: *MCQs testing knowledge of subject–verb agreement, adjective agreement and comparative structures in Spanish*

Circulate and listen

Go around the classroom listening in to students while they complete a pair speaking activity and then act on any misconceptions, mispronunciations or grammatical mistakes.

Use of mini whiteboards (MWBs)

Using mini whiteboards allows you to receive instant feedback on students' understanding of the material being taught. They should be used regularly in every lesson. Students can write answers and then hold up their boards for you to see. This immediate visibility allows you to quickly gauge whether students grasp the concepts, enabling real-time adjustments to the lesson plan. It makes the learning process more interactive and ensures that all students are involved in the activity. Because each student is required to respond on their whiteboard, it encourages even the more reluctant or shy students to participate, providing a safer, less intimidating way in which to contribute to the class. MWBs are a low-stakes tool that encourages students to take risks with their answers. Students can easily erase and correct their mistakes, promoting a growth mindset where errors are seen as a natural part of the learning process. This method is time-efficient in providing a quick check of student understanding across the entire class. You can swiftly identify areas of misunderstanding or confusion and address them promptly within the lesson, thereby optimising instructional time. However, what is key is to ensure that you have a clear system in place to use MWBs. Using the 'show me boards' technique (Sherrington and Caviglioli, 2020, pp. 94–95) provides the perfect structure for it.

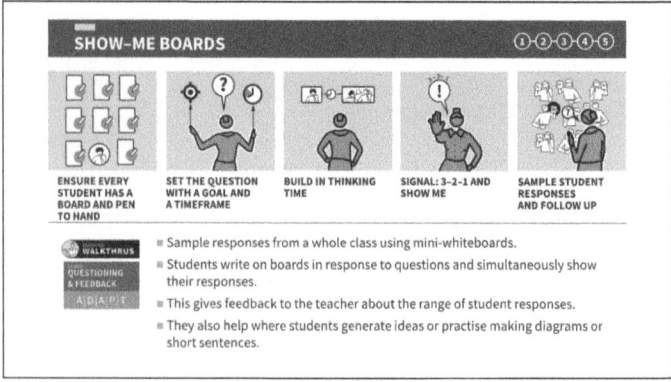

FIGURE 7.4: *Image created by Tom Sherrington and Oliver Caviglioli, taken from the Walkthrus members' site that schools and colleges can join to support the design of their professional development programmes via walkthrus.co.uk*

Diagnostic testing

These help you to identify specific areas where students are struggling, such as grammatical structures or vocabulary usage. Diagnostic questions present one correct answer alongside multiple incorrect answers to check where students are making mistakes. In a French class, you might use diagnostic questions to assess comprehension of verb conjugations. For instance, asking students to quickly conjugate a verb in different tenses can provide immediate insights into their grasp of French grammar. Similarly, in a German class, diagnostic questions might focus on case endings in sentences, helping you to identify who needs more practice.

For example, at the beginning of Year 10, when you get a new class with students whom you have never taught before, a diagnostic test to see what students can remember in terms of grammar is very powerful.

Y10: Present tense

Question	Answer A	Answer B	Answer C	Answer D	Answer E
1. Brigitte _____ du vélo.	a	fait	fais	as	est
2. Mon frère et moi _____ un match.	regarde	regardez	regardent	regardons	regardes
3. Quel âge _____ vous?	êtes	sont	est	avez	avons
4. Les filles et moi _____ intelligentes.	sont	ont	avons	sommes	est
5. Ils _____ fatigués?	sont	êtes	est	ont	avez
6. Nous _____ quinze ans.	sommes	avons	est	avez	sont
7. Je _____ aux cartes.	perd	perde	perdis	perds	pert
8. Nous _____ des frites et un hamburger.	mangons	mangeons	mangissons	mangez	mange
9. 'Ils' est...	singulier	masculin	féminin	pluriel	neutre
10. Chantal _____ trois enfants.	avoir	est	a	ai	as
11. Marc _____ au telephone.	répondez	réponds	répondre	répond	répondent
12. On _____ des cartes pour ma fête.	choisis	choisissons	choisissez	choisit	choisir
13. Nous _____ à apprendre l'espagnol.	commence	commencons	commençons	començons	comencons
14. Tu _____ trop paresseux.	as	êtes	est	être	es
15. Elles _____ le bus.	attend	atendent	attendent	attende	attendez

FIGURE 7.5: *Example of a diagnostic test for Y10 French*

Peer assessment

Students learn from each other through structured peer feedback sessions, which can enhance collaborative learning and increase linguistic exposure.

Matrix

Use the matrix adapted from Dylan Wiliam and Marnie Thompson's (2007) ideas on formative assessment to illustrate how different roles (teacher, peer and learner) interact with three key questions of learning: where the learner is going, where the learner is now and how to get there.

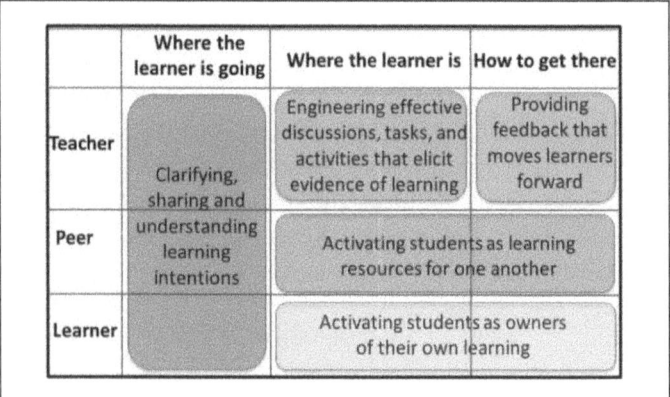

FIGURE 7.6: *Image courtesy of Dylan Wiliam and Marnie Thompson (used with permission)*

In the context of modern foreign languages lessons, this framework can be particularly effective, due to the interactive and cumulative nature of language learning. Here's how each part of the matrix can be applied:

1. Teacher's role:

- **Clarifying, sharing and understanding learning intentions:** You clearly define the learning objectives, such as new vocabulary, grammatical structures or communication skills. This might involve outlining specific targets for a lesson or a series of lessons.

- **Engineering effective discussions, tasks and activities that elicit evidence of learning:** This could involve designing activities that require students to use new language structures in conversations, or tasks that assess comprehension and fluency – for example, role-plays, group discussions or written exercises.

- **Providing feedback that moves learners forward:** Feedback in MFL needs to be immediate and constructive, helping students to adjust their pronunciation, choice of vocabulary or grammatical accuracy. This feedback is crucial for helping students to refine their language skills and become more confident speakers.

Peer's role:

- **Activating students as learning resources for one another:** This is particularly beneficial in language learning, where peers can practise conversational skills together, correct each other and share learning strategies. Peer interactions can provide a less intimidating environment for learners to try out new language skills.

Learner's role:

- **Activating students as owners of their own learning:** In MFL, this might involve students setting personal goals for language proficiency or seeking out additional resources, such as films, music or books in the target language. This encourages a more personalised and engaged learning experience.

Using this matrix, you can more effectively plan and deliver lessons that are interactive, responsive to student needs and supportive of peer and self-directed learning. These strategies help to build a dynamic learning environment where students not only learn a new language but also develop skills in self-assessment and peer feedback, which are valuable beyond the language classroom.

Written feedback

Detailed comments on written work highlight strengths and areas for improvement, focusing on grammatical accuracy and the use of language in context.

Knowledge checkers

These are designed to be quick and targeted, allowing you to gauge the retention of specific facts, concepts or skills and to identify areas where students might need more support or additional instruction. The goal is to ensure that all students have a firm grasp of the key content as they progress through their studies and to adjust teaching methods or review material as necessary, based on the results of these checks.

As you can see from the example above, the last two tasks are translation, which will check whether students can apply their knowledge and understanding. Sometimes students understand the rules but cannot apply them, so it is important to also check that students can do both.

Year 8 Spanish Quiz – Comparativo

___/20

1. How do you say 'more than' in Spanish?	
a) mejor que….	b) menos…. que
c) tan…. como	d) más… que

2. How do you say 'as…as' in Spanish?	
a) tan…como	b) peor que
c) menos…que	d) mejor que

3. How do you say 'Music is more creative than history.' in Spanish?	
a) La música es menos creativo que la historia.	b) La música es menos creativo que la historia.
c) La música es más creativa como la historia.	d) La música es más creativa que la historia.

4. Which word is masculine?	
a) religión	b) informática
c) tecnología	d) inglés

5. How do you say 'Maths is as important as science' in Spanish?	
a) Las matemáticas es tan importantes como las ciencias.	b) Las matemáticas son tan importantes como las ciencias.
c) Las matemáticas son tan importantes que las ciencias.	d) Los matemáticas son tan importante que las ciencias.

6. If you want to say "I study technology" in Spanish, which phrase would you use?	
a) Estudias la tecnología.	a) Estudia la tecnología.
c) Estudiar la tecnología.	c) Estudio la tecnología.

7. How do you say 'English is more interesting than chemistry' in Spanish?	
a) El inglés es menos interesante que la química.	b) El inglés es más interesante como la química.
c) El inglés es mas interesante que la química.	d) El inglés es más interesante que la química.

8. How do you say 'Spanish is better than art' in Spanish?	
a) El español es mejor que el dibujo.	b) El espanol es más que el dibujo.
c) El espanol es major que el dibujo.	d) El español es mejor como el dibujo.

9. What are inglés, francés and español?	
a) masculine, singular	b) feminine, singular
c) masculine, plural	d) feminine, plural

10. What are ciencias, lenguas, idiomas?	
a) singular	b) masculine
c) feminine	d) plural

Now translate this into English: (5 marks)

Estudio el francés y la educación física. Me encanta la educación física porque es más interesante y menos aburrida que el francés.

....

....

Then translate this into Spanish: (5 marks)

I study drama and English. Music is more creative than history.

....

....

FIGURE 7.7: *Example of a knowledge checker for Year 8 Spanish*

Knowledge checkers can also be used to check any grammar points and also work on phonics, so that you can check whether students can apply the phonics rules taught. For example:

Are the following words pronounced properly? Tick if yes and cross if not (7 marks)

1. chat
2. nord
3. mais
4. deux
5. trois
6. français
7. petit

FIGURE 7.8: *Example of a knowledge checker to check pronunciation in Year 7 French*

The above example is to check the silent final consonant. If you say *nord* pronouncing the -d (which is not correct), students need to put a cross next to it, but if you say it without pronouncing the -d, then students have to put a tick next to it. It is very easily marked and allows you to check what students can remember.

Think-pair-share

This is an interactive formative assessment technique developed by Frank Lyman in 1981 that involves students in the process of thinking, discussing and sharing ideas or solutions with each other. It's an effective strategy to engage students actively and to assess their understanding in real time. You can quickly gauge students' comprehension of the material being taught. As students discuss their thoughts with a partner, you can listen in and identify any misunderstandings or misconceptions that need to be addressed. It encourages all students to participate, not just the ones who are quickest to raise their hands.

This provides a more complete picture of the class's overall understanding and progress.

Think-pair-share can be used in different ways in MFL lessons:

- **Vocabulary building:** Use think-pair-share when introducing new vocabulary. After demonstrating new words, have students think of sentences using those words, pair up to compare sentences and share a few examples with the class. This can help to solidify vocabulary usage in a practical context.

- **Cultural context discussions:** When discussing cultural elements related to the language, use the technique to have students first reflect on their knowledge or assumptions, then discuss these with a peer and finally share their findings. This can deepen their cultural understanding and enhance language learning.

- **Grammar practice:** After a grammar lesson, give students a few practice sentences to work through individually, then discuss their answers with a partner to explain their reasoning. Finally share their conclusions with the class for corrective feedback if needed.

- **Role-play:** This is a great way in which to practise conversational skills. Students can think of responses in a given scenario, practise with a partner and then perform or share highlights with the class. This helps not only with language fluency but also with gaining confidence in speaking.

- **Error correction:** Use think-pair-share for peer correction activities, where students write a short piece, exchange it with a partner to identify and discuss errors and then share their corrected versions with the class. This encourages attention to detail and reinforces learning from peers' mistakes as well.

Research by Black and Wiliam (1998, pp. 139–148) has demonstrated that effective formative assessment leads to significant learning gains. Despite its benefits, formative assessment in MFL is not without challenges. Issues such as the subjective nature of language assessment, the time required to provide meaningful feedback and the need for ongoing professional development for teachers can impact its efficacy. Implementing formative assessment requires thoughtful planning and consistent application.

Summative assessment

Unlike formative assessments, which are continuous and occur in every lesson, summative assessments are evaluative and designed to measure student learning at the end of a topic, a unit of work, a term or an academic year. These assessments are generally more formal and include tests, exams or projects. They aim to evaluate overall language proficiency across listening, speaking, reading and writing skills. Summative assessments are essential for determining grades, assessing the effectiveness of instructional strategies and informing future educational planning.

Criteria for summative assessments

It's vital to ensure that these evaluations not only align with the intended learning outcomes and comprehensively cover all language skills but also mirror the structure and content of the standardised exams that students will ultimately face. For instance, in England, the reformed GCSE emphasises particular skills such as reading aloud and dictation. Therefore, incorporating these elements into summative assessments from early on becomes crucial. This alignment helps students to become accustomed to the types and formats of tasks that they will encounter in their final exams, thereby increasing their confidence and proficiency. It is important to develop assessments that reflect the exam's criteria, fostering a more effective and seamless preparation process. This approach ensures that your assessments are not only a measure of learning but also a constructive part of ongoing student preparation for significant academic milestones.

Developing clear and consistent grading criteria that assess both language proficiency and content understanding is important. It's also helpful to consider the impact of test anxiety and aim for a balanced approach that incorporates a variety of assessment methods.

The four skills

Summative assessments should cover the four primary language skills: listening, speaking, reading and writing. Here are some examples for each:

Listening

End-of-unit listening exam:
Students listen to several audio recordings in the target language, ranging from dialogues to monologues, and then answer comprehension questions. This can assess their ability to understand spoken language in various contexts and accents.

Question 1

Listen to the words and write them down in French. Think about the phonics sounds you've covered so far and how these link to the correct spelling of these words.

You will hear each word 3 times.

5 MARKS

Question 2

Listen to the following extract and answer the questions

1 mark per correct answer. No half marks

1. How do you spell her name?
2. a) How is she?

    b) Why?

3. How old is she?
4. When is her birthday?

5 MARKS

FIGURE 7.9: *Example for Year 7, based on a French listening exercise*

EFFECTIVE ASSESSMENT AND FEEDBACK 177

Section A: Listening

1. What do these people like about their town? Write the correct answer. /3

Description
1. The beach with people swimming and playing volleyball.
2. A busy market with fresh fruits and vegetables.
3. A large park with children playing and families having picnics.
4. A sports centre with people playing basketball and tennis.
5. A bowling alley with friends enjoying their time.
6. A nature path with trees and a calm river.

A)

B)

C)

2. Where do these people live? Write the correct answer. /3

Description
1. A coastal town with a beach and cliffs.
2. A traditional village with historic buildings.
3. A snowy mountain area with chalets.
4. A modern city with tall buildings and busy streets.
5. A rural area with farms and animals.
6. A caravan park with mobile homes.

D)

E)

F)

2. Listen to these people talking about their towns. Choose an advantage and a disadvantage of each town. /4

1. Beautiful
2. Calm
3. Small
4. Polluted
5. Expensive
6. Lively
7. Industrial
8. Crowded

	Advantage	Disadvantage
A		
B		

3. Fill in the gaps with the words you hear. /4

Ex. J'aime mon quartier parce qu'il est très *tranquille*.

1. Ma ville est très _____ parce qu'il y a beaucoup de voitures.

2. Le centre est assez _____, il y a beaucoup de magasins et de restaurants.

3. Je n'aime pas mon quartier parce qu'il est un peu _____.

4. La place est très _____ l'après-midi, il y a toujours beaucoup de gens.

FIGURE 7.10: *Example in French for the topic of towns*

Q4. Dictation section. Fill in the missing gaps with the word you hear.

1 Vivo en un pueblo en el _____ del país.

2 Me encanta donde vivo _____ es atractivo.

3 Vivo en un _____ pueblo en la _____.

4 En mi ciudad hay un _____ pero no hay una _____.

(Total 6 marks)

FIGURE 7.11: *Example in Spanish for the topic of towns: Dictation*

Speaking

Oral proficiency interview:

Conducted by you, this interview assesses the student's ability to engage in conversation, describe experiences, give opinions and use appropriate register and vocabulary. This can be

EFFECTIVE ASSESSMENT AND FEEDBACK

structured as a one-on-one interaction or as a role-play scenario, allowing students to demonstrate their proficiency in spoken language, understanding of grammar and cultural knowledge.

Speaking and Pronunciation

Name: _____

Speaking

¿Qué tal? ¿Por qué?

¿Cómo te llamas?

¿Cuántos años tienes?

¿Cuándo es tu cumpleaños?

| | 10 |

9-10	Answer all questions clearly with as much detail as possible. 10 = asked teacher a question.
7-8	Answer 3 questions clearly and extend some answers
5-6	Answer 2 questions clearly and give some extended answers OR answer all 4 with no extension
3-4	Answer 2 questions understandably or 3 questions with no extension
1-2	Answer 1 question with no/ limited detail
0	No answers given

Top of the box = ask teacher a question

Pronunciation : Read out the following passage. Your teacher will listen and give you a mark for all of the key sounds you pronounce correctly. There are 20 key sounds indicated on the teacher's copy. You don't know which they are and so have to try to pronounce everything as well as you can!

Hola, tengo once años. Mi cumpleaños es el quince de junio.
Me llamo P-E-D-R-O. ¿Cómo te llamas?
Me llamo S-O-F-I-A.
¿Qué tal? Estoy fatal, porque no dormí bien.
Tengo los ojos azules el pelo pelirrojo y rizado.
Quiero un chocolate. ¡Qué rico!
¡Hasta luego!

| | 20 |

FIGURE 7.12: *Example in Spanish for Year 7: speaking and reading aloud*

For the reading aloud task, you have the same text as the one in the picture but with 20 of the words highlighted, and you give a mark for every word highlighted that students pronounce correctly.

Reading

Cumulative reading test:

This test includes texts that students have not previously seen, requiring them to use their cumulative vocabulary knowledge and reading strategies to understand, interpret and analyse texts. Questions may include MCQs, short-answer questions or questions that focus on vocabulary, main ideas, inference or critical analysis.

Holiday Reading Assessment

Read the text and answer the questions by writing the correct letter for each box. /4

"Durante las vacaciones, me encanta ir a la montaña con mis amigos. Vamos en coche y pasamos una semana en una cabaña. Me gusta mucho caminar por los senderos y sacar fotos de los paisajes. Sin embargo, no me gusta cuando llueve porque no podemos salir. Cada tarde, jugamos al fútbol y cocinamos juntos. Mañana vamos a visitar un pueblo cercano en bicicleta."

1. **Where do they stay?**
   A. Hotel
   B. Cabin
   C. Campsite

2. **How do they travel?**
   A. By train
   B. By car
   C. By plane

3. **What do they do every afternoon?**
   A. They play tennis
   B. They play football
   C. They swim in the river

4. **How are they going to visit the town tomorrow?**
   A. By car
   B. By bike
   C. On foot

FIGURE 7.13: *Example in Spanish for the topic of holidays*

5. Read the postcards and for each person write what is their least favourite aspect of their holiday. / 4

Carlos:	*María:*
"Fui una semana a la costa en coche con mi familia. Me gustó mucho nadar en el mar y tomar el sol en la playa, pero no me gustaron las tiendas porque eran muy caras."	"Pasé cinco días en un camping cerca de un lago. Viajé en autobús con mis amigos. Me encantó sacar fotos del paisaje y pasear en bicicleta, pero había muchos mosquitos y no podía dormir bien."
Jorge:	*Lucía:*
"Mis padres y yo fuimos en avión a un parque temático durante cuatro días. Me gustó mucho subir a las atracciones y sacar fotos, pero las colas eran muy largas y hacía mucho calor."	"Viajé en tren con mi mejor amiga a una ciudad histórica durante tres días. Visitamos muchos monumentos y saqué muchas fotos, pero había mucho ruido por las noches y no podía dormir."

1. Carlos
2. María
3. Jorge
4. Lucía

FIGURE 7.14: *Example in Spanish for the topic of holidays*

Writing

Integrated writing task:

This task could involve students reading a short article or listening to a presentation in the target language, followed by a prompt asking them to write a paragraph based on the information provided. This assesses their ability to write coherently and correctly, while also incorporating information from another medium.

> You are going to write up to 80 words on the topic of school
>
> You will need to cover the following bullet points:
> - A description of your school
> - A description of your teachers
> - What your ideal school would be like
>
> You must cover all 3 bullet points to achieve maximum marks

FIGURE 7.15: *Example of a writing task.*

> **Example in Spanish – translation for the topic of town:**
>
> Q3. Translation section Translate A–C into English and D–F into Spanish.
>
> a) Vivo en una ciudad moderna en Alemania.
>
> b) Vivimos en un pueblo que está en el suroeste de Inglaterra.
>
> c) Pienso que mi zona es moderna y limpia.
>
> d) He lives in a big city which is called Madrid.
>
> e) I don't like my town because it is ugly and dirty.
>
> f) In my town there is a swimming pool but no castle.
>
> (12 marks)

FIGURE 7.16: *Example in Spanish – translation for the topic of towns*

It has also proved beneficial to assess students on the grammar taught during the course. For instance, when teaching French, you might introduce a variety of regular *-er* verbs and their usage with trigger phrases such as *je peux* (I can), *je dois* (I must), *je voudrais* (I would like) and *je vais* (I am going), to ensure comprehensive understanding and application.

> Question 1 to 6: choose the correct answer out of the five options.
>
> | Question | Answer A | Answer b | Answer C | Answer D | Answer E |
> |---|---|---|---|---|---|
> | 1. to travel | travailler | voyage | travail | voyager | travailé |
> | 2. to wear | habiter | porter | laver | discuter | jeter |
> | 3. to study | studier | éluder | étude | etuster | étudier |
> | 4. voler | theft | robber | to steal | I stole | to cheat |
> | 5. essayer | to try | to cry | to shout | to wear | to work hard |
> | 6. trouver | finding | treasure | to find | to threaten | to discuss |
>
> Question 7 to 15: Write the English for the following words:
>
> 7. embrasser
> 8. détester
> 9. nager
> 10. pleurer
> 11. chasser
> 12. acheter
> 13. travailler
> 14. dessiner
> 15. intimider
>
> Question 16 to 25: Write the French for the following words:
>
> 16. to live
> 17. to eat
> 18. to watch
> 19. to play
> 20. to visit
> 21. to listen
> 22. to think
> 23. to love
> 24. to prepare
> 25. to talk
>
> Question 26 to 35: How do you say the following in French:
>
> 26. I can think
> 27. I have to listen
> 28. I like to hunt
> 29. I would like to watch
> 30. I am going to study
> 31. We are going to love
> 32. We are not going to find
> 33. I cannot eat
> 34. I am not going to download
> 35. I would not like to surf

FIGURE 7.17: *Example of an assessment to test -er verbs in French*

Final projects can be used for a more creative summative assessment; students might be tasked with designing a tourist brochure in the target language, which requires them to apply their writing and design skills, while also showcasing their vocabulary and grammatical accuracy.

Marking and feedback

Effective marking and feedback are pivotal elements in enhancing educational outcomes. They serve as crucial channels through which students receive insights and guidance on their performance. The Education Endowment Foundation (EEF) offers comprehensive research into the best practices in feedback that significantly influence student learning and achievement.

Feedback, as explored in the EEF's 2021 report, is information given to the learner about their performance that aims to reinforce positive behaviours and correct mistakes. EEF research suggests that high-quality feedback can add up to eight additional months of educational progress over a year. Feedback can take various forms, including written comments, verbal feedback or peer feedback, each with different impacts on learning. The effectiveness of feedback largely depends on how it is delivered – its timing, clarity and relevance to the task.

The EEF report reminds us that what matters 'is what learners do with it' and that 'the most important decisions taken in classrooms are not taken by teachers but rather by learners'(2021, p. 5).

Principles of effective marking

Marking, a standard method of providing feedback, involves annotating student work. The EEF (2021) notes that while students and parents often find detailed comments helpful, their impact on learning varies greatly. Effective written feedback, including comments, marks and scores, can enhance student achievement. However, it's important to consider the timing of feedback to maximise its impact. The amount of feedback provided should be balanced; too much can overwhelm or demotivate students. Additionally, focusing on the most relevant aspects of the students' work is crucial for improving their performance. Effective marking should:

- **Be meaningful:** Provide clear, specific comments that help students to understand how to improve.
- **Be manageable:** You should employ strategies that optimise time and effort, ensuring a sustainable workload.
- **Be motivating:** Feedback should be constructive and help to build confidence and interest.

Optimising feedback

To optimise feedback, you should align your methods with the following EEF strategies (2021):

- **Timelines:** Immediate feedback can be more impactful, but the optimal timing can vary based on the complexity of the task.
- **Specific:** Feedback should be specific enough to be actionable, guiding students on how to improve.
- **'Feed forward':** Feedback should not only address the present task but also advise on how to apply the learning to future work.

Ineffective feedback

Feedback may well be ineffective when it contains some of the following characteristics:

- **Marking as the principal or only method:** Marking, when used as the sole method of feedback, often lacks the interactive and constructive elements that promote deeper learning. The EEF report (2021) suggests that feedback should be more than just corrective; it should also provide guidance that leads students to enhance their understanding and capability. Sole reliance on marking can be limited in scope and fail to engage students in reflective thinking or discussion that could fortify learning and application of concepts.

- **Uses a universal feedback stamp (e.g. 'Excellent!'):** This type of feedback is typically generic and non-specific. It fails to tell students what exactly they did well, nor does it guide them on how to improve or continue their success. The EEF (2021) emphasises that effective feedback should be specific and clear, guiding students towards improved understanding and performance. Generic praise like 'Excellent!' does not achieve this goal.

- **Vague or general feedback (e.g. 'Include more details'):** Vague feedback does not provide enough information for students to act upon. It lacks specificity and can leave students confused about what actions to take next. According to the EEF (2021), feedback should be precise and link directly to the learning objectives, enabling students to understand exactly what they need to do to improve.

- **Focuses on the person rather than the piece of work:** When feedback is person-focused rather than task-focused, it can lead to fixed mindsets, where students may begin to believe that their abilities are innate and unchangeable, rather than something that they can develop through effort and learning. The EEF report (2021) recommends focusing feedback on the specific tasks or processes related to the work at hand, rather than on the individual's character or abilities.

- **Does not allow students to act on it:** If feedback is given in a way that does not allow for students to make improvements (for example, if it is given after a project is completed and there is no further opportunity to engage with the task), then it becomes ineffective. Effective feedback involves not only identifying areas for improvement but also providing opportunities for students to apply this feedback. This reiterative process of applying feedback to subsequent tasks is essential for deep learning.

- **There is too much to think about at once:** Overloading students with too much feedback at one time can be overwhelming and counterproductive. The EEF (2021) suggests that feedback should be manageable and focused, targeting key aspects for improvement one at a time. This approach helps to avoid cognitive overload and allows students to concentrate on making meaningful changes incrementally.

Strategies that can help to reduce teacher workload

- Immediate feedback, delivered in the lesson, is timely and can be done with the whole class to focus on a general misunderstanding or exploration of how to improve. The teacher can model alternative approaches, suggest a variety of answers and illustrate common errors. You can use a visualiser for live feedback by marking two or three books with the class, talking through your marking with reference to the success criteria or asking the class questions about errors that they spot. As you go through the process with the visualiser, students can correct their own work as they recognise some of the mistakes that they have made. Feedback will include vocabulary ideas/corrections, grammar points to review (especially tenses) and phonics to revisit if it was a spoken piece of work. Specific feedback on these points is just as important for our students as the overall comments on tests.

- Following speaking tests, targeted feedback followed by targeted practice is important, so that students have the opportunity to practise what they did not say/pronounce correctly. The example below is a homework task following a reading aloud test, and students have specific phonics to practise. Some will only have one sound to practise and others might have two or three.

Phonics	SFC	SFE	A	EU
	I	Eau	Q	
Targets	Revise these sounds:			
	SFC – petit / grand / croissant / cafard / dans			
	SFE – aime / petite / demie / ensuite / comme			
	A – salade / malade / ca va / animal / salle			
	Eu – bleu / lieu / peu / deux / feu			
	I – midi / demi / ici / petit / fini			
	Eau – peau / cadeau / château / eau / manteau			
	Q – que / quelle / quand / qui /quoi			

FIGURE 7.18: *Example of follow-up task (credit to Charlotte King)*

- Why correct the same mistake in 20 different books when you could use a whole-class feedback sheet instead? Whole-class feedback acknowledges that many students experience similar problems and gives greater scope to explain and expand on comments.

- Try using marking codes – for example, w.o. = word order or sp. = spelling. Marking codes are designed to pinpoint specific areas that need attention, which can make the feedback clearer and more direct for students. For instance, a particular code might indicate a recurring grammatical error or the need for more evidence in an argument. This precision helps students to focus on specific areas for improvement without ambiguity.

- Require students to check their work before submission, training them to proofread. Having a checklist to use can be powerful. For example:

Have you...	Tick
underlined your date and title?	
included an answer for bullet point 1?	
included an answer for bullet point 2?	
included an answer for bullet point 3?	
used a range of vocabulary to avoid repetition?	
checked the spelling of 'ennuyeux' / 'cependant' / 'malheureusement' / 'restaurant'?	
checked adjectives endings for accuracy? (What happens if it's feminine? What happens if it's plural?)	
used the present tense?	
used the past tense? (Have you got the auxiliary verb?)	
included opinions?	
ensured that opinions are justified as much as possible?	
checked word order?	

FIGURE 7.19: *Example of a student checklist for areas of improvement*

- Dylan Wiliam's 'find it, fix it' (2018, p. 145) strategy is a form of formative assessment and feedback technique designed to improve student learning by identifying specific errors and addressing them directly. The core idea is to encourage students to actively engage with their mistakes and learn how to correct them, thus deepening their understanding and mastery of the subject matter. After a written piece of work, you collect the work and identify common grammatical errors made by the students. Instead of correcting these errors, you highlight them and hand the assignments back to the students. Students are tasked with finding out why each highlighted section is wrong and must correct the errors themselves. This can be done individually or in pairs to encourage discussion and peer learning. Students learn to recognise frequent grammatical mistakes and understand the rules more thoroughly, which is crucial in language learning.

- For oral feedback, consider technology – tools like voice memos are easy to use. You can use the Vocaroo or Qwiqr websites (both free) to give students personalised feedback on their pronunciation and the quality of their answer. The voice memo is converted into a QR code that students now have in their books, so that they can re-listen when they need to.

- For feedback on the finished piece of work, the PiXL 'correct and perfect' strategy can be an effective approach. When addressing student errors, it is important to distinguish between simple mistakes and those that indicate deeper misunderstandings. While straightforward errors may only require identification, misunderstandings are better tackled through prompts or questions that guide students toward the correct concepts.

Feedback should be given when it will move students on, in a form that they can understand and act upon. You should also give time for students to respond, maybe by redrafting their work or following up on your suggestions in terms of grammar and pronunciation practice.

If you ask a question in your feedback, try to make sure that it stimulates thinking and allows your students to make progress to the next level. Students should spend longer responding to your feedback than you spend giving it. Make sure that you plan the time (in lessons or home learning) for students to respond and make the improvements. If they don't get the DIRT (Directed Improvement and Reflection Time), then you have wasted your marking time.

Feedback plays a key role in helping students to make progress. Whether it's verbal, written or peer-to-peer, good feedback helps students to understand what they're doing well and what they need to work on. It doesn't have to be time-consuming or complicated – even small, clear pointers can build confidence and help your students progress.

REFLECTIVE QUESTIONS

- What does success look like for your students in MFL?
- What are the main purposes of the assessments that you use in your classroom?
- How do you ensure that your assessments are meaningful and beneficial to both students and yourself?
- What assessment strategies have you found most effective in accurately and fairly evaluating student performance in MFL? How do you balance formative and summative assessments to support real learning?
- What methods do you employ to provide effective, specific and timely feedback? How do you ensure that the feedback you give

is constructive and helps to guide learners towards targeted improvements?
- How do you use the information from assessments to adjust your teaching strategies?
- How do you ensure that students actively engage with the feedback provided?

CASE STUDY

Case study: Using the 20 Keys to achieve effective assessment and feedback
Contributor: Elena Díaz, Regional Northern Adviser for United Learning

What was the issue?

Grammar was just *too much*. Before implementing the 20 Keys framework, I often encountered students overwhelmed by 'too many rules', perceiving grammar as an impossible system to master. They could only use structures within specific topics and frequently forgot them shortly after learning them.

This fragmented approach hindered their ability to transfer grammatical knowledge across topics, recycle key language and use language spontaneously. Frustratingly, students could only say what I had taught them, and not what they wanted to express.

The issue became evident during assessments, where students struggled to demonstrate cohesion between skills. For example, while they might recognise grammatical structures in listening and reading tasks, they often failed to use them accurately in speaking or writing. There was a clear need for a system that streamlined grammar, promoted retention and enabled students to create rather than merely reproduce language.

How did we resolve it?

To address this issue, I designed and implemented the 20 Keys framework: a system for teaching grammar that distils it into 20 categories – or keys – such as the simple future, comparisons or negatives. The 20 Keys aims to make grammar memorable, transferable and useable creatively across topics and skills. This framework became the foundation for restructuring both curriculum design and assessment practices.

Embedding the 20 Keys into the curriculum

- I structured the curriculum around the 20 Keys, introducing them gradually and early in students' language-learning journeys, and then revisiting them regularly.

- Each student received a mat with five examples of each key, which were then used to create lesson activities.

- The keys and their examples acted as a consistent thread across all year groups, helping students to view grammar as a cohesive and accessible system rather than an overwhelming collection of ever-changing rules.

Innovative assessment strategies with the 20 Keys at the centre

- **Receptive skills:** In reading and listening tasks, students identified and interpreted the 20 Keys in context. This raised the profile of the keys and modelled their practical use for students.

- **Productive skills:** By testing the same 20 Keys in different vocabulary contexts, assessments highlighted that grammar is useful, recyclable and finite and can be mastered through practice and repetition.

Feedback rooted in the 20 Keys

- **Feedback to increase motivation:** Speaking and writing assessments credited communication as well as the number of keys that students included. Students were rewarded for incorporating keys.
- **Promoting grammar ownership:** Feedback consistently referenced the 20 Keys. I highlighted correct examples in students' work and asked them to identify which key matched the example. This motivated students, who frequently aimed to use more keys than they had previously.
- **Feedback variety:** Immediate feedback during low-stakes activities (e.g. matching a word with a key) reinforced the transferability of the 20 Keys. Meanwhile, delayed feedback on writing tasks encouraged deeper reflection on key usage.

Retrieval practice

- Retrieval activities at the start of each lesson focused on the 20 Keys.
- Students tested themselves and each other using examples from the 20 Keys regularly, reinforcing retention and recall.

What was the impact?

The implementation of the 20 Keys has significantly enhanced both student outcomes and teaching practices:

- **Retention and transfer:** Students now see grammar as manageable and confidently apply the 20 Keys across topics and tasks, demonstrating adaptability and improved retention. They can create spontaneously.
- **Growth through feedback:** Feedback linked to the 20 Keys has developed students' metacognitive skills, enabling them to self-correct, improve their work and work independently.
- **Engagement:** Students find the 20 Keys clear and empowering, while teachers appreciate the framework's practicality in connecting grammar across skills.

The 20 Keys framework has transformed grammar teaching from a daunting and fragmented process into a cohesive and empowering experience. By focusing on these keys, we have not only improved grammatical accuracy but also equipped students with the tools to use grammar creatively and confidently across all four language skills.

Chapter summary

In this chapter, we have explored how assessment and feedback can support meaningful progress in language learning across listening, speaking, reading and writing.

- Assessment in MFL serves two key purposes: to inform teaching and to help students to embed and apply what they've learned. Effective planning starts with clarity about what success looks like and what knowledge should be retained in the long term.

- Formative assessment techniques, such as questioning, diagnostic tasks, mini whiteboards, hinge questions and peer feedback, offer timely insight into student understanding and support responsive teaching. These methods help to identify misconceptions and allow teachers to adapt instruction in the moment.

- Summative assessment remains important for checking progress over time and preparing students for final exams. Well-designed summative tasks reflect key skills and exam formats, while maintaining a focus on genuine language use and communication.

- Feedback plays a central role in helping students to improve. Whether verbal, written or peer-based, good feedback is timely, specific and focused on what learners can do to get better. Strategies such as whole-class feedback, marking codes, DIRT time and the use of technology can make feedback more effective, while keeping workload manageable.

- By embedding purposeful assessment and clear, constructive feedback into everyday practice, teachers can help students to deepen their understanding, build confidence and make sustained progress in all four language skills.

Further reading

- *Embedded Formative Assessment* by Dylan Wiliam (2018) is a foundational text that explores how formative assessment, when embedded into daily classroom practice, can significantly boost learning outcomes and inform more responsive teaching.

- The EEF's 'Teacher feedback to improve pupil learning' (2021) summarises research into what makes feedback effective, offering practical, evidence-based guidance for schools looking to improve how students respond to and use feedback.

- *Making Good Progress? The Future of Assessment for Learning* by Daisy Christodoulou (2016) is a thought-provoking analysis of assessment in schools, challenging common misconceptions about formative assessment and arguing for a more structured, subject-specific approach to tracking progress over time.

- Evidence Based Education's 'Designing great assessment' (n.d.) is a practical and accessible guide that outlines key principles for creating high-quality assessments, with a strong emphasis on validity, reliability and clear purpose to support effective teaching and learning.

8

Enrichment inside and outside the language classroom

Introduction

Many students have yet to explore life beyond their local surroundings. As language teachers, what can you do to provide all your students with as many opportunities and experiences as possible? Cultural capital is very important, especially for those students who come from disadvantaged backgrounds. Even if this isn't a challenge in your school, we all know that not all students enjoy learning languages. However, culture and how you teach it, can be a great way in which to spark their interest and motivation.

Culture as the fourth pillar of language learning

Language learning extends far beyond the traditional classroom setting, encompassing a variety of enriching activities that can significantly enhance students' linguistic skills and cultural understanding.

Mastering a language involves more than just acquiring vocabulary and grammar, as Cortés (2007, p. 230) explains: 'The process of teaching a foreign language should imply teaching the cultural aspects connected to such a language and not just its grammar and vocabulary.' Cultural immersion plays a crucial role in deepening language comprehension and fluency. The incorporation of cultural knowledge not only enhances the learning experience but is also essential in fostering a genuine connection with the language. While the Ofsted research review (2021) emphasises the three pillars of progression – phonics, vocabulary and grammar – there is a compelling argument for considering culture as a fourth indispensable pillar. Cultural enrichment in language learning does not merely supplement the educational framework; it transforms it, offering students insight into the nuanced ways language operates within various social contexts.

Incorporating culture into MFL lessons offers several distinct advantages that enhance both the educational experience and the outcomes for students. Here are some key benefits:

- **Enhanced engagement and motivation:** By incorporating elements of culture such as music, film, cuisine and traditions, lessons become more interesting and engaging for students. This engagement can lead to increased motivation to learn the language, as students see its relevance to real-world experiences.

- **Improved language proficiency:** Cultural context helps students to understand not just the 'what' of language, but the 'why'. This deeper understanding can improve their ability to use the language appropriately in different social contexts, improving their overall proficiency and fluency.

- **Cultural competence and sensitivity:** Exposure to different cultures fosters respect and empathy. Students learn to appreciate differences and similarities between their own culture and others, which is crucial in our increasingly globalised world. This cultural competence is not only a key skill in personal development but also highly valued in the professional realm.

- **Critical thinking and perspective-taking:** Discussing cultural norms and values encourages students to think critically about their own beliefs and those of others. It challenges them to view the world from different perspectives, enhancing their overall cognitive flexibility and problem-solving skills.

- **Preparation for real-life interactions:** Understanding cultural nuances prepares students for real-life interactions with native speakers. This preparation can be crucial for students who travel, work or study abroad, providing them with the confidence to communicate effectively and appropriately.

- **Supports multilingual identity development:** Integrating culture helps students to see language learning as a process of identity expansion, rather than simply a school subject. This can lead to a more profound personal connection to the language and an ongoing interest in its study.

When considering the enhancement of the MFL curriculum, it's essential to critically evaluate where and how cultural elements can be integrated across the curriculum. This means looking beyond the conventional confines of the language itself and exploring a broad spectrum of cultural contexts. For instance, while teaching French, it's crucial to expose students to the diverse cultures of the entire Francophone world from France, Belgium and Swizerland to Canada, the Caribbean and African countries such as, for example, Senegal, Cameroon, Madagascar or Côte d'Ivoire. It recognises the equal importance and rich contributions of all French-speaking communities in a decolonising curriculum. Similarly, when teaching Spanish, attention should be given to the distinct cultural characteristics and traditions of Spain, as well as those of Latin American countries like Mexico, Argentina and Peru. When teaching German, it is important to include cities, landmarks, food, customs and traditions of other German-speaking countries, such as Austria, Switzerland and Lichtenstein.

This comprehensive approach encourages students to appreciate the rich variety of cultural expressions and historical contexts that influence how languages are spoken and used differently across regions. By incorporating a wide range of cultural perspectives, students gain a more nuanced understanding of the language and its global footprint. This not only enriches their learning experience but also prepares them for real-world interactions where cultural sensitivity and awareness are paramount. Examining the MFL curriculum with a focus on maximising cultural exposure ensures that language learning is both deep and broad, reflecting the true diversity of the world's language-speaking communities.

In-class enrichment activities

Enrichment within the MFL curriculum involves activities that complement and enhance the standard language learning syllabus without requiring additional class time or resources. An effective strategy includes integrating cultural content directly into language lessons. For example, during a lesson on food vocabulary, introducing a French cooking demonstration not only helps students to learn the names of different dishes but also immerses them in the cultural practices related to the cuisine.

Literature and film are valuable resources for in-curriculum enrichment. For instance, reading a short story can deepen understanding of language history, societal norms and cultural values through discussions about character motivations and themes. Watching a film and analysing its cultural context enhances listening skills and cultural literacy. Chapter 2 includes several film study suggestions suitable for Key Stage 3.

Integrate books, magazines, podcasts and shows in the target language into your curriculum. This exposure helps students to understand various dialects and regional nuances within the language and to discuss content that is culturally and contextually rich.

It is crucial to critically evaluate how and where cultural elements are integrated into the curriculum. Discussions with your MFL department should address what 'culture' means in your context and how and when to incorporate it. Consider whether cultural elements are best introduced in stand-alone lessons, as homework, integrated throughout the curriculum or covered in one-off sessions. It's also important to define the strategies used to teach these elements.

Examples of practical ideas

- In Year 7, when teaching *comment ça va?* in French, you could teach your class how French people greet each other.

Greetings in France

- Greetings are important in France. Thus, it is necessary to greet others correctly to make a good impression.
- Handshakes are the norm in a business setting or with acquaintances. It is expected that you will shake hands with everyone present when arriving and leaving.
- Among friends and relatives, the most common greeting is the *la bise* (kiss on both cheeks).
  The *la bise* consists of placing one's cheek against another's, making a kiss noise, then repeating it on the opposite side. A *la bise* is sometimes accompanied with an embrace.
- People generally kiss twice during a *la bise*; however, this varies depending on the region in France. In this instance, follow your French counterpart.
- One should remove their sunglasses and/or hat when doing a *la bise*.
- Respect is shown in verbal greetings by referring to the person as "Madame," ('Mrs') "Monsieur"('Mr') or "Mademoiselle". Madame is only used to refer to a married woman, while Mademoiselle is reserved for unwed women.
- https://www.youtube.com/watch?v=d4V0aD2PF14

FIGURE 8.1: *Example of teaching French greetings and cultural etiquette*

- When you teach phonics, practise by using French cities (SFC: Paris, Nantes, Montréal) or French names (Julien, Géraldine, Amadou, Théo, Jérôme, Angélique, Malik). You can do the same in Spanish with specific sounds (Barcelona, Valencia, Murcia) or in German (Wien, Weimar, Wiesbaden, Heidelberg).

- You can also teach idioms with certain topics: *il est malin comme un singe* when teaching personality or *ça coûte un bras* when talking about something that is expensive, etc.

- When teaching the topic of family, tell students that French people call their mum *maman* and their dad *papa*; in German, children call their grandma *Oma* and grandpa *Opa*, etc. In Spanish, use the Spanish royal family to describe family members. Alternatively, you can also ask students to look at the story of Diego Maradona and his family for homework.

- For the topic of food, use recipes. This can be done as reading comprehension, you can link with food tech and students could cook a dish or you can even set it for homework.

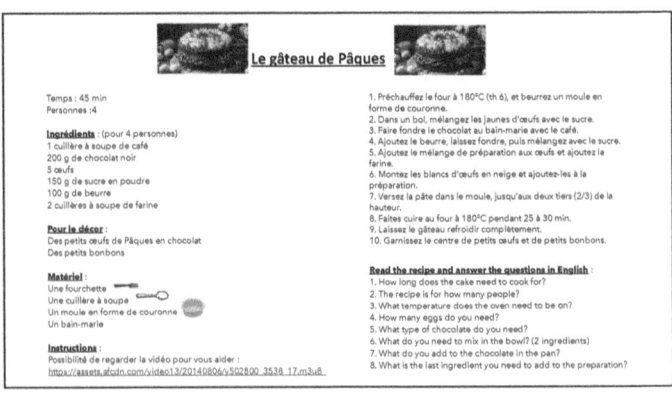

FIGURE 8.2: *Example of a recipe and comprehension questions*

ENRICHMENT INSIDE AND OUTSIDE

- When teaching the topic of school, talk about the uniform, the school day, school reports and the subjects taught, as these vary from one country to another. Students are always captivated by the fact that, for example, in France, students do not wear a uniform; they don't study subjects such as religious studies or food tech; and students in France and Germany can resit the year.

- When describing houses, use a real estate website and ask students to search for different houses using different criteria. When going on school trips, I always collect leaflets, so that I can share the cultural capital with my students back at home.

Go to the website: **https://immobilier-genas.nestenn.com**

Look at the website and answer the following questions in French

1. Find and name a house with 4 bedrooms.
2. Find and name an office for rent.
3. Find and name an apartment with 2 bathrooms, 3 bedrooms and a garage.
4. Describe the rooms in the apartment that costs 235 000 euros.
5. How big is the most expensive house?
6. Which property is new on the market?
7. If you had a budget of 450 000 euros, which house/ apartment would you choose? Give reasons in French.
8. Pick an apartment and a house of your choice and describe them in French (include the rooms, extra details, price, give opinions -use your knowledge organiser for the vocab).
9. What is the estate agency's phone number?
10. Name the differences between the apartment that costs 395 000 euros and the one that costs 650 000 euros. Write the differences in French (use your knowledge organiser to help you).

FIGURE 8.3: *Example of real estate webquest*

- When teaching the topic of pets, use a video of the Zoo de Beauval (one of the most famous French zoos) and ask students to answer some comprehension questions. https://youtu.be/RVwDYWdDcmg?si=4mYntwo5ry5gvo6s

- When covering the topic of towns, you can use a range of virtual tours for different cities, museums or famous landmarks. For example:
  - a flight over Paris landmarks in 3D: https://youtu.be/CbYpaNcILl8?si=aSkhfmxuy_VpCP3p
  - a virtual tour of Lyon in France: www.blog-in-lyon.fr/visite-virtuelle/index.html
  - Les Grottes de Lascaux: https://archeologie.culture.gouv.fr/lascaux/fr/visiter-grotte-lascaux
  - Camp Nou in Barcelona: www.youvisit.com/tour/campnou

All sorts of activities could be planned. For example:

- true or false
- treasure hunt
- description of the city
- you describe an area of the town or a monument in the target language and students have to find which one it is
- students choose an area of the town or a monument and they pretend to be a tour guide, describing it for a group of tourists in the target language
- create an advertisement to encourage people to go there
- use famous paintings – for example, when learning about bedrooms, use Van Gogh's painting.

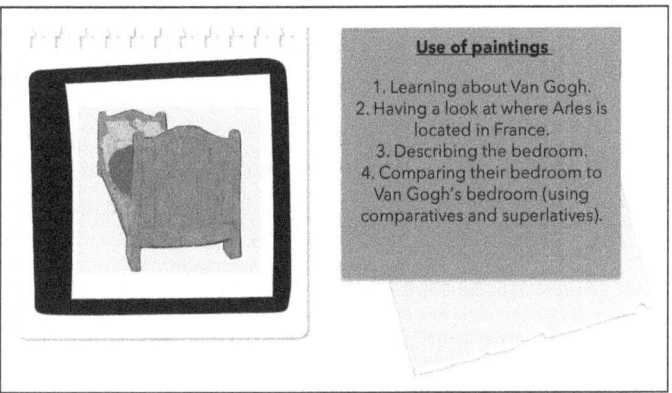

FIGURE 8.4: *Example using Van Gogh's painting*

- Look at famous poems and, as an activity, students can then write their own. For example, for '*Un hombre sin cabeza*' by Armando José Sequera, students can rewrite the poem changing all the infinitives.

Or, if using the poem '*Dans Paris*' by Paul Éluard, students can change all the nouns when writing their own poem and pick the French city of their choice. This encourages creative writing.

- Authentic materials can be used with every single topic taught. There are many useful websites for this, including:

  - **Periodico El Gancho** offers engaging, age-appropriate news articles in Spanish, helping young learners to improve their language skills, while staying informed about current events: www.periodicoelgancho.com

  - **Muy Interesante** provides fascinating and accessible articles on science, technology, history and culture, which is ideal for expanding vocabulary and general knowledge in Spanish: www.muyinteresante.com

- **TodoELE** offers a wide selection of Spanish songs with activities, making language learning more engaging through music and cultural context: www.todoele.net/contenido-cultural/canciones
- **Deutsche Welle**: www.dw.com/de/themen/s-9077
- **Goethe-Institut**: www.goethe.de
- **1jour1actu**: www.1jour1actu.com
- **le Petit Quotidien**: https://lepetitquotidien.playbacpresse.fr
- **Extra!** https://youtube.com/playlist?list=PLpcO4gjCbvuXXF78atzT-LK6ofPa66aC_&si=M2mi0vl2Jw_H7rAE
- **TeachVid**: www.teachvid.com

- It's important to plan the festivals and celebrations that you wish to cover in Key Stage 3, ensuring that students are exposed to a diverse range. For instance, while you might include a Christmas lesson each year, it's crucial to coordinate with your department to define distinct activities for each year group, to avoid repetition. In Year 7, students might explore Christmas celebrations using resources from Euroclub Schools (www.euroclub-schools.org). In Year 8, they could learn a Christmas song in the target language, and in Year 9, they might complete a quiz about Christmas traditions.

Le carnaval de Québec
Fin janvier à mi-février

Où est le Québec?

 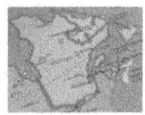

Le saviez-vous?: au Québec, on parle français.

La ville de Québec a introduit le Carnaval de Québec avec Bonhomme Carnaval en 1954.

Il porte un chapeau rouge et une ceinture multi-couleurs.

> Ce festival est de fin janvier à mi-février comme la fête de la Nouvelle Orléans qui s'appelle Mardi Gras, et le Carnaval de Rio de Janeiro.
>
> **Activités pendant le carnaval**
>
> 1. Dégustation de crêpes avec le sirop d'érable.
> 2. La sculpture sur neige.
> 3. Le tournoi international de hockey pee-wee.
> 4. Le Bal de la Reine.
> 5. Glissades sur neige.
> 6. Spas.
> 7. Bain de neige.
> 8. Course en canot.
> 9. Le Palais de Bonhomme.
> 10. Promenade en carriole.
> 11. Promenade en traîneau à chiens.
>
>

FIGURE 8.5: *Example: French with Year 7 when teaching them about the carnival in Québec*

Out-of-class enrichment activities

School events

Extra-curricular activities offer greater flexibility and creativity for enrichment initiatives. Events like Languages Day present ideal opportunities for extensive cultural activities that engage the entire school, thereby enhancing students' appreciation for and excitement about learning languages. For instance, on the Languages Day, you could organise a language fair, where each class sets up a booth representing different countries. Students might prepare presentations, wear national costumes and offer samples of traditional foods. These activities encourage students to explore and share diverse cultural insights, which not only makes language learning fun but also fosters a sense of community. Additionally, you could involve colleagues from various departments to contribute a few words in different languages that they know. Consider organising a themed bake-off, where students bake cakes representing a country or their own heritage/community language. You could also create a quiz with three questions related to languages sent daily to all form tutors during that week. The first form to submit the most correct answers each day wins a prize. Examples of questions to ask include:

- What day is the European Day of Languages celebrated every year?
- In which European country would you hear people speaking Gaelic?
- What is the capital city of Austria, where German is the official language?
- Name one of the Romance languages spoken in Latin America.
- In which African country is Swahili an official language?
- Name two languages that are official in Belgium.
- In which South American country is Guaraní a co-official language with Spanish?
- What is the capital city of Portugal?
- Which African country has 11 official languages, including Zulu and Xhosa?
- Which European language is known for having many cases, including nominative, accusative, and genitive?

- Which Latin American country's official language is Portuguese?
- What is the official language of Cyprus?
- Which African country recognises Arabic, Berber, and French as important national languages?
- Which European country has the longest alphabet, consisting of 33 letters?
- How many official languages are there in the European Union?

World Book Day is also the perfect opportunity to raise the profile of languages. Well-known books that students know in their own language can be looked at in MFL. With younger students, you could look at *The Very Hungry Caterpillar* in different languages, books such as *We're Going on a Bear Hunt* or even famous tales. For older students, it's a great opportunity to study famous authors from the language that they learn. For example, in French, they could look at an extract of *Le Petit Prince* by Antoine de Saint-Exupéry. Interactive activities like language-based scavenger hunts or storytelling workshops can also be integrated, where students create simple stories in another language.

Collaborating with the school canteen is another effective way in which to increase cultural awareness among students. For instance, implementing a themed food day that celebrates the diverse nationalities represented at the school can be very engaging.

Clubs

You can offer a rich array of extra-curricular clubs that enrich students' learning experiences and broaden their cultural horizons. For example:

Conversation club

This focuses on improving students' speaking and listening skills through regular practice sessions. Students engage in discussions, role-playing games and conversational activities that mimic real-life interactions, making language learning more practical and less intimidating.

Duolingo club

Students select a language that they wish to learn and progress through lessons on Duolingo. The school can enhance motivation by maintaining a leaderboard to track and celebrate students' achievements. It's especially encouraging for students when teachers from various subjects participate, demonstrating widespread interest in language learning across the school community.

Drama club

Leverage famous plays to teach students how to perform in the target language, presenting their acts to primary students. Collaborate with your school's drama teacher to access necessary props, costumes and performance guidance. For instance, a Nativity play could be organised before Christmas. Other effective selections include *The Gruffalo*, *Cinderella* and *The Three Little Pigs*. These well-known stories are already familiar to primary students in English, which helps them to grasp the storyline when it is presented in a new language.

Film club

This is an opportunity to showcase films from various countries whose languages are taught at the school. This exposes students not only to different dialects and accents but also to diverse cultural contexts and cinematic styles. Post-viewing discussions can enhance critical thinking and language skills, as students express their opinions and analyse the films in the language of study.

Into Film Clubs (www.intofilm.org) offer students the opportunity to watch, discuss and review films. This is complemented by Into Film+, a streaming service specifically designed for educational settings, providing a wide range of films along with educational resources and activities. The organisation also hosts the Into Film Festival, the world's largest free youth film festival, which provides cinema experiences intended to inspire and educate young viewers. Into Film is dedicated to inclusivity and diversity, ensuring a broad representation in the films selected for their catalogue. This includes films from various cultures, languages and perspectives, which helps in fostering a greater understanding of diverse societies and issues among students.

Year 9 teaching in primary

You could consider training Year 9 students – or other groups – to teach in your feeder primary schools, although Year 9 is ideal since it's their option year. One possible project could be organising a Christmas-themed day. Depending on the number of participating students, you could form several groups, each focusing on different activities: one could teach Christmas-related vocabulary, another might host a quiz on Christmas traditions in the country whose language is being taught, a third could teach a Christmas song in the target language and another could lead a session using Blooket or Kahoot. This club requires extensive practice and hard work, but the rewards are immense. Imagine the pride that you'll feel watching your Year 9 students effectively teach a full class at a primary school! At the end of the academic year, consider hosting a French/German/Spanish Day, where different groups could lead various activities. For instance, one group could teach the primary students how to order food in a café – and then actually have them order and taste items like pain au chocolat, croissants, Brezels or crêpes. Another group could introduce a popular game from France, such as '*La clé de Saint Georges*', or lead a quiz about French culture. This hands-on approach not only enhances learning but also enriches the students' cultural understanding.

Spelling bee club

The purpose of a spelling bee club is to enhance students' vocabulary, pronunciation and orthographic skills in the target language. Students are challenged to correctly spell a variety of words, which helps to deepen their understanding of the language's phonetics and spelling rules. This can be especially helpful in languages where the spelling and pronunciation differ significantly from one's native language. Activities in this club include regular practice sessions and internal spelling competitions, and you could also compete in larger, inter-school events (for example, if your school is in a trust). The club can be a fun and engaging way for students to immerse themselves in the language and improve their fluency and linguistic confidence.

Cooking club

This explores the cuisine of countries where the target language is spoken. Students cook dishes together while practising language skills by following recipes and discussing in the target language.

Travel and cultural club

This focuses on the customs, traditions and history of countries where the target language is spoken. Activities might include planning virtual trips, learning about landmarks and celebrating cultural festivals.

Language immersion programme

Language immersion programmes are a step beyond traditional learning environments, placing students in a setting where they must use the target language exclusively. This approach is highly effective for rapid language acquisition. Immersion can occur within the school environment, where certain subjects are taught entirely in the target language, or through full immersion programmes abroad, where students live and study in a country where the language is spoken natively. This not only bolsters linguistic proficiency but also helps students to understand cultural nuances first-hand.

The Language Immersion Challenge from the British Council, known as 'The Great Languages Challenge', is an educational initiative designed to enhance language learning through a series of engaging and creative activities. This challenge encourages students to immerse themselves in the target language and culture in a variety of ways. Activities include cooking dishes from countries where the target language is spoken, learning phrases in a language with a different script and changing social media settings to the language being studied, among others. This programme aims to make language learning interactive and fun, pushing students to use the language in practical, everyday contexts and thereby deepen their understanding and proficiency.

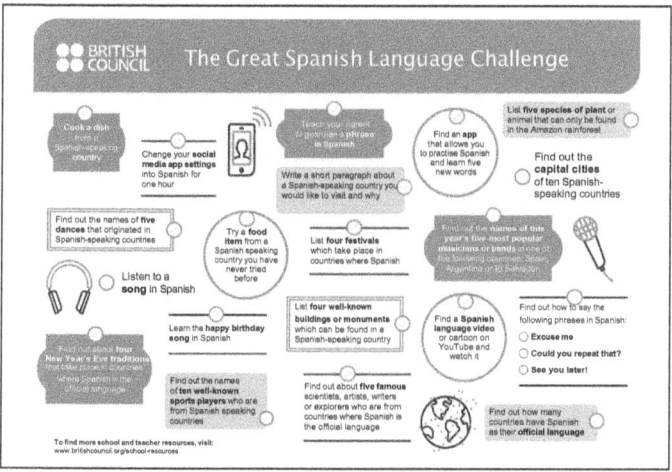

FIGURE 8.6: *Image courtesy of the British Council*

Competitions

Language competitions provide students with an excellent opportunity to showcase their language skills and compete against their peers. These events motivate students to set specific goals and can greatly improve their language proficiency and quick thinking in the target language. Such competitions also encourage students to refine their grammar, vocabulary and pronunciation.

You can organise these competitions within your school or extend them across your trust to allow students to compete with their peers from other schools. For example, you might set up a writing competition on a topic of your choosing. One idea is to have students create a postcard describing their holiday. This task would require not only writing in the target language but also designing and decorating the postcard. In the classroom, you can conduct other competitions like a vocabulary quiz. Similar to a spelling bee, this quiz would focus on the definition and usage of words, offering a fun way in which to learn new vocabulary. Another option is a translation challenge, where students translate sentences or short paragraphs from one language to another. For older students, consider hosting a debate on a pertinent issue, requiring them to prepare and present arguments in the target language – excellent practice for developing fluency and rhetorical skills. A pronunciation contest could also be effective, focusing on the accurate pronunciation of challenging words or phrases. Additionally, you can include language-based games like Pictionary, Charades or Scrabble, adapted to the language being studied.

Additionally, there are national competitions available for broader participation:

- '*Poésiæ*', created by Jérôme Nogues, offers a unique cross-curricular activity that uses language learning through the medium of poetry. This project is particularly beneficial for less confident or multi-talented students, providing them with an alternative way in which to express their understanding of selected or suggested poems. '*Poésiæ*' merges the art of poetry with language learning, helping students to enhance their linguistic and cultural comprehension. For more information, visit: www.poesiae.com

- 'Gimagine Award' is a digital learning programme from the Goethe-Institut UK, designed for young learners aged 13 to 18. It combines German language learning (20 modules) with global topics (five out of 19 modules) on areas like sustainability, arts and future skills. Participants earn an official certificate from the Goethe-Institut London, which can support CVs, university applications and the Duke of Edinburgh Award. The programme is flexible and open to individuals and groups, and includes interactive activities. For more details or to sign up, visit: gimagine.uk

- 'The French Pop Video Competition' is a national competition organised by Francophonie UK, in association with the Institut Français du Royaume-Uni and supported by TV5Monde. Since 2019, the competition has revealed many talented young singers and encouraged students to engage with French in a creative way. From the writing of a song to its singing (or rapping!) and video shooting, former participants have expressed how empowered the contest has made them feel. See the Institut Français website for more details.

- 'Celebrate speaking' is a celebration of languages in education and community through speaking and performance. To encourage students to practise the language that they are learning, or that they use in their community, they are invited to prepare either:

  - a short poem in the target language (written by themselves or by another author)
  - a short presentation
  - a short sketch
  - a short dialogue.

  This can be a solo or joint performance but should be no longer than 90 seconds in total. The students will record themselves delivering their performance; however, participants aged under 16 should use PowerPoint slides, Bitmoji or other pictures or video imagery, rather than showing their faces. For more information, visit: www.britishcouncil.org/school-resources/languages/celebrate-speaking – a helpful site with resources to support language learning and speaking activities.

- The European Day of Languages Annual Competition, organised by ALLNE and NfLNE is to celebrate linguistic diversity and language learning. The competition varies but often included creating posters, writing texts or participating in quizzes. For more information, please visit the Association for Language Learning website (https://www.all-languages.org.uk/).

Exchanges and trips

Trips abroad

These real-world experiences serve as invaluable pedagogical tools, providing students with immersive opportunities that enhance linguistic proficiency and cultural understanding. Organising international exchanges allows students to live with host families and attend local schools, thereby engaging directly with the language in its natural context. This not only bolsters their speaking and listening skills but also deepens their cultural appreciation, helping them to grasp nuanced expressions and regional dialects that classroom settings may not fully capture.

How to organise an exchange

Before initiating any plans, it's crucial to define what you want to achieve through the exchange. Consider the age of the students involved, the duration of the exchange and the key learning outcomes. Decide whether it will be a reciprocal visit, with students from both schools visiting each other's countries. Begin by presenting the idea to school leadership. You'll need to outline the educational benefits, costs and logistical considerations. Gaining the support of parents and the school board early on is also essential, as they will play a critical role in funding and approving the programme.

Finding a school

- **Networking:** Utilise existing contacts within your educational network who might have connections with schools in France, Spain or Germany.
- **E-Twinning:** This is a platform for schools in Europe that facilitates the establishment of educational partnerships.
- **The British Council:** This can also help you to find partner schools.
- **Embassies and cultural attachments:** Contact the cultural or educational attaché at the embassies of France, Spain or Germany for recommendations and support in finding a partner school.

Vetting potential schools

- Look for schools that have a strong language programme and are enthusiastic about cultural exchange.
- Consider the location, size and demographic of the partner school to ensure compatibility with your school.

Once you have a partner school, plan logistically. Work with a reputable travel agency that specialises in educational trips, or directly with airlines and coach companies for group bookings. Ensure that all travel documents and visas (if necessary) are in order. Decide whether students will stay with host families or in a dormitory/hostel setup. If opting for host families, students will have a real exposure to the language, culture and tradition. However, you will have to conduct thorough checks and briefings to ensure student safety. Secure comprehensive travel insurance that covers health, accidents and cancellations. Familiarise yourself with the healthcare system of the host country and communicate this information to parents and students.

Develop a balanced schedule that includes educational activities, cultural outings and some free time. Educational activities might involve attending classes at the partner school, while cultural outings could include visiting historical sites and museums.

Develop a clear communication plan to keep parents informed throughout the exchange. This should include emergency contact information and regular updates during the trip.

Organising a school exchange requires careful planning and a proactive approach, but the rewards in terms of student development and international understanding are immeasurable. Similarly, educational trips to countries where the target language is spoken can be transformative. By planning activities that include historical site visits, cultural workshops, visits to a local school and interaction with local peers, teachers can create dynamic learning environments that encourage spontaneous language use and foster a genuine connection with the culture. These experiences help to demystify foreign languages, turning abstract classroom lessons into tangible, memorable interactions.

Furthermore, the anticipation and preparation for these trips often motivate students to engage more deeply with the language in their regular studies, knowing that they will soon use their skills in real-world scenarios. To maximise the benefits, it is important that you carefully plan these activities to align with curricular goals and ensure that all students are prepared and supported throughout these experiences, thereby making language learning both enjoyable and effective.

There are many agencies that can help you to plan your trip, such as Edventure Travel, NST and Halsbury Travel.

Enrichment without leaving the country

While organising an exchange or a trip abroad is beneficial, there are effective alternatives that don't require travel. One such way is setting up a pen pal programme with a school in another country. Students can write letters in the language that they are studying and exchange them with a partner school abroad. Participating in a few letter exchanges each year not only boosts motivation but also gives students a practical reason to use and improve their language skills. This approach ensures that all students can engage, unlike trips abroad, which may not be accessible to everyone.

Beyond pen pal programmes, you can engage in collaborative online projects with schools in countries of the target language. These could be research projects on specific cultural aspects, joint art exhibitions or science projects, allowing students to interact and learn collaboratively through digital platforms.

You could also organise practical language use experiences, such as a visit to a tapas restaurant for students learning Spanish, where they must order and communicate in Spanish. Additionally, institutes like the French, Spanish and German (Goethe) Institute often host a variety of cultural events and theme days that are beneficial for students. Contact them to explore current offerings.

For film enthusiasts, you could consider arranging a movie outing where films are shown in the target language with English subtitles. Some venues offer a comprehensive cultural experience by screening a film followed by a study session about it – for example, HOME Manchester or Ciné Lumière in Institut Français Royaume-Uni organise such events.

You can also invite native speakers or cultural experts to your class to talk about different aspects of their culture, cuisine, daily life or special holidays. Workshops could include cooking classes, dance lessons or traditional crafts, which provide hands-on learning opportunities without the need for travel.

Organising or participating in language café events, where students can practise speaking with native speakers in a relaxed setting is another fantastic way of bringing culture into the classroom. Additionally, attending local cultural festivals that celebrate different cultures can be a great way for students to immerse themselves in the language and customs of the countries whose languages they are studying.

You can also invite companies such as Onatti Productions or Mingalaba.

- Onatti produces fantastic plays and films to inspire students who are learning foreign languages, giving teachers a fantastic teaching resource. Onatti has an incredible reputation for creating exciting and modern stories to enthuse students. They come to school to perform the play and they offer a range of plays for different age groups. To reduce the cost, you could invite other schools so that the price can be split.

- Mingalaba delivers exciting, innovative projects that enthuse young people to learn a language through the medium of football. They also offer outreach services to schools, including motivational talks, workshops, football and language sessions, and fun, engaging learning resources. Football is the common thread in everything that they do. It's their tried-and-tested engagement tool, particularly for those who wouldn't normally engage with learning a language.

Enrichment activities in and outside the MFL classroom help to bring language learning to life. Things like clubs, trips, themed days or even simple games and projects can boost motivation, build confidence and even spark curiosity about other cultures. When students see how languages connect to the real world, they're more likely to stay engaged and enjoy the journey.

REFLECTIVE QUESTIONS

- How do you currently integrate cultural elements into your language teaching and how might you expand these efforts to enhance students' engagement and cultural understanding?
- Is culture planned in your schemes of work to ensure consistency across your department?
- Reflect on the enrichment activities that you have tried in the past. What has been successful and what could be improved?
- Reflect on the types of authentic materials that you currently use in your lessons. How could you expand this to include more diverse media (e.g. podcasts, films, magazines) to enhance linguistic and cultural exposure?
- What are some in-class and out-of-class enrichment activities that you could implement to make language learning more engaging and relevant for your students?
- Reflect on how the cultural components of your lessons have influenced student motivation. What changes could you make to further enhance their interest and participation?
- How do extra-curricular activities complement your curriculum in promoting language proficiency and cultural understanding? Can you think of new clubs or events that could further these goals?

CASE STUDY

Case study: Finding time for cultural enrichment: Little and often and going for gold
Name of school: Cundall Manor School
Contributor: Suzi Bewell, Head of Languages

What was the issue?

A significant hurdle for MFL educators is the effective incorporation of cultural elements within the time constraints of typical lessons. The necessity of covering core language skills and exam content often marginalises cultural exploration, potentially leading to a superficial understanding and hindering the development of genuine intercultural competence. Enrichment, both within and beyond the classroom, risks becoming secondary, diminishing the motivational and connective power of cultural understanding in language acquisition.

How did we resolve it?

To tackle this, I adopt a dual strategy: integrating brief cultural insights 'little and often' into regular lessons and offering optional 'going for gold' cultural homework for students demonstrating a strong interest in the target language culture.

The 'little and often' method involves seamlessly weaving short, engaging cultural snippets into the lesson's fabric. Instead of dedicated cultural lessons, which can be challenging to schedule, I regularly introduce small, interesting cultural elements linked directly to the lesson's content. For instance, when teaching French food vocabulary, we might briefly explore regional specialities through images or short audio clips, e.g. comparing breakfast in several Francophone countries. Similarly, discussions on Spanish daily routines could include insights into mealtimes or siesta practices. Authentic resources like brief online videos or social media posts prove invaluable here. I have also found that realia acquired from a French-speaking country, e.g. Sénégal, can spark curiosity.

Complementing this in-class integration is voluntary 'going for gold' cultural homework. This extension activity caters to students with a keen interest in deeper cultural exploration. Moving beyond standard language exercises, it offers a range of creative tasks, such as researching non-traditional Francophone sports, translating up-to-the-minute chart lyrics or even preparing a simple meal or dessert following a target language recipe. These tasks promote independent learning, critical thinking and a more profound connection with personally relevant cultural aspects. While not traditionally graded, completed work is acknowledged and celebrated in class through sharing sessions or displays, and house points are awarded.

What was the impact?

This two-pronged approach has yielded notable positive outcomes. The 'little and often' strategy has successfully embedded cultural learning within language acquisition, moving it away from being a separate entity. Regular exposure to cultural nuances fosters a gradual development of cultural awareness and understanding. Anecdotally, students show increased engagement and curiosity during these brief cultural moments, prompting more questions about the target language world.

Furthermore, the 'going for gold' cultural homework has provided a valuable avenue for passionate students to pursue their cultural interests in more depth. The voluntary nature of the tasks fosters high motivation, resulting in creative and insightful work. This cultivates a sense of ownership over their learning and a more personal connection with the target culture. Sharing their discoveries enriches the learning experience for peers, offering engaging exposure to diverse cultural facets. In fact, everyone benefits.

In conclusion, by integrating cultural elements in manageable chunks within lessons and providing optional, enriching homework, I have established a more sustainable and engaging method for cultivating intercultural understanding in my MFL students. This ensures that cultural enrichment is recognised not as an optional extra but as a golden thread that weaves through all language lessons.

Chapter summary

This chapter looked at the importance of enrichment, both in and beyond the classroom, and how it can bring language learning to life for our students.

- Giving learners a window into different cultures can really shift their attitude towards languages, especially for those who don't see the subject as 'for them'.

- Enrichment doesn't have to be complicated or expensive. Using real-life materials such as menus, adverts, property listings or watching clips of films in the target language can all be done in class. Celebrating festivals or doing creative projects linked to culture can make a big impact too.

- Outside the classroom, consider trips, exchanges, clubs and themed days. Not every school can offer a trip abroad, but there are still many ways in which to give students that 'real world' connection.

- Clubs and competitions are great ways in which to give students something extra.
- Enrichment isn't just 'nice to have'. It plays a big role in boosting motivation, widening students' horizons and helping them to see language learning as something exciting, relevant and real.

Further reading

- *From Foreign Language Education to Education for Intercultural Citizenship* by Michael Byram (2008) explores how language teaching can go beyond grammar and vocabulary to develop learners' intercultural understanding, promoting global citizenship through meaningful engagement with culture.
- *Interculturality in International Education* by Jane Jackson (2020) offers an in-depth exploration of how intercultural learning happens through international experiences, making it a valuable read for educators planning exchanges or aiming to embed global perspectives.
- *Intercultural Language Teaching and Learning* by Anthony Liddicoat and Angela Scarino (2013) provides a strong theoretical and practical foundation for integrating intercultural understanding into language lessons, helping students to connect language to identity, context and culture.
- Suzi Bewell's Polly Glot Languages shares practical MFL teaching ideas, cultural activities and enrichment suggestions: https://pollyglotlanguages.wordpress.com/author/suzibewell

9

Personal professional development

Introduction

Professional development is a cornerstone of effective teaching, especially for language teachers, whose work requires both strong teaching skills and a deep understanding of language. This chapter looks at how personal and professional growth can benefit language teachers, offering strategies and resources to support ongoing improvement. By reflecting on your teaching, setting achievable goals, joining professional learning communities, participating in CPD opportunities and seeking mentorship, you can consistently develop your skills and create meaningful learning experiences for your students.

Reflective practice

Reflective practice is a valuable tool that helps language teachers to grow professionally and personally. By taking the time to think about and evaluate your teaching experiences, you can gain insights into what works, what doesn't and how to improve your approaches to better support your students.

Reflection allows you to focus on successes, identify areas for improvement and explore innovative approaches to teaching. For example, after a lesson, you might reflect by asking yourself:

- What went well in this lesson?
- Were my instructions clear and accessible to all students?
- How did my students respond to the activities and what does this say about their engagement or understanding?

You can make reflective practice more structured by keeping a self-reflection diary, discussing your experiences with peers or using reflection tools like Gibbs' reflective cycle (1988), which guides you through a step-by-step process. Reflecting isn't just about finding gaps; it is also about celebrating what you are doing well and building on your strengths.

Examples of reflective practice in action

- **Self-reflection diary:** Keeping a weekly diary allows you to reflect on your lessons in a systematic way. For instance, after a lesson on the subjunctive mood, you might realise that your explanation was too abstract for your students to fully grasp. As a result, you decide to incorporate concrete, real-life examples next time, such as planning an imaginary holiday, to make the concept clearer and more relatable.

- **Lesson recording:** Recording your lessons (using Swivl or IRIS Connect) can give you a clearer view of how they unfold. For example, after recording a French lesson on the past tense, you might notice that quieter students didn't get involved as much as others. To address this, you plan to use strategies like cold-calling and group activities designed to encourage broader participation, ensuring that every student stays engaged.

- **Student feedback/student voice:** Seeking feedback directly from your students can offer valuable insights. For example, you might ask them which activities helped them to better understand adjectival agreements. Their responses could lead you to retain certain strategies or activities, while adjusting written exercises to make them either more engaging or appropriately challenging.

Why reflective practice matters

Reflective practice is essential because it fosters continuous growth. It helps you to adapt to the needs of your students, refine your teaching and build confidence in your ability to deliver effective lessons. By combining thoughtful reflection with actionable strategies, you can ensure that your teaching evolves in ways that have a lasting, positive impact on your students' learning outcomes.

Goal-setting and action planning

Setting clear and achievable goals is crucial for growth in any profession, and language teaching is no exception. Goals help you to stay focused, giving you a sense of purpose and direction in your work. Whether you are looking to improve your teaching approaches, strengthen your language skills or advance your career, setting the right goals can make all the difference.

For language teachers, professional goals can take many forms. You might aim to refine specific teaching strategies, such as better supporting students with different learning needs or integrating more technology into your lessons. Or you could focus on personal development goals, like becoming more fluent in your second or third language or expanding your knowledge of cultural contexts to enrich your teaching. Career advancement goals might include earning a qualification, attending workshops or taking on leadership roles within your school or professional network.

Achieving these goals starts with making them clear and manageable. Instead of vague targets like 'get better at classroom management', try specific, measurable goals like 'develop a new seating plan and use consistent routines to improve classroom dynamics by the end of the term'. Breaking large goals into smaller steps can also make them easier to achieve, keeping you motivated as you see progress.

Tracking your progress is another important step. Use tools like checklists to see how far you have come and where you might need to adjust. Sharing your goals with a mentor, coach or trusted colleague can also provide valuable guidance and encouragement.

Setting goals isn't just about personal development; it directly benefits your students. As you grow more skilled and confident, your teaching becomes more effective, helping your students to learn better and achieve more.

To make goals actionable, you can adopt the SMART framework (Doran, 1981), ensuring that your objectives are:

- **Specific:** Clearly define what you aim to achieve, focusing on a distinct area of improvement or development. For example, 'Integrate three new authentic resources into lessons over the next term' is more precise than 'Use more authentic materials'. A specific goal narrows your focus and provides direction.

- **Measurable:** Include criteria to assess progress and success. This might involve using tools like student feedback forms, lesson observations or a self-reflection diary. For example, you could measure the effectiveness of your authentic materials by tracking student engagement or performance in tasks linked to those resources.

- **Achievable:** Set objectives that are realistic within your current capacity, considering your time, resources and skills. Stretching your limits is productive but goals should remain attainable. For instance, instead of planning to overhaul all lessons with new materials, aim to adapt a few key topics.

- **Relevant:** Ensure that the objective ties into your broader teaching goals, curriculum priorities or specific needs of your students. For example, if students struggle with a particular grammar concept, such as verb conjugation, your goal to incorporate authentic resources should focus on tasks that support the understanding and application of this concept. Using short texts or dialogues that naturally model verb conjugations in context can make grammar more accessible and engaging for students.

- **Time-bound:** Define a clear deadline or timeframe to maintain focus and motivation. For example, you might aim to trial new resources over a half term or assess their impact within a term. Deadlines encourage consistent effort and provide opportunities for review and reflection.

Creating an action plan with clear steps to achieve your goals can help you to stay focused and make steady progress. For example, if your goal is to strengthen your classroom management skills, you could break it into actionable steps. Start by setting a timeline: first, read a book, work with a coach or mentor or attend a CPD session on effective classroom management strategies. Then, practise specific strategies in your lessons, such as setting clear expectations or using positive framing. Finally, evaluate their impact and adjust your approach, based on what works best for you and your students. This structured approach ensures that you not only set goals but also take concrete actions to achieve them, keeping you on track and motivated along the way.

Other examples of goal-setting in CPD

- **Improving language skills:** Building your skills in your second or third language is a great way in which to grow, both personally and professionally. To do this, take a well-rounded approach. Join subject enhancement classes for structured learning, ensuring that you cover the key areas that you need to improve. Each week, practise speaking with a language partner, focusing on everyday conversations. Make time for daily practice by reading newspapers in the target language for 15 minutes, helping you to pick up new words and understand the culture better. These regular activities will help you to become more confident and fluent over time.

- **Using technology:** Adding more digital tools to your teaching can make lessons more interesting and engaging. To do this, break the process into small steps. In the first month, focus on learning one tool, like Vidnoz, by watching tutorials and practising its features. Use it to create short videos for your lessons. By the second month, move onto creating interactive videos with quizzes. Step-by-step, build your confidence with technology and find new ways in which to make your lessons more dynamic and effective.

- **Career development:** If you are aiming to become a subject leader, it is important to prepare yourself step-by-step. Start by shadowing the current subject leader, observing how they manage the team, solve problems and handle their responsibilities. This gives you a clear idea of what the role involves. Attend leadership training sessions to learn the skills that you will need, such as leading teams and managing change. To formalise your progress, work towards a leadership qualification, like the National Professional Qualification for Leading Teaching (NPQLT). These steps give you the experience and knowledge to feel ready for the role and succeed in it.

Professional learning communities

Collaboration with colleagues is a vital component of professional development. Professional learning communities (PLCs) provide a platform for teachers to share best practices, exchange ideas and discuss challenges in a supportive environment.

Language teachers like you can benefit greatly from engaging with PLCs within their schools or multi-academy trusts (MATs) or through external networks like subject associations. These communities often focus on specific themes, such as improving speaking skills or exploring innovative assessment methods.

For instance, participation in an Association for Language Learning (ALL) regional hub, Institut Français, Consejería de Educación or Goethe-Institut teacher network can connect you with peers who share the same passion for language education as you. These networks not only provide practical resources but will also keep you informed about the latest research and policy developments in the field. Members of these teachers networks often also benefit from free subject specific CPD offerings.

Examples

- **Within a MAT:** Collaborating within a MAT allows teachers from different schools to work together and share successful strategies. For example, you and your colleagues meet monthly to discuss ways in which to improve vocabulary instruction at Key Stage 3. During one meeting, you explain how using retrieval practice has helped your students to remember vocabulary more effectively. Show examples of how you have used this approach, such as regular, interleaved and spaced retrieval quizzes, and share the positive impact that it has had on retention. Inspired by your success, other teachers in the group might decide to try it in their own classrooms. Over time, these shared ideas create a stronger, more cohesive approach to vocabulary teaching across the trust.

- **Subject associations:** Joining a professional organisation like ALL (https://www.all-languages.org.uk/) gives you access to a wealth of resources and support. For example, you or your department might decide to become a member and attend an online session focused on teaching languages to students with SEND. In the session, you learn practical strategies, such as breaking tasks into smaller steps, using visual aids or providing more structured scaffolding for language practice. Afterwards, you apply these ideas to your own teaching, making your lessons more inclusive and accessible to all students. By sharing what you have learned with your colleagues, you also help to create a more supportive learning environment across your department.

- **Global networks:** Becoming part of a global network, like the Global Schools Alliance, opens up opportunities to work on international projects and bring diverse perspectives into your classroom. For instance, your school might collaborate with teachers in other countries on cultural exchange projects, such as joint virtual pen pal activities or shared research tasks. These collaborations allow students to interact with peers from different cultures, practising their language skills in real-world contexts. For teachers, it means access to new resources, ideas and teaching methods that enrich your lessons. By making language learning more engaging and culturally relevant, your students gain a deeper understanding of the world, while developing essential communication skills.

By collaborating in these communities, you can contribute to a collective knowledge base, while also growing individually through shared insights.

Continuing professional development

Ongoing learning is a hallmark of effective teaching. CPD opportunities allow language teachers to deepen their knowledge, refine their skills and stay current with evolving educational trends. CPD can take many forms:

- **Conferences:** Attending conferences is a great way in which to stay updated on new teaching practices and build connections with other professionals. Events like the annual Language World conference, the Language Show or local training days bring together language teachers to share innovative ideas and strategies. These events also provide the chance to meet other teachers, exchange ideas and build professional networks. You leave inspired and equipped with fresh approaches to try in your classroom, making your teaching more engaging and effective.

- **Online courses:** Online platforms such as the Chartered College of Teaching or the Ambition Institute offer flexible, high-quality professional development opportunities. Online courses allow you to learn at your own pace, making them an ideal option for busy teachers. By applying what you learn, you can strengthen your teaching practice and stay up to date with the latest trends in education. The NCLE's Language Educators Online (LEO) platform – https://ncle.ucl.ac.uk/language-educators-online/ – is another excellent free resource dedicated to the professional development of language teachers, offering flexible CPD courses you can complete whenever it suits you.

- **Webinars and podcasts:** Subject associations, language organisations and professionals, such as ALL, Linguascope, Languagenut and Sanako or the Motivated Classroom podcast, regularly offer free webinars and podcasts designed specifically for language teachers. For instance, a webinar might focus on using authentic resources to enhance listening skills, while a podcast could include interviews with experienced teachers sharing practical tips for curriculum design. These resources are flexible and easy to access, whether at home or on the go, and they offer actionable strategies that you can quickly implement in your teaching.

Other examples

- **Workshops:** Attending workshops can be a practical way in which to learn new teaching techniques. For example, you attend a session on French phonics and discover creative methods to help your students to improve their pronunciation. The session introduces strategies like breaking words into syllables, focusing on common sound patterns and using rhymes or songs to practise tricky sounds. Back in the classroom, you apply these strategies, integrating them into warm-up activities or pronunciation drills. Over time, you notice your students becoming more confident in speaking French, with clearer pronunciation, intonation and improved fluency. This success encourages you to explore more workshops to further enhance your teaching.

- **Online learning:** Online courses offer a flexible way in which to stay updated with curriculum changes and teaching approaches. For example, you enrol in a course about delivering the new GCSE and learn about the updated specification, assessment objectives and changes in the examination format. The course also provides tips for preparing students effectively, such as focusing on specific grammar points or refining listening and speaking skills. By the end of the course, you feel more confident about teaching the new GCSE. You use what you have learned to plan lessons aligned with the new requirements, ensuring that your students are well prepared for the changes, as well as feeding back the gained knowledge to your department.

- **TeachMeets:** Attending TeachMeets can provide valuable insights and opportunities for professional growth. For example, you attend a TeachMeet where an Ofsted inspector explains what makes a strong, well-sequenced MFL curriculum. The session highlights key features such as clear progression in language skills, regular revisiting of vocabulary and grammar and embedding cultural knowledge. Armed with this knowledge, you return to school and share what you have learned with your colleagues in a department meeting. Together, you review your current curriculum, identify areas for improvement and make adjustments to ensure that it meets high standards. This collaborative approach strengthens the overall quality of language teaching at your school.

Engaging in CPD will not only benefit your teaching practice but also signal a commitment to lifelong learning – a quality that resonates with your students and colleagues alike.

Mentorship and coaching

The guidance of a mentor or coach can have a powerful impact on a teacher's professional development, regardless of their career stage. In my school, we run an instructional coaching programme using StepLab. This programme is carefully structured, with timetabled coaching sessions for every teacher in the school – whether they are an ECT, an experienced classroom teacher, a subject leader or a member of the senior leadership team (SLT). These sessions provide personalised professional development, where coaches share their expertise, offer constructive feedback and help teachers to overcome challenges and grow to achieve their goals.

For ECTs or teachers stepping into new roles, having a mentor can be transformative. Mentors provide practical help, like refining lesson plans, navigating curriculum updates or building confidence in using innovative techniques. For example, mentors might help the new teacher to implement strategies such as cold-calling to engage students, circulating the classroom to monitor learning or checking for understanding to ensure that students are learning. They might also support the teacher in fine-tuning their questioning techniques, maintaining a good lesson pace or embedding routines such as signal/pause/insist to keep students focused.

Instructional coaching focuses on specific, actionable goals. For instance, a coach might work with a teacher on improving their presence in the classroom, helping them to consistently gain and hold students' attention, or on developing strategies for addressing low-level disruptions effectively. This targeted approach helps teachers to make measurable improvements in key areas of their practice.

Strong mentorship and coaching relationships are built on trust and open communication. To make the most of these opportunities, it is important to actively engage with mentors and coaches. This can happen through formal programmes like those within schools or subject associations or through informal networks. These relationships will not only support you in your immediate challenges but also help you to build the confidence and skills needed for long-term success in your career.

Examples

- **ECT mentoring:** If you are an ECT, mentoring is a statutory requirement that provides you with essential support during your first two years in the classroom. You will be paired with a mentor who will guide you through challenges and help you to develop your teaching skills. For example, if you are planning a GCSE lesson on extended writing but feel uncertain about structuring it, your mentor can offer practical advice. They might suggest breaking the task into smaller, manageable steps or using live modelling with a visualiser to demonstrate effective writing strategies. These strategies will not only boost your confidence but also help your students to build their writing skills in a clear, structured way.

- **Instructional coaching:** Instructional coaching is a focused way in which to refine specific aspects of your teaching practice. During a coaching session, your coach might observe a lesson and notice that pair work isn't running smoothly. Rather than just giving you solutions, they will probe – ask thoughtful questions to help you to identify the root of the issue and brainstorm improvements. Together, you might explore how to assign clear roles to your students, like 'speaker' and 'note-taker', so that each student stays actively engaged. Your coach will also work with you to script and deliberately practise these strategies, ensuring that you feel prepared to manage pair work effectively in future lessons. This deliberate practice will help you to feel more confident and capable in your classroom.

- **Peer mentoring:** Peer mentoring gives you the opportunity to collaborate with colleagues who have expertise in specific areas. For instance, if you want to use digital tools in your lessons, a tech-savvy peer can guide you. They might show you how to use apps like Wordwall to create interactive language activities. By meeting regularly, you can share tips, plan lessons together and build your skills. This kind of mentoring not only increases your confidence but also enriches your lessons, making them more engaging and enjoyable for your students.

Professional development is a journey that helps you to grow both personally and professionally. It is about finding ways in which to improve your skills, stay up to date with educational research and meet the changing needs of your students and the education system.

By engaging in continuing professional development, you learn new ideas and strategies that can make your teaching more effective. It gives you the chance to think about what you are doing well and what you could do better, helping you to grow as a teacher. Whether you join workshops, work with colleagues, take online courses or get coaching, each experience adds to your knowledge and builds your confidence in the classroom.

Professional development isn't just about improving your teaching – it also helps you to grow as a person. It teaches you to be more reflective, adaptable and focused on your goals. As you try new ideas and overcome challenges, you will feel more connected to your students and your work. In the end, professional development helps you to become the best teacher that you can be, so that you can make a positive difference for your students.

REFLECTIVE QUESTIONS

- Which personal and professional development strategies stood out to you and why?
- How often do you reflect on your teaching and how can you improve this process to learn more?
- Have you set clear goals for your growth? How can you use the SMART framework to make them better?

- How can you get more involved in professional learning communities to share and learn with others?
- Which CPD opportunities have helped you the most and what new ones could you try to improve your teaching?
- How could seeking or offering mentorship and coaching help you to grow professionally?

CASE STUDY

Case study: Empowering educators: Personal development for lifelong learning
Contributor: Crista Hazell, International Education Consultant (Teaching and Learning, Behaviour and MFL), Specialist Leader in Education for MFL, author of Independent Thinking on MFL and Development Manager for The Association for Language Learning

What was the issue?

To succeed as an MFL teacher, engaging in ongoing personal and professional development is vital. Our educational institutions provide us with whole-school professional development, in line with the school vision, action plan and/or development plan, but it is our responsibility to seek out our own so that we continue to develop knowledge, skills and understanding from a languages perspective in order to remain relevant, engaged and motivated. This could be upskilling language ability, learning another language, understanding how to lead an overseas educational visit, becoming an examiner, engaging with action research or engaging with the wider language learning community, to mention a few.

How did we resolve it?

As a leader, it is important to ensure that we support colleagues so that they can access professional development too, and we need to signpost this. I worked with the teams that I line-managed and one thing that I encouraged annually was to choose a 'personal development project'. This project was in addition to the annual appraisal target, but it was a personal goal – a free choice that would allow them to consider deeply what aspect they wanted to improve that would have an impact on themselves and on their classroom and which they could share with others.

I asked the following questions, which provided a framework to monitor and track:

- What do you want to learn/improve/develop? Why this and why now?
- What do you need in order to complete this project successfully?
- Who can help you to do this?
- What will success look like and what will the impact be:
  - for you?
  - for your classroom?
  - for your department/family?
  - for your professional journey as a languages teacher?
- What is your timeframe for completion?

Staff should be prepared to give updates at departmental meetings on their projects. This framework provided a safe environment for teachers to be honest about their personal and professional development needs, for which they would be responsible.

The point/goal was to ask the teachers to stop and think deeply about themselves. What did they want to develop and achieve? But rather than just 'dream' it, they needed to make it a reality, so that they could improve their skill set and toolkit as a teacher/leader/human. Then they needed to consider the different elements required to take them out of their comfort zone to engage with others – perhaps a coach or other teachers – and to seek out and attend training that would help them to achieve their goal. This could be seeking support from exam boards and reputable external providers or engaging more with their subject association and the wider language learning community, to find commonality and to develop their community of practice beyond their immediate department. All of this was in order to allow inspiration and curiosity to engage but also to provide support and signposts to allow the individual to grow – such as subject association membership, which gave access to a range of events, both local and national, and to periodicals as well as research journals. I also aimed to improve access to forums and discussion groups, so that the teacher could build their skill set, toolkit or repertoire but also learn from others.

What was the impact?

Teachers at all stages of their career and levels of leadership have improved in confidence and communication skills, as well as navigating potholes along the way, learning to find alternative solutions in achieving their project aims. My purpose was to ensure that teachers were looking and learning beyond the department and school in which they work, but also for them to take ownership of their own professional development, in order that this was a process done *by* them rather than a process done *to* them – ergo a positive experience. Timetabling opportunities to share their project progress at departmental-level meetings proved powerful, as colleagues were sharing their practice freely but also learning from others openly.

> This developed to such an extent that individuals were sharing across departments and beyond the school, on social media and at network events, TeachMeets and conferences.
>
> The impact of this included:
>
> - increased knowledge, skills and understanding
> - an increased repertoire
> - improvements in confidence, communication, creativity, problem-solving and project management
> - deeper and wider reading
> - engaging more deeply with pedagogy and research in their professional practice
> - putting learning and their learners at the heart of their development.
>
> Everyone who engaged with this benefitted because they chose their own project and made it a success.

Chapter summary

In this chapter, we have explored key strategies for supporting the professional development of language teachers.

- Reflective practice enables teachers to evaluate their teaching experiences, celebrate strengths and identify areas for improvement, through structured reflection.

- Setting clear, specific and achievable goals (using the SMART framework) helps teachers to focus their growth and take actionable steps to improve their teaching or language skills.

- Joining PLCs encourages collaboration, sharing of best practices and mutual support among language teachers.

- CPD opportunities such as conferences, online courses, webinars and podcasts keep teachers informed and equipped with fresh ideas and strategies.
- Mentorship and coaching provide personalised guidance, constructive feedback and targeted support, helping teachers to build confidence and develop effective teaching practices.

Further reading

- *Independent Thinking on MFL* by Crista Hazell (2020) offers strategies and experiences from the MFL classroom how to make modern foreign language teaching exciting, inclusive and relevant.
- *Get Better Faster: A 90-Day Plan for Coaching New Teachers* by Paul Bambrick-Santoyo (2016) is a brilliant read, offering a practical and structured coaching plan designed to accelerate new teachers' development within their first 90 days in the classroom.
- *The Definitive Guide to Instructional Coaching: Seven Factors for Success* by Jim Knight (2023) is an accessible guide outlining key principles and practical steps for building effective instructional coaching programmes in schools.
- *Teaching WalkThrus 3: Five-Step Guides to Instructional Coaching* by Tom Sherrington and Oliver Caviglioli (2022) is a practical resource offering bite-sized coaching strategies to support teacher development through focused classroom observation and feedback.

10

Developing your language teaching team: Strategies for growth and collaboration

Introduction

Language teaching works best when it is a team effort. Building a strong and united teaching team not only makes teaching more effective but also helps teachers to feel supported, appreciated and motivated. This chapter explores ways in which you can grow and collaborate as a team, focusing on building a culture of collaboration, identifying strengths and areas for improvement for your team, working together on lesson plans and resources and supporting each other through peer support, coaching and mentoring.

Building a culture of collaboration

Set shared targets and vision

Collaboration starts with having a common vision. To build a successful language teaching team, you can begin by working together to define your goals. Make sure that these goals align with the school's priorities and meet the needs of your students. Organise departmental meetings where you and your colleagues can talk about:

- **your curriculum and pedagogy:** your evidence-informed teaching approaches
- **your assessment, feedback and marking policy:** the purpose of it and the outcomes that you want for your students
- **your behaviour and culture policy:** based on high expectations for all
- **CPD:** professional development opportunities such as NPQs.

Listen to everyone's input so that the vision and goals reflect the team's collective ideas. When everyone feels like they have contributed, they will be more committed to achieving these shared goals.

Once you have set your targets, revisit them regularly to make sure that they are still relevant and adjust them if needed. It is also a good idea to document your targets in a shared space so that you and your team can refer back to them easily. My department and I use SharePoint, but there are other platforms that you could consider using.

Promote open communication

Strong collaboration depends on clear and respectful communication. To ensure this, set up channels that make it easy for you and your team to talk and share ideas. Some ways in which to improve communication include:

- scheduling regular departmental meetings with clear and specific agendas
- using online platforms like Google or Microsoft Teams for ongoing conversations
- providing anonymous feedback tools so that team members can share their thoughts or concerns freely.

Make it a habit to actively listen and respond constructively when team members share their input. Listen to hear and not just to respond! By creating a space where everyone's ideas are valued, you help to build trust and transparency within the department.

Build an inclusive environment

An inclusive environment helps everyone in your team to feel valued and motivated to contribute. Celebrate the diverse backgrounds and experiences of your team members by:

- organising team-building activities to strengthen team bonds, like a shared meal or eventing out as a department
- encouraging teaching approaches that highlight different cultural perspectives
- ensuring equal opportunities for training, development and leadership roles.

It is also important to address unconscious biases within the team, offering training or workshops to increase awareness and ensuring that every member feels respected and understood. When people feel included, they are more likely to bring their best to the table.

Make decisions together

When you involve your team in making important decisions, you tap into a wider range of perspectives. Whether it is choosing new resources, choosing exam boards, revising the curriculum or planning workshops, group decisions are often more effective and ensure that everyone feels invested in the outcomes.

Use structured decision-making processes like voting or reaching a consensus to ensure fairness. When your team has ownership over decisions, they are more likely to follow through with them.

Identifying strengths and areas for growth

Assess skills

Understanding your team's strengths and areas for growth helps you to make the most of everyone's abilities. Use tools like surveys (Microsoft or Google Forms), self-assessments or lesson drop-ins to:

- highlight individual skills, such as proficiency in specific languages or innovative teaching approaches
- identify areas where additional training or support is needed
- create a skills chart to visualise the strengths and gaps within your team. This will help you to assign classes, roles and responsibilities more effectively and plan professional development opportunities.

Observe and give feedback

Classroom observations, learning walks or drop-ins are an excellent way in which to support growth within your team. Have a scheduled time to visit your teams (I use my Outlook calendar for this) but also each other's lessons, and follow up with one-on-one feedback to:

- celebrate effective teaching practices
- offer constructive feedback for improvement
- ensure that teaching strategies align with department and school policies.

When giving feedback, focus on being supportive. Offer specific examples and actionable suggestions and follow up to discuss progress. This approach makes feedback feel like an opportunity for development rather than criticism.

Set targets for development

Encourage your team members to set individual targets for their professional development. These targets should align with both their personal interests and the department's objectives. Examples of development targets could include:

- having an effective entry and dismissal routine
- creating more opportunities for speaking practice
- developing effective questioning strategies to check for understanding.

Provide resources, coaching or mentorship to help your team to achieve these targets. Celebrate milestones to keep everyone motivated and encourage team members to share their achievements to inspire others.

Encourage peer feedback

Peer feedback is another valuable tool for growth. Create opportunities for informal classroom visits or peer review sessions, where teachers can share lesson plans or teaching materials. This not only builds trust but also provides fresh perspectives on teaching practices.

Collaborative lesson planning and resource sharing

Create a shared resource library

A shared resource library is a great way in which to make teamwork easier. Use online tools like Google Drive, SharePoint or One Drive to:

- store and organise lesson plans, PowerPoints, activities and assessments
- categorise resources by phase, language, key stage, unit or topic
- enable team members to update and improve materials collaboratively.

It is important to keep the library well organised and up to date, ensuring that its content is regularly refreshed so that it stays useful. You can either manage this yourself or appoint someone to take charge of its maintenance. Encourage everyone involved to actively contribute, whether by adding new resources, reviewing existing ones or suggesting improvements.

Plan lessons together

Set aside dedicated time to plan lessons as a team. Collaborative planning sessions allow you and your colleagues to:

- brainstorm creative ideas for engaging lessons
- support your new colleagues and ECT
- align objectives across different classes and levels
- tailor shared lesson plans to suit individual teaching styles
- reduce workload.

These sessions help to maintain consistency, while also encouraging creativity and autonomy and offering support when necessary. They provide a great chance to address challenges, whether it is a difficult concept to teach or issues with classroom management, and to work together to find solutions.

Use technology to collaborate

Technology can simplify collaboration. Use tools like Padlet, Wakelet and Canva to:

- plan lessons visually
- share multimedia resources
- track progress and assign tasks as a team.

Offer training so that everyone feels confident using these tools. Stay open to exploring new apps and platforms that could enhance your team's productivity.

Test and improve resources

After trying out shared lesson plans, PowerPoints or materials in your classroom, gather feedback from your team by:

- discussing what worked during departmental meetings
- reviewing student performance
- reflecting on your own experience.

Use this feedback to refine and improve resources. By encouraging a culture of experimentation, you allow your team to innovate and learn from both successes and challenges as well as supporting teacher autonomy.

Mentoring and peer support

Start a mentoring or coaching programme

A mentoring or coaching programme (as mentioned in Chapter 9) is a great way in which to support new teachers, while giving experienced teachers an opportunity to share their knowledge. To set up a successful programme, you might:

- define clear expectations for mentors and mentees
- schedule regular meetings for guidance and advice
- set achievable targets, such as improving classroom management or enhancing classroom circulation.

Pair mentors and mentees thoughtfully, matching their strengths and needs. Create a feedback loop to ensure that the programme is meeting its objectives.

Encourage peer observations

Peer observations provide an opportunity for teachers to learn from one another. You could organise classroom visits where teachers can:

- observe effective teaching strategies
- offer constructive feedback
- reflect on how to apply new ideas in their own classrooms.

Frame these informal observations as learning experiences rather than evaluations. Provide guidelines to ensure that they are productive and focus on growth.

Create professional learning groups

Professional learning groups (PLGs) are a valuable way in which to encourage collaboration and ongoing development. As discussed in Chapter 9, these communities and groups can:

- focus on specific areas like assessment strategies or integrating effective feedback in lessons
- include workshops, discussions or collaborative research projects
- share best practices and successful strategies from individual experiences to inspire others.

PLGs create a supportive environment where you and your team can innovate and stay updated on the latest teaching trends.

Celebrate achievements

Recognising achievements is crucial, not only for your students but also for boosting morale and fostering a positive team culture within your department. You could celebrate by:

- sharing successes during departmental meetings
- highlighting achievements in newsletters or at school events
- sending personal notes of appreciation.

Celebrations show your team that their hard work is appreciated and help to foster a sense of pride and belonging. Consider organising an annual event to recognise your team's collective achievements. This could be as simple as going out for a meal together.

Building a strong, collaborative language teaching team takes effort but it is worth it. Remember that the strength of your team and department lies in how well you work together, respect each other and aim for shared success. Keep learning, celebrate progress and stay connected to ensure your team's long-term success.

REFLECTIVE QUESTIONS

- How well are you fostering a sense of collaboration within your team? Are there specific actions that you can take to strengthen your teamwork?

- Do you know the strengths and areas for growth within your team? What tools or strategies could you use to gain clearer insights?
- Are you creating enough opportunities for shared lesson planning and resource sharing? Could this process be made more efficient or inspiring?
- How are you supporting mentoring and peer feedback in your department? How can you ensure that these initiatives are meaningful and effective?
- How do you ensure that communication is open and inclusive across your team? Are there ways in which to improve how you facilitate communication?
- How are you celebrating your team's achievements and maintaining morale? Are there more ways in which you could show appreciation and keep the team motivated?

CASE STUDY

Case study: Keeping the team moving in the right direction
Name of school: United Learning, Peterborough
Contributor: Adam Lamb, Trust-wide director of MFL and examiner

What was the issue?

As someone who has spent years navigating the complexities of MFL education as a head of faculty and now a trust-wide director of MFL, I've seen first-hand how recruitment and retention challenges can impact schools. The 2024 House of Commons report predicted that 40 per cent of MFL teachers may leave the profession within five years. While recruitment often grabs the spotlight, I firmly believe that retaining and developing the incredible talent that we already have is just as vital.

In my experience, empowering team members through thoughtful and targeted professional growth can transform not only their individual trajectories but also the resilience and success of the entire team. The real challenge? Understanding and supporting each colleague's unique aspirations and development needs.

How did we resolve it?

I believe that the resolution to this issue revolves around three key strategies: meaningful performance management, tailored professional development and consistent follow-ups to ensure growth.

1. Reframing performance management

Performance management meetings can often feel like a tick-box exercise, focused solely on outcomes. I changed this narrative by starting these conversations with the teacher's own aspirations. A simple set of questions can unlock invaluable insights:

- Where do you see yourself in one, three or five years?
- What support do you need to get there?
- Who could guide or mentor you along the way?
- How will you know when you've reached your goal?

These honest conversations didn't just help me as a leader; they empowered the teacher to take ownership of their journey. Sometimes, they led to unexpected revelations – like a desire to leave teaching or relocate. While those moments were challenging, they provided clarity and allowed for strategic future planning.

2. Tailored professional development

Once aspirations were clear, we worked together to chart a path forward. This might involve reviewing professional development programmes like the NPQs or identifying internal promotion opportunities. For example, I supported a teacher who wanted to move into middle leadership. Together, we reviewed job descriptions for similar roles and pinpointed areas for growth. We identified opportunities, like shadowing department leaders or organising extra-curricular activities, to build the necessary skills and experiences. These concrete steps gave them the confidence and the roadmap that they needed to move closer to their goal.

3. Consistent check-ins and support

Regular follow-ups were crucial for maintaining momentum and demonstrating commitment. I scheduled periodic check-ins to discuss progress and provide encouragement. For instance, a casual reminder, such as 'Have you spoken to the head of Year 7 about shadowing parental meetings?', reinforced my investment in their growth. This ongoing engagement built trust and accountability, while ensuring that staff felt supported in their journey.

What was the impact?

This personalised approach transformed my team. By putting aspirations and professional growth at the heart of performance reviews, teachers felt seen, valued and supported. They gained clarity about their career paths and our team culture shifted to one of collaboration and trust. The ripple effect was undeniable: confident,

> motivated teachers inspired and engaged their students, leading to better outcomes all around.
>
> In conclusion, addressing the challenges of retention in MFL wasn't just about solving a staffing problem; it was about nurturing the people who made our schools thrive. By rethinking performance management, offering tailored development opportunities and staying committed to ongoing support, I was able to support building teams that were resilient and motivated.

Chapter summary

In this chapter, we have explored how building a collaborative and supportive language teaching team can lead to more effective teaching and greater staff wellbeing.

- Establishing a shared vision, promoting open communication and creating an inclusive environment help to build a strong culture of collaboration.

- Identifying team strengths and areas for growth, through feedback, observations and peer support, enables targeted professional development.

- Collaborative lesson planning and resource sharing promote consistency, creativity and efficiency, while supporting teacher autonomy.

- Mentoring, coaching and peer observations foster a culture of growth, enabling teachers to learn from and support one another.

- Celebrating individual and collective achievements boosts morale, builds team spirit and reinforces a positive departmental culture.

Further reading

- The Ambition Institute's *Mentor Handbook: Everything You Need to Help You Apply the Early Career Framework* (2020) is an easy-to-use guide packed with tools and prompts to help mentors to support ECTs effectively through the early career framework (ECF).
- *Mentoring Languages Teachers in the Secondary School: A Practical Guide* (Mentoring Trainee and Early Career Teachers) by L. Molway and A.L. Gordon (2025) supports mentors in developing effective skills, offering evidence-based strategies, practical tools and essential guidance to help beginning teachers thrive.
- *Mentoring in Schools: How to Become an Expert Colleague* by Haili Hughes (2021) is a practical book that supports mentors in developing meaningful relationships grounded in professional dialogue and trust.
- 'Improving mentoring practices through collaborative conversations' by Rachel Lofthouse (2017) is a fantastic and thought-provoking article advocating for mentoring as a dialogic and reflective practice, grounded in professional collaboration.

11

Leading your language department: Strategies for effective leadership

Introduction

Leading a modern foreign languages department poses unique challenges, from meeting curriculum standards to managing diverse student needs. As globalisation increases, the demand for multilingual communicators escalates, underscoring the critical role of MFL teachers. It requires a thoughtful blend of visionary leadership and practical management skills. By establishing a clear vision, fostering strong relationships, empowering teachers, strategically managing resources and actively advocating for the department, leaders can create an environment that not only promotes language learning but also prepares students for the challenges and opportunities of a globalised world. Through these detailed strategies, MFL leaders and their teams can effectively enhance both educational outcomes and the overall profile of their departments, making a lasting impact on their students' lives and careers.

Setting a clear vision and mission

Establishing a clear vision and mission in an MFL department is essential for setting long-term educational goals and strategies. This requires taking an active role in defining a vision that highlights the importance of language learning in a globalised world. A strong vision might centre around producing confident, culturally aware students who can communicate effectively in more than one language. It could even be as ambitious as aiming to be the most inspiring department in the school!

It's essential to involve the whole department from the start. They need to be engaged in the process so that they will be more likely to support the vision as they understand it and have contributed to it. Ownership at all levels is important. As a subject leader, it is key to look at the school's vision and priorities and see how these can be linked to your own department.

The vision and mission of your department need to be regularly reviewed. Reflecting and updating them when needed keeps you responsive. Using student performance data, staff feedback and current educational trends can help to refine and adjust the department's direction effectively.

Examples

A compelling vision for an MFL department might be: 'We want our students to become confident communicators who can navigate a multilingual world with ease.' The vision needs to mean something to the people in your department. A statement like this helps to steer the ship and reminds everyone why language learning matters. The mission should build on that – perhaps focusing on creating rich, engaging lessons that combine real-world language use with cultural understanding.

It could, for example, be: 'to provide engaging, culturally rich language education that equips all students with the linguistic skills and cultural awareness necessary for global success'. But none of this works without solid leadership. And leadership isn't just about having a title; it's about having the right mix of skills to bring people with you. Here's a detailed look at the essential skills needed:

- **Thinking ahead:** You need to be able to zoom out and look at where things are going. What do students need now and what will they need in five years? What's changing in education? What's happening in the world outside school that affects language learning? Strategic thinking means being able to juggle all of that and still make a clear plan. Not everything has to be revolutionary; sometimes it's just about knowing which small changes will make a big difference.

- **Leadership and decision-making:** There are times when you'll need to make calls that won't please everyone. That's just part of the job. Good leaders know when to ask for opinions and when to take the reins. It's about balancing consultation with decisiveness and being clear on why you're doing what you're doing. However, it's key to always communicate your rationale so that everyone in your team understands the decision made and why it has been made. Above all, it's about being someone whom your team trusts to lead with purpose.

- **Communication skills:** You might have a brilliant vision, but if you can't explain it clearly, it won't go far. How you communicate matters and is essential to gaining buy-in from all stakeholders, including teaching staff, students, parents and senior leaders. This requires excellent oral and written communication skills. It's not just what you say; it's how you say it. People need to hear the message in a way that feels real, relevant and motivating.

- **Collaborative skills:** Some of the best ideas come from the people around you. Developing a vision and mission should be a collaborative effort, involving input from a variety of stakeholders. Involving your team in shaping the department's direction isn't just smart; it builds buy-in and energy. That said, collaboration isn't always neat. It takes patience, a willingness to listen and consensus-building to integrate diverse perspectives and create a shared vision to which everyone is committed.

- **Adaptability and flexibility:** Things change – timetables, policies, exam specifications, even the students themselves. You need to be able to adapt without losing sight of the bigger picture. Flexibility doesn't mean having no plan; it just means being able to bend without breaking. Leaders must be adaptable: able to adjust their vision and mission in response to changes in the external and internal school environment.

- **Empathy and cultural competence:** Language teaching is rooted in culture, identity and human connection. So, empathy isn't optional – it's essential! When you understand where your students and colleagues are coming from, you're better placed to lead in a way that's inclusive, respectful and genuinely meaningful, which is crucial for crafting a vision and mission that promotes inclusivity and cultural awareness.

- **Analytical skills:** Results, feedback, progress tracking – all of this helps you to figure out where things are working and where they're not. Analysing current resources, capabilities and the educational environment is essential for setting realistic and impactful goals. This includes the ability to assess the department's strengths and weaknesses, evaluate the effectiveness of current programmes and identify areas for development.

Leading difficult conversations

No matter how well your language department gets along, tough conversations are going to crop up now and then. Whether it's addressing underperformance, tackling friction between colleagues or pushing back on a decision that affects the team. Whatever the case, dealing with those moments head-on with clarity, empathy and a bit of backbone is part of what makes a subject leader effective.

Why these conversations matter

Putting off difficult conversations might feel easier in the short term, but it doesn't take long before problems start growing roots. Left alone, issues can start to drag down team morale, impact the students and quietly chip away at the culture that you're trying to build. But when these conversations are handled properly – even if they're awkward – they can strengthen trust, set clearer boundaries and get things back on track.

Strategy 1: Prepare but don't over-rehearse

Going into a difficult conversation cold without thinking it through is a bad idea. Take time to gather your thoughts and pull together any relevant information: drop-ins evidence, feedback from parents or students, missed deadlines – whatever applies. Know what you want to come out of the conversation. That said, don't write a script and cling to it. Conversations are messy. You've got to stay flexible.

It is also worth thinking about where and when you have the conversation. Grabbing someone in the corridor right before lunch? Not ideal. Quiet room, end of the day, no interruptions? Much better.

Strategy 2: Focus on the problem, not the person

It's easy to sound like you're making it personal if you're not careful. The goal is to talk about actions and impact, not personality. Using phrases like 'I've observed… ' or 'One issue that's been raised is… ' can make it easier for the other person to hear what you're saying without getting defensive.

Instead of 'You're always behind on stuff', try: 'I've noticed that Key Stage 3 assessments haven't been uploaded by the deadline in the past two terms.' This is a small shift, but it makes a big difference in how it lands. This approach encourages problem-solving rather than blame.

Strategy 3: Listen to hear

A difficult conversation should never feel like a lecture. Once you've said your part, let the other person talk. You might find out something that completely changes how you see the situation – or maybe not. Either way, give them space. Ask open questions. Don't interrupt. Active listening shows respect, even if you don't agree with everything that they say. Useful phrases include:

- Can you walk me through what happened from your side?
- Thanks for being honest. Let's work out what the next steps might look like.

Strategy 4: Be clear about what needs to change

This is where people often slip up. You've had the conversation; it wasn't awful and now everyone just wants to move on. But unless you've clearly agreed on what's going to be different and when, you're probably going to have the exact same conversation again in a few weeks. What are the expectations? What's the timeframe? What support is on offer?

A tough conversation isn't just about pointing out what's wrong; it's about helping someone to get better at what they do.

Strategy 5: Keep your cool – even if they don't

It's normal for people to get emotional when receiving feedback, especially if it catches them off guard. As a leader, your job is to stay calm and keep your tone level. Stick to the key points and don't let it spiral into something personal.

These conversations won't ever be easy. But they don't have to be combative or cold either. If you come in prepared, stay respectful and genuinely want to help things to improve, you'll build a stronger, healthier team in the long run, even if the process is a bit uncomfortable.

Effective learning walks and departmental review

As a subject leader, it is essential to do some drop-ins or learning walks so that you know what is happening in your department. You cannot assume that because you have been through something with your team it will necessarily be implemented effectively. It's not about catching anyone out; it's just about seeing how things are landing in real time. You notice little things: students really engaged in a task or someone trying something new with their teaching. Sometimes it just gives you a better sense of what support a colleague might need or what's working from which others could learn. And when it's informal, it feels more like part of normal school life and not some big performance.

Effective lesson feedback

When you're leading a department, one of the most valuable things that you can do is to give feedback that genuinely helps teachers to grow, not just tick boxes or point out flaws. The way in which you deliver that feedback can make all the difference between someone feeling supported or just... scrutinised.

First off, timing matters. Feedback shouldn't arrive weeks later, when the moment's passed. If you've just sat in on a lesson, try to offer your thoughts while everything's still fresh for both of you. And don't feel like it all needs to be formal. A well-timed conversation over a coffee can sometimes be more powerful than a typed-up document.

Always start with what went well – not in a 'sandwich' way that feels forced, but because recognising strong teaching helps to reinforce what's working. Maybe the questioning was sharp or the students were clearly confident using the target language. Whatever it is, say it plainly.

Then, be honest but constructive about what could be stronger. Don't just say 'improve engagement'. That's vague. Be specific: 'It might help to get more students to talk in pairs.' or 'You could try building in a quick recap to help students to consolidate vocab.'

Also, avoid making it all about what you would do. Focus on the impact that you noticed and offer ideas rather than prescriptions. People appreciate suggestions that they can try out, not theory-heavy jargon.

Tone also matters. Feedback should feel like a professional conversation and not an appraisal. If you approach it as a chance to reflect together, it opens the door to real dialogue. That's when people start sharing what they've been trying, what they're stuck on and what support they'd find helpful. And don't forget the value of peer observations. Encouraging teachers to visit each other's lessons – not just for accountability but for inspiration – builds a culture where feedback isn't something to dread. It becomes part of how the team learns and evolves.

In the end, feedback isn't about finding fault. It's about supporting people to keep getting better because none of us are ever done learning.

Department review

When you know that a departmental review is on the horizon, it's easy to feel the pressure. But instead of seeing it as something to dread, it helps to approach it as a chance to reflect, collaborate and celebrate what's going well.

Start by being upfront with your team. Let them know what the review is about, what it will involve and why it matters – not in a way that creates stress, but more as an opportunity to highlight the good work that's already happening. Framing it as a positive and professional development moment sets the tone early on.

It's also a good idea to bring everyone together before things kick off. Hold a team meeting to talk through the process and the criteria that reviewers will be using. Make space for questions, concerns and any suggestions. It's not just about giving information; it's about building a sense of shared purpose, so that no one feels like they're going it alone.

On the practical side, get your documents in order. That includes your curriculum intent, long-term plans, schemes of work, department improvement plan... basically, anything that helps to explain the why behind what your team does. Be ready to talk through the department's strengths and areas that you're still working on and make sure that you can explain the rationale behind them. You'll also want to be clear on what reviewers might see in lessons or student books or hear through student voice.

Don't forget to have a list of enrichment activities and extra-curriculars that your department offers; it's often these things that paint a fuller picture of your team's impact.

If you find yourself feeling nervous when the day arrives, having all this to hand can really ground you. It's a lot easier to talk confidently about your department when you've taken the time to reflect and prepare ahead of time. You're not scrambling for details; you're ready!

Keep the lines of communication open throughout the process. Check in with your team, offer support where needed and make sure that everyone feels like you're in it together. If a reviewer brings up something that they didn't observe, be ready to point to where and how it is happening, whether that's in another class, in students' books or through something that a student says.

After the review, don't let the feedback sit in a drawer. Share it with your team in a way that's honest but constructive. Focus on what went well and on any actions that you'll take together moving forward. When a review is managed as a team effort, and not just a leadership task, it has the power to bring a department closer and not just feeling more accountable.

Supporting your team with behaviour management

As a subject leader, you're not expected to have all the answers, but your team will look to you when they're struggling.

Strategy 1: Follow the school behaviour policy

Consistency is key. If each teacher in school is managing behaviour differently, then students quickly learn where the boundaries are flexible. Use the school's behaviour system and refer to it in meetings, take the time to practise/rehearse. Work with your team to establish shared routines for entry, settling the class, use of target language, transitions and end-of-lesson procedures.

Even something as simple as a standard expectation – e.g. 'Students stand behind chairs and wait silently at the start' – can create a powerful sense of order when it is upheld by all members of the team.

Strategy 2: Know when to step in

Sometimes, a colleague will face behaviour issues that escalate beyond classroom strategies. Rather than leaving them to 'deal with it', be proactive in offering support. This might mean observing a lesson to offer feedback, co-planning a seating plan or entry routine, or liaising with SLT about particular students. Subject leaders should act as a bridge between their team and the wider pastoral system. Make sure that you're aware of which students are on behaviour reports, what support plans exist and how your team can feed into those structures.

Strategy 3: Use department time to build skills

Behaviour management is often assumed to be innate; you've either 'got it' or you haven't. But, like any professional skill, it can be developed. Use department meetings to share strategies and discuss challenges. Consider dedicating time each half-term to a 'case study', where one team member brings a behaviour challenge and others offer ideas.

You might also invite a colleague from another department with strong practice to deliver a short input, especially useful if your department includes less experienced teachers or ECTs.

Strategy 4: Balance accountability with empathy

If a team member is struggling with behaviour, resist the urge to jump straight to performance concerns. Poor behaviour can erode confidence quickly; what might look like 'low expectations' is often the result of a teacher who feels overwhelmed. Ask open, non-judgemental questions: 'What feels the hardest at the moment?', 'How can I help?'.

Once you've listened, work together on one or two practical changes that they can try.

Strategy 5: Celebrate behaviour wins

Behaviour management isn't just about sanctioning the negatives; it's also about reinforcing the positives. Encourage your team to celebrate students who are showing resilience, kindness or improvement. Share success stories in meetings.

Example: Supporting a new colleague

When Simon joined the department as an ECT, he found Year 9 French particularly difficult. The class was noisy, homework was rarely completed and he often left lessons feeling defeated. Rather than waiting for him to raise it formally, the subject leader checked in informally after noticing several corridor incidents involving the same group.

They sat down and identified some patterns. Students were arriving late, seating was unstructured and transitions were chaotic. Together, they designed a clear entry routine, reworked the seating plan based on prior data and introduced a reward system tied to positive class contributions. The subject leader also arranged for Simon to observe that specific Year 9 class with a more experienced colleague.

Within three weeks, the atmosphere in Simon's lessons had shifted: there were still challenges, but his confidence and control had grown noticeably. Crucially, Simon felt supported rather than judged. That made all the difference.

Behaviour management doesn't belong to individual classrooms; it's a collective responsibility. As a subject leader, your influence lies not just in enforcing expectations but also in building a department culture where your team feels equipped, encouraged and empowered to lead their classrooms with calm authority and compassion.

Advocating for the department

Advocacy is crucial in ensuring that the importance of MFL is recognised, both within the school and in the broader community. This advocacy is essential to ensure that the department receives the necessary support and resources from the leadership team and also to highlight the value of language learning to students and parents.

Implementation strategies

- **Resource allocation:** Effective advocacy ensures that the MFL department receives a fair share of school resources, including funding, technology and teaching materials. By presenting the needs and successes of the department clearly and compellingly, you can secure essential resources that might otherwise be allocated to other departments. Present curriculum bids to your headteacher to obtain necessary resources.

- **Enhancing enrolment:** Active promotion of the benefits of learning foreign languages can boost students' desire to study a language for their GCSE or A level or at university. Demonstrating the practical and cultural benefits of language skills, like enhanced career opportunities and improved cognitive abilities, can attract more students to the department.

- **Increasing engagement:** Advocating for the subject helps to boost student interest and engagement. When students understand the value and applications of what they are learning, their motivation and participation in class can significantly increase.

- **Building confidence:** Effective communication about the successes of the MFL department and its students can build confidence. Sharing success stories of past students or current achievements can inspire current students and elevate the status of the department within the school.

- **Community engagement:** Initiate programmes that involve the community, such as language days and cultural festivals, to highlight the value of learning foreign languages. These events showcase the practical value of language learning and cultural exposure.

- **Lobbying for resources:** Actively seek support from school leadership for adequate resources, highlighting the benefits of language learning.

- **Support from home:** Engaging parents and helping them to understand the value of language learning ensures their support, which is crucial for students' success. Informed parents are more likely to encourage their children to take up and persist with language studies.

- **Promoting success stories:** Share successes of the department and its students, such as student achievements in lessons or for language competitions or successful cultural exchange programmes/trips, through newsletters and social media to enhance the department's profile.

Good behaviour doesn't come from a single policy or poster. It comes from a team culture where teachers are trusted, supported and not made to feel ashamed when things go wrong. As a leader, your influence lies in the day-to-day: the quiet conversations, the shared strategies and the belief that everyone deserves a calm classroom, even when it takes a while to get there.

REFLECTIVE QUESTIONS

- Have you established a clear and meaningful vision and mission for your MFL department?
- Do you effectively involve your team in shaping and committing to your department's direction?
- How do you handle difficult conversations in a way that maintains trust and promotes improvement?
- How do you support teachers struggling with behaviour management without making them feel judged?
- How prepared are you for departmental reviews and do you involve your team in this process?
- Are you actively advocating for the importance of MFL within the school and to the wider community?

CASE STUDY

Scenario 1: Addressing lesson visit feedback when perceptions differ

Unfortunately, as a head of department, you might end up in a situation where a member of your team has a completely different opinion of how the lesson went. To fully prepare for that kind of scenario, we would advise the following.

During the lesson, make detailed time-stamped notes of what the teacher says and does, as well as how the students respond and engage. This allows you to refer to specific examples during the feedback session. For example, you can say, 'I noticed that you said… ' or 'I observed that students responded by… ', grounding your discussion in specific observations so that nobody can argue with them as you are using concrete evidence.

We would also encourage to use prompts like:

- Tell me about…
- I noticed…
- What impact did… ? How could we… ?
- How could we build on that? Are there strategies that could further support student learning?

These prompts are non-judgemental and solution-focused, which encourages reflection. Then suggest collaborative strategies:

- co-planning future lessons together
- conducting practice sessions before teaching the material
- arranging opportunities for the teacher to observe, alongside you, some colleagues who demonstrate strong practice in that area, so that you can show them

what you discussed during the lesson that you are observing. Ask questions such as 'Look here, what has the teacher just done? What is the impact on students?'

We would also make it explicit that you'll revisit the classroom to see how the strategies are being implemented and to provide further support, but emphasise that it is not 'formal' and that the aim is to keep improving. As Dylan Wiliam says (2012), 'Every teacher needs to improve, not because they are not good enough, but because they can be even better.'

CASE STUDY

Scenario 2: Addressing missed deadlines and unanswered emails

You might also be in a situation where a member of your team consistently misses deadlines or doesn't respond to emails in a timely manner. To handle this situation, we would do the following.

Have concrete examples that you can bring up during your discussion. For example, you can say, 'I noticed that the report due on… wasn't submitted until three days later' or 'I observed that the email about… went unanswered.' This way, you are referring to clear and factual evidence.

Have the conversation in a one-to-one meeting in a supportive environment (not rushing it between lessons and not in the corridor). Begin the conversation with open-ended prompts to encourage reflection and self-awareness:

- I've noticed that a few deadlines have been missed recently and some emails haven't been responded to. How have you been finding your workload?

- What challenges are you facing at the moment that might be impacting communication?
- Is there anything that I might not be aware of that's affecting your ability to meet deadlines?

These prompts are non-judgemental and solution-focused, allowing the staff member to express any difficulties that they might have.

Once you have listened to them, it's important to outline clear expectations moving forward. For example, you can say:

- For our department to run smoothly, it's really important that deadlines are met and emails are answered in a timely manner. This ensures that everyone is kept in the loop and projects move forward as planned.
- Would it be helpful if we set specific response times for emails and a calendar for key deadlines?

You can also suggest practical strategies such as:

- using calendar reminders for important deadlines
- allocating time each day specifically for responding to emails
- prioritising tasks to make sure that critical deadlines are not missed.

Tell your member of staff that you'll check in: 'I'll check in with you in a couple of weeks to see how things are progressing. Let me know if there's anything I can do to help in the meantime.' If there is still no improvement after providing support and clear expectations, it may be necessary to have a more formal discussion.

CASE STUDY

Scenario 3: Addressing a lack of team collaboration

In any department, it's really important that everyone pulls their weight, especially when it comes to planning and sharing lesson materials for their year group. When one person keeps falling behind, it can cause a lot of frustration for the rest of the team. People end up waiting for lesson plans, sending reminder emails and feeling the pressure of not being able to plan ahead.

Before you speak to the person, it's a good idea to have your facts straight. Keep a note of when lesson plans are late, how often people are chasing them up and any times where it's caused issues. For example:

- Last term, Year 8 lesson plans were late three separate times and other staff were left waiting.
- There were several follow-up emails needed before the resources were finally shared.

Having these specific examples helps to make the conversation clearer. It's not about opinions; it's about what is happening.

Then arrange a time to speak with them one-on-one. It's really important to do this in a relaxed, private setting and not rushed in the corridor or squeezed in between lessons. The aim is to understand what's going on and share your concerns calmly. You could start with some open questions to get them talking:

- I've noticed that there have been a few times when the Year X lesson plans were running late and others had to follow up. Is there anything that's been making it difficult to get them done on time?

- How are you finding the workload for your year group? Are there any challenges that have been getting in the way?

This gives them a chance to explain if there's something going on that you might not know about. If there are genuine reasons, this is where you can find out and figure out how to support them.

Once you've listened, it's important to explain how these delays are affecting the rest of the team. You might say something like:

- When the lesson plans are late, it means that other staff are stuck waiting and can't move forward with their own planning. It puts a lot of pressure on them.
- For us to work smoothly, it's important that everyone has the materials that they need when they need them.

The idea is to help them to understand that it's not just about them; it's about the whole team staying on track.

After you've talked about the impact, be clear about what needs to change:

- From now on, the lessons for Year X need to be ready by [specific day] each week. That way, everyone else can plan their own lessons without having to wait.
- Would it be helpful if we set up some reminders or had quick check-ins each week to make sure that everything is running smoothly?

It's important to show that you're there to support them and not just setting rules. Working together to solve the problem is the goal.

Let them know that you'll check in regularly to see how things are going. A simple 'I'll catch up with you every couple of weeks to see how things are going – if you need any help, just shout' shows that you're committed to helping them to succeed.

> If things don't improve after a couple of check-ins and support, it might be time for a more formal conversation. That's the last step, but sometimes it's necessary if the rest of the team is being held back. Ideally, though, catching it early and talking it through can help to fix things before it gets to that stage.

Chapter summary

In this chapter, we have explored the key principles of effective leadership in a language department.

- A clear and shared vision helps to guide decision-making and supports team cohesion.
- Strong leadership includes offering support with behaviour, modelling high standards and being visible.
- Open and honest conversations, when handled professionally, build trust and encourage growth.
- Learning walks and departmental reviews should be used as tools for development, and not just accountability.
- Advocating for your subject raises its profile and helps to secure support from the wider school community.

Further reading

- *The Power of Teams: How to Create and Lead Thriving School Teams* by Samuel Crome (2023) is a practical and insightful guide that explores what makes school teams work well, with a strong focus on collaboration, clarity of purpose and building a positive culture across departments.

- *Successful Middle Leadership in Secondary Schools: A Practical Guide to Subject and Team Effectiveness* by Peter Fleming (2019) offers clear, realistic advice for middle leaders looking to improve subject leadership, manage teams effectively and lead change with confidence and integrity.

- *Middle Leadership Mastery: A Toolkit for Subject and Pastoral Leaders* by Adam Robbins (2021) is a comprehensive, user-friendly resource packed with strategies, templates and case studies to support new and experienced middle leaders in navigating the challenges of the role.

- *Is Leadership a Race?* by Samuel Strickland (2024) challenges traditional ideas of leadership by examining how identity, equity and inclusion intersect with leadership roles in education, encouraging deeper reflection on representation and belonging in school leadership.

References

Agarwal, P. and Bain, P. (2019), *Powerful Teaching: Unleash the Science of Learning*. Hoboken, NJ: Jossey-Bass.

Ambition Institute (2020), *Mentor Handbook: Everything You Need to Help You Apply the Early Career Framework*, www.lrtshub.org.uk/attachments/download.asp?file=10&type=pdf

Ashbee, R. (2021), *Curriculum: Theory, Culture and the Subject Specialisms*. Abingdon: Routledge.

Baddeley, A. and Logie, R. (1999), 'Working memory: The multiple-component model'. In: A. Miyake and P. Shah (eds), *Models of Working Memory*. Cambridge: Cambridge University Press, pp. 28–61.

Bambrick-Santoyo, P. (2016), *Get Better Faster: A 90-Day Plan for Coaching New Teachers*. San Francisco: Jossey-Bass.

Bambrick-Santoyo, P. (2018), *Leverage Leadership 2.0: A Practical Guide to Building Exceptional Schools*. San Francisco: Jossey-Bass

Benati, A. (2017), 'The role of input and output tasks in grammar instruction: Theoretical, empirical and pedagogical considerations', *Studies in Second Language Learning and Teaching*, 7, (3), 377–397.

Bilbrough, N. (2011), *Memory Activities for Language Learning*. Cambridge: Cambridge University Press.

Bjork, R. (1988), 'Retrieval practice and the maintenance of knowledge'. In: M. Gruneberg, P. Morris and R. Sykes (eds), *Practical Aspects of Memory II*. London: Wiley, pp. 396–401.

Bjork, R. (2011), 'On the symbiosis of learning, remembering, and forgetting.' In: A. S. Benjamin (ed.), *Successful Remembering and Successful Forgetting: A Festschrift in Honor of Robert A. Bjork*. London: Psychology Press, p. 1–21.

REFERENCES

Black, P. and Wiliam, D. (1998), *Inside the Black Box: Raising Standards Through Classroom Assessment*. London: King's College London.

Bloom, B. S. (1956), *Taxonomy of Educational Objectives: Cognitive and Affective Domains*. New York: David McKay.

British Council (n.d.), 'Where will languages take me?', www.britishcouncil.org/school-resources/languages/where-will-languages-take-me

Broady, E. (2014), 'Foreign language teaching: Understanding approaches, making choices. In: N. Pachler and A. Redondo (eds), *A Practical Guide to Teaching Foreign Languages in the Secondary School*, 2nd edn. Abingdon: Routledge, pp. 1–10.

Brookfield, S. D. (2017), *Becoming a Critically Reflective Teacher*, 2nd edn. San Fransisco: Jossey-Bass.

Brown, H. D. (2007), *Principles of Language Learning and Teaching*, 5th edn. White Plains, NY: Pearson ESL.

Busch, B. and Watson, E. (2019), *Science of Learning: 77 Studies That Every Teacher Needs to Know*. Abingdon: Routledge.

Byram, M. (2008), *From Foreign Language Education to Education for Intercultural Citizenship: Essays and Reflections*. Clevedon: Multilingual Matters.

Chiles, M. (2020a), *The Feedback Pendulum: A Manifesto for Enhancing Feedback in Education*. London: Hachette Learning.

Chiles, M. (2020b), *The Craft of Assessment: A Whole School Approach to Assessment for Learning*. Woodbridge: John Catt.

Christodoulou, D. (2016), *Making Good Progress? The Future of Assessment for Learning*. Oxford: Oxford University Press.

Cortés, C. (2007), 'Language meeting culture in the foreign language classroom: A comparative study', *Interlingüística*, 17, 230–237.

Coe, R., Aloisi, C., Higgins, S. and Major, L. E. (2014), 'What makes great teaching? Review of the underpinning research', The Sutton Trust, www.suttontrust.com/wp-content/uploads/2014/10/What-Makes-Great-Teaching-REPORT.pdf

Coyle, D., Hood, P. and Marsh, D. (2010), *CLIL: Content and Language Integrated Learning*. Cambridge: Cambridge University Press.

Crome, S. (2023), *The Power of Teams: How to Create and Lead Thriving School Teams*. Woodbridge: John Catt.

Deci, E. L. and Ryan, R. M. (2000), 'The "what" and "why" of goal pursuits: Human needs and the self-determination of behavior', *Psychological Inquiry*, 11, (4), 227–268.

Department for Education (DfE) (2013), 'National Curriculum in England: Languages programmes of study', www.gov.uk/government/publications/national-curriculum-in-england-languages-progammes-of-study

Department for Education (DfE) (2015), 'Special educational needs and disability code of practice: 0 to 25 years', https://assets.publishing.service.gov.uk/media/5a7dcb85ed915d2ac884d995/SEND_Code_of_Practice_January_2015.pdf

Department for Education (DfE) (2019), 'Early career framework', https://assets.publishing.service.gov.uk/media/60795936d3bf7f400b462d74/Early-Career_Framework_April_2021.pdf

Department for Education (DfE) (2021), 'Teachers' standards: Guidance for school leaders, school staff and governing bodies', https://assets.publishing.service.gov.uk/media/61b73d6c8fa8f50384489c9a/Teachers__Standards_Dec_2021.pdf

Department for Education (DfE) (2022), 'Modern foreign languages: GCSE subject content', https://assets.publishing.service.gov.uk/media/6389fb628fa8f569f55c9833/GCSE_subject_content_modern_foreign_languages.pdf

Doran, G. T. (1981), 'There's a S.M.A.R.T. way to write management's goals and objectives', *Management Review*, 70, 35–36.

Dörnyei, Z. (2001), *Motivational Strategies in the Language Classroom*. Cambridge: Cambridge University Press.

Dufour, R., Dufour, R., Eaker, R. and Many, T. (2016), *Learning by Doing : A Handbook for Professional Learning Communities at Work*, 3rd edn. Bloomington, IN: Solution Tree Press.

Dweck, C. S. (2007), *Mindset: The New Psychology of Success. How We Can Learn to Fulfil Our Potential.* New York: Random House.

Eaton, J. (2022), 'Moving from "differentiation" to "adaptive teaching": What does adaptive teaching mean for Education South West?', Education Endowment Foundation blog, https://educationendowmentfoundation.org.uk/news/moving-from-differentiation-to-adaptive-teaching

Ebbinghaus, H. (1885), *Memory: A Contribution to Experimental Psychology*, trans. 1913 by H. A. Ruger and C. E. Bussenius. New York: Teachers College.

Ellis, R. (2005), 'Principles of instructed language learning', *System*, 33, (2), 209–224.

Evidence Based Education (n.d.), 'Designing great assessment: The case for using multiple choice questions for accurate assessment', https://f.hubspotusercontent30.net/hubfs/2366135/Designing%20Great%20Assessment%20eBook-1.pdf

Facer, J. (2024), *The ResearchEd Guide to Professional Development: An Evidence-Informed Guide for Teachers.* Woodbridge: John Catt.

Fleming, P. (2019), *Successful Middle Leadership in Secondary Schools: A Practical Guide to Subject and Team Effectiveness.* Abingdon: Routledge.

Fletcher-Wood, H. (2018), *Responsive Teaching: Cognitive Science and Formative Assessment in Practice.* Abingdon: Routledge.

Gibbs, G. (1988), *Learning by Doing: A Guide to Teaching and Learning Methods.* Oxford: Oxford Polytechnic.

Goodrich, J. (2024), *Responsive Coaching: Evidence-Informed Instructional Coaching that Works for Every Teacher in Your School.* Woodbridge: John Catt.

Government Equalities Office and Equality and Human Rights Commission (2010), 'Equality Act 2010: Guidance', www.gov.uk/guidance/equality-act-2010-guidance

Halsbury Travel (2025), '5 reasons to study languages', www.halsbury.com/resources/5-reasons-to-study-languages

Hazell, C. (2020), *Independent Thinking on MFL*. Independent Thinking Press.

Howard, K. and Hill, C. (2020), *Symbiosis: The Curriculum and the Classroom*. Woodbridge: John Catt Educational.

Hughes, H. (2021), *Mentoring in Schools: How to Become an Expert Colleague*. London: Crown House Publishing.

Ingram, G. (2008), *Meeting the Needs of Your Most Able Pupils: MFL*. London: David Fulton Publishers.

Jackson, J. (2020), *Interculturality in International Education*. Abingdon: Routledge.

Jones, K. (2019), *Retrieval Practice: Research & Resources for Every Classroom*. Woodbridge: John Catt.

Jones, K. (2021), *Wiliam & Leahy's Five Formative Assessment Strategies in Action*. Woodbridge: John Catt.

Kennedy, M. M. (2016), 'How does professional development improve teaching?', *Review of Educational Research*, 86, (4), 945–980.

Knight, J. (2023), *The Definitive Guide to Instructional Coaching: Seven Factors for Success*, UK edn. Woodbridge: John Catt.

Krashen, S. D. (1982), *Principles and Practice in Second Language Acquisition*. Oxford: Pergamon Press.

Krashen, S. (2020), 'Webinar with Dr Stephen Krashen', British Council Morocco, www.youtube.com/watch?v=hSnGEGoUfL0

Lemov, D. (2021), *Teach Like a Champion 3.0: 63 Techniques that Put Students on the Path to College*. Hoboken, NJ: Jossey-Bass.

Liddicoat, A. J. and Scarino. A. (2013), *Intercultural Language Teaching and Learning*. Oxford: Wiley-Blackwell.

Little, D., Damm, L. and Legenhausen, L. (2017), *Language Learner Autonomy: Theory, Practice and Research*. Clevedon: Multilingual Matters.

Lofthouse, R. M. (2017), 'Improving mentoring practices through collaborative conversations', *CollectivED Working Papers*, 1, 10–11, https://eprints.leedsbeckett.ac.uk/id/eprint/5253/1/CollectivEd%20Dec%202017%20Issue%201.pdf

Lush, V. (2023), *Building Your Inclusive Classroom: A Toolkit for Adaptive Teaching and Relational Practice*. Abingdon: Routledge.

Maxwell, J. (2019), *Making Every MFL Lesson Count: Six Principles to Support Modern Foreign Language Teaching*. London: Crown House.

Mazenod, A., Francis, B., Archer, L., Hodgen, J., Taylor, B., Tereshchenko, A. and Pepper, D. (2018), 'Nurturing learning or encouraging dependency? Teacher constructions of students in lower attainment groups in English secondary schools', *Cambridge Journal of Education*, 49, (1), 53–68.

McLean, A. (2024), *Educational Collateral Damage: Disadvantaged Students, Exclusion and Social Justice*. Bristol: Policy Press.

Mansworth, M. (2021), *Teach to the Top: Aiming High for Every Learner*. Woodbridge: John Catt.

Molway, L. and Gordon, A.L. (2025), *Mentoring Languages Teachers in the Secondary School: A Practical Guide* (Mentoring Trainee and Early Career Teachers). Routledge.

Macaro, E., Graham, S. and Woore, R. (2015), *Improving Foreign Language Teaching: Towards a research-based curriculum and pedagogy*. Abingdon: Routledge.

Mould, K. (2020), 'Five evidence-based strategies to support high-quality teaching for pupils with SEND', Education Endowment Foundation blog, https://educationendowmentfoundation. org.uk/news/five-evidence-based-strategies-pupils-with-special-educational-needs-send?utm_source=/news/five-evidence-based-strategies-pupils-with-special-educational-needs-send&utm_medium=search&utm_campaign=site_search&search_term=send

Myatt, M. (2018), *The Curriculum: Gallimaufry to Coherence*. Woodbridge: John Catt.

Myatt, M. and Tomsett, J. (2021) *Huh: Curriculum Conversations Between Subject and Senior Leaders*. Woodbridge: John Catt.

Myatt, M. and Tomsett, J. (2023), *SEND Huh: Curriculum Conversations with SEND Leaders*. Woodbridge: John Catt.

Nation, I. S. P. (2007), 'The four strands'. *Innovation in Language Learning and Teaching*, 1, (1), 2–13.

Nation, I. S. P. (2008), *Teaching Vocabulary: Strategies and Techniques*. Boston, MA: Heinle.

Nation, P. (1989), 'Improving fluency', *System*, 17, (3), 377–384.

National Association for Gifted Children (NAGC) (2009) 'Myths about gifted students', www.nagc.org/myths-about-gifted-students

Nuthall, G. (2007), *The Hidden Lives of Learners*. Wellington: New Zealand Council for Educational Research Press.

Ofsted (2021), 'Research review series: Languages', www.gov.uk/government/publications/curriculum-research-review-series-languages/curriculum-research-review-series-languages

Pollard, A., Black-Hawkins, K., Cliff Hodges, G., Dudley, P., James, M., Linklater, H., Swaffield, S., Swann, M., Turner, F., Warwick, P., Winterbottom, M. and Wolpert, M. A. (2018), *Reflective Teaching in Schools*. London: Bloomsbury.

Reis, S. M. and McCoach, D. B. (2000), 'The underachievement of gifted students: What do we know and where do we go?', *Gifted Child Quarterly*, 44, (3), 152–170.

Robbins, A. (2021), *Middle Leadership Mastery: A Toolkit for Subject and Pastoral Leaders*. London: Crown House.

Rosenshine, B. (2012), 'Principles of instruction: Research-based strategies that all teachers should know', *American Educator*, 36, (1), 12–39.

Ryan, R. M. and Deci, E. L. (2000), 'Self-determination theory and the facilitation of intrinsic motivation, social development, and well-being', *American Psychologist*, 55, (1), 68–78.

The Schools, Students and Teachers Network (SSAT), Association for School and College Leaders (ASCL) and National Foundation for Education Research (NFER) (2017), 'Refocusing assessment: Modern foreign languages', https://webcontent.ssatuk.co.uk/wp-content/uploads/2017/03/17154926/Refocusing-Assessment-MFL-FINAL.pdf

Servini, N., Shanks, D., Hameed, L. and Violette, J. (2025), *Secondary Languages in Action*. Woodbridge: John Catt.

Sherrington, T. and Caviglioli, O. (2020), *Teaching WalkThrus: Five-Step Guides to Instructional Coaching: Visual Step-by-Step Guides to Essential Teaching Techniques*. Woodbridge: John Catt.

Sherrington, T. and Caviglioli, O. (2021), *Teaching WalkThrus 2: Five-Step Guides to Instructional Coaching*. Woodbridge: John Catt.

Sherrington, T. and Caviglioli, O. (2022), *Teaching WalkThrus 3: Five-Step Guides to Instructional Coaching*. Woodbridge: John Catt.

Shimamura, A. (2018), 'MARGE: A whole-brain learning approach for students and teachers', shimamurapubs.files.wordpress.com/2018/09/marge_shimamura.pdf

Smith, A. and Conti, G. (2021), *Memory: What Every Language Teacher Should Know*. Independently published.

Stephen, M. and Warwick, I. (2015), *Educating the More Able*. London: SAGE.

Strickland, S. (2024), *Is Leadership a Race?* Woodbridge: John Catt.

Toward, A., Henley, C. and Cope, A. (2016), *The Art of Being a Brilliant Middle Leader*. London: Crown House.

Vygotsky, L. (1978), *Mind in Society: The Development of Higher Psychological Processes*. Cambridge, MA: Harvard University Press.

Wajnryb, R. (1990), *Grammar Dictation*. Oxford: Oxford University Press.

Warren, D. (n.d.), 'Morgan MFL teaching resources', https://morganmfl.weebly.com

Warren, D. (2019), 100 Ideas for Secondary Teachers: Outstanding MFL Lessons. Bloomsbury Education.

Whittaker, T. (2020), *What Great Teachers Do Differently: Nineteen Things That Matter Most*. Abingdon: Routledge.

Wiliam, D. (2006), 'Assessment: The bridge between teaching and learning', *Voices from the Middle*, 21, (2), 15–20.

Wiliam, D. (2018), *Embedded Formative Assessment*, 2nd edn. Bloomington, IN: Solution Tree Press.

Wiliam, D. and Thompson, M. (2007), 'Integrating assessment with learning: What will it take to make it work?' In: C. A. Dwyer (ed.), *The Future of Assessment: Shaping Teaching and Learning*. New York: Routledge, pp. 53–82.

Glossary

ADHD attention deficit hyperactivity disorder
AI artificial intelligence
AimTLP activating intentional monitoring through lesson preparation
A level Advanced Level (16–18 years old)
ALL Association for Language Learning
ALLNE Association for Language Learning North East
AR augmented reality
ASD Autism Spectrum Disorder
AST advanced skills teacher
CI comprehensible input
CPD continuing professional development
DfE Department for Education
DIRT directed improvement and reflection time
EAL English as an additional language
ECF early careers framework
ECT early career teacher
EEF Education Endowment Foundation
EHCP education, health and care plan
ESL English as a second language
FLA foreign learning assistant
GCSE General Certificate of Secondary Education (11–16 years old)
HA higher attainer
HOD head of department
KS2 Key Stage 2 (9–11 years old)
KS3 Key Stage 3 (11–14 years old)
KS4 Key Stage 4 (14–16 years old)
LEO Language Educators Online, CPD platform
MAT multi-academy trust
MCQs multiple-choice questions
MFL modern foreign languages
MWBs mini whiteboards

NCLE National Consortium for Language Education
NfLNE Network for Languages North East
NPQ National Professional Qualification
NPQLT National Professional Qualification for Leading Teaching
PLCs professional learning communities
PLGs professional learning groups
Q&A question and answer
SDT self-determination theory
SEND special educational needs and disabilities
SL subject leader
SLA second language acquisition
SLE specialist leader of education
SLT senior leadership team
T&L teaching and learning
TA teaching assistant
TAP transfer-appropriate processing
TL target language
VR virtual reality

Index

achievements, recognising and celebrating 19, 124, 256
adaptive teaching 89–91, 105, 119, 163
    challenges of 92–3
    considerations after lesson 95–6
    constructive feedback 101–2
    diagnostic questioning 97–8
    early career framework (ECF) guidance on 90–1
    effective assessment in 92
    exit ticket 95, 97
    formative assessment 95
    grammar, checking for understanding and application of 96–7
    guided vocabulary revision 103–4
    intentional monitoring 106–9
    misconceptions of 91–2
    multiple-choice questions 99
    online collaborative tools 104–5
    probing questions 99–100
    real-time adaptations 89–90
    self-questioning before lesson 93–4
    strategies during lesson, use of 94–5
    technology and 91–2
    using AimTLP framework 107–9
    using visualisers 102–3
    of vocabulary instruction 103–4
adaptive technologies 21
Adeniji, Wendy 123, 153
AimTLP framework 107–9
assessment
    in adaptive teaching 92
    effective framework for 159–62
    formative 95, 159, 162–73
    of language teaching team skills 250
    peer 168
    purpose of 161–2
    'refocusing assessment' framework 159–61
    summative 173–80
    20 Keys framework 188–91
authentic materials 16, 32, 54–5, 134, 139, 143, 150, 204–5

BEEP reading activity 45
Bewell, Suzi 222
Bjork, Robert 64
Black, Paul 162, 173

INDEX

Bloom's taxonomy 142–3
the British Council 213, 217
Brown, H. Douglas 7
bubble translation 52
buzzed dictation 53

Caviglioli, Olivier 94, 136, 153, 166
Celebrate speaking 215–16
choral repetition 73–4
clubs 209–12
coaching 238–41, 254
co-construction models 70
cognitive science 24–6
collaboration 19, 104–5, 119, 247–50
collaborative lesson planning 253
comparison models 70, 71
competitions 214–16
comprehensible input (CI) 8
conferences, professional development 236
constructive feedback 10, 19, 101–2, 181
contextual learning 4, 16–17
continuing professional development (CPD) 232–8, 248
conversation club 209
cooking club 212
Cortés, C. 196
creative writing 150, 204
critical thinking 197
cultural competence 196–7, 266
cultural enrichment 196–8, 221–3
    'going for gold' cultural homework 222–3
    in-class activities 198–207
    'little and often' strategy 222–3
    out-class activities 207–12
cultural immersion 196
culturally responsive teaching 125
cumulative reading test 177–8
curriculum 29–31
    film studies 32–3
    for higher attainers 137
    impact 37–8
    implementation 34–7
    intent 31–3
    lesson sequencing 38–41
    phonics 34–5
    review and evaluation 55–6
    revisiting, at regular intervals 37
    skills and content integration 42–55
    systematic grammar instruction 36–7
    topics in, number of 32
    vocabulary 35
    Year 7 32

Deci, E. L. 15
deconstruction models 70
delayed dictation 53
'describe your partner' routine 11
diagnostic questioning 97–8, 167
Díaz, Elena 188
dictation 53, 76–7
Dictogloss 77
digital literacy 23
digital tools 22–3
distraction-free classroom 6

drama club 210
drills 76
dual coding 8, 16
Duolingo club 210

Ebbinghaus, H. 64
ECT mentoring 239–40
Education Endowment Foundation (EEF) 180, 181, 182, 183
Ellis, Rod 7
end-of-unit listening exam 174–5
error detection and correction activity 12–14, 46, 172–3
E-Twinning 217
The European Day of Languages 216
Everett, Vincent 128
exam-style questions 80–1
exchanges 216–21
extrinsic motivation 7

fast translations/questions 66–7
feedback 74, 180, 187, 229, 248
   constructive 10, 19, 101–2, 163, 181
   feed forward 181
   'find it, fix it' strategy 185–6
   of formative assessment *see* formative assessment
   ineffective 182–3
   to language teaching team 251, 252
   lesson 270–1
   live 20, 90, 97, 125, 165, 181, 183–4
   marking 180–1, 182
   optimisation 181
   oral 163, 186
   peer 168, 252, 255
   peer-to-peer 55
   person-focused and task-focused 183
   PiXL 'correct and perfect' strategy 186
   positive reinforcement 125
   specific 181, 184
   teacher workload reduction strategies for giving 183–6
   timing and amount of 181, 183
   20 Keys framework 188–91
   universal feedback stamp 182
   using marking codes 185
   vague 182
   written 170, 181
film club 210–11
film studies 32–3, 143, 198–9
'find it, fix it' strategy 185–6
flashcards 66
forgetting curve 64
formative assessment 95, 159, 162, 173
   circulation and listening to students 165
   diagnostic testing 167
   'find it, fix it' strategy 185–6
   implementation strategies 163–73
   knowledge checkers 170–1
   oral feedback 163
   peer assessment 168
   principles of 163
   questioning 164–5
   think-pair-share 171–3

INDEX

using matrix 168–70
using mini whiteboards 165–6
written feedback 170
4, 3, 2 technique 78–9
free recall session 66
The French Pop Video Competition 215

gamification 21
gap fill activity 46, 75
Gimagine Award 215
global educational networks 235
goal-setting 229–30
   action planning of 231–2
   for career development 233
   for language skills 232
   SMART framework 230–1
   using technology 232–3
grammar curriculum 36–7
grammar transference skills 146
The Great Languages Challenge 213
greetings routine 10, 140
guided practice 73
   choral repetition 73–4
   dictation 53, 76–7
   drills 76
   gap fill activity 46, 75
   oral scaffolds and guided conversations 74
   using sentence starters 74–5
guided vocabulary revision 103–4

Hazell, Crista 242
higher attainers 134–5
   authentic materials into lessons, incorporating 139–40, 143
   characteristics 134–5
   curriculum for 137
   first letter of each word activity 145–6
   grammar challenge activities 146–7
   independent learning of 148–51
   mastering grammar for 140
   mixed-ability MFL classes for 153–5
   mixed-attainment classes for 137
   motivation 151–2
   Puissance 5 activity 141–2
   as risk-averse 136
   routines for, use of 140
   scaffolding for 137
   sentence extension activity 145
   stretching and challenge of 136–40, 153–5
   synopsis, activity using 143–4
   target language of 140
   'teaching to the top' approach for 137, 138
   Torture Tenses activity 147–8
   underachievement of 135–6
   using secret mission cards 144
hinge questions 164

i+1 language learning 8
immersive virtual environments 21

INDEX

implicit learning 26
in-class cultural enrichment activities 198–207
inclusive classroom 125–7
inclusive language learning 57–61, 125–7
independent learning 148–51
independent practice 78
    exam-style questions 80–2
    4, 3, 2 technique 78–9
    Q and A 50, 79–80
    translations 79
information hunt activity 42–3
instructional coaching 239, 240
integrated writing task 178–9
intentional monitoring 106–9
interaction language 10–12
interactive activities 6, 17, 20, 209
'in the style of....', reading aloud (activity) 44
Into Film Clubs 210–11
intrinsic motivation 7

knowledge checkers 170–1
Krashen, Stephen 8

Lamb, Adam 257
language exchange platforms 22
language fluency 14
    activities 18
language form 12–14
language immersion programme 212–13
language practice 18–19
    digital tools for 22
Languages Day 207
language skills 20, 30, 31
    integration with content 42–55
language teaching team development 247, 257–9
    achievements, recognising and celebrating 19, 124, 256
    collaboration among 247–50
    collaborative lesson planning 252–4
    decision-making processes 250
    inclusive environment, building 249
    mentoring/coaching programme 254
    observations and giving feedback 251
    open communication, promoting 248–9
    peer feedback 252
    peer observations 255
    professional learning groups (PLGs) 255
    resource sharing 252–4
    shared resource library 252
    shared targets and vision, setting 247–8, 251
    skill assessment 250
    strengths and areas for growth, identifying 250–2
leadership of MFL department 263
    adaptability and flexibility 266
    advocacy of 275–7
    analytical skills 266–7
    behaviour management 272–5

collaborative skills 266
communication skills 265–6
decision-making 265
department review 271–2
difficult conversations, leading 267–9
effective learning walks 269–71
effective lesson feedback 270–1
empathy and cultural competence 266
thinking ahead 265
vision and mission, setting 264–7
learning roadmap 39
lesson recording 228–9
lesson sequencing 38–41
listening activities 46–9
live modelling 68–9
long-term memory 4, 68, 93, 161
low-stakes quizzes 64–5
Lyman, Frank 171

marking 180, 182
  principles of effective 180–1
Maxwell, James A. 138
meaningful input activities 8–9, 16–17
meaningful output activities 9–12, 17–18
memory 4–5
mentoring programme 254
mentorship 238–41
metacognitive skills 149
Mingalaba 221
mini whiteboards (MWBs) 97, 98–9, 165–6
missing words activity, spotting 17
mixed-ability MFL classes 153–5
mixed-attainment classes 137
mnemonics 4, 5
modelling 67–8, 83–6
  co-construction models 70
  comparison models 70, 71
  deconstruction models 70
  models of excellence 70, 72
  thinking aloud 69
  worked examples 69–72
models of excellence 70, 72, 139
motivation 6–7, 151–2, 196
  extrinsic 7
  higher attainers 151–2
  for independent learning 149
  intrinsic 7
  self-determined 15
  of students with SEND and struggling learners 124–5
multi-academy trusts (MATs) 234
multiple-choice questions (MCQs) 65, 99–100, 164–5
Myatt, Mary 133–4

narrow reading 43
Nation, Paul 7, 78
native speakers, online learning platforms for 21, 22

Onatti Productions 220–1
online collaborative tools 104–5
online courses, professional development 236, 237

online language learning
  platforms 20–1
oral feedback 163, 186
oral proficiency interview 176–7
oral scaffolds and guided
  conversations 74
out-class cultural enrichment
  activities
  clubs 209–12
  competitions 214–16
  exchanges and trips 216–21
  language immersion
    programme 212–13
  school events 207–9

peer assessment 168
peer feedback 168, 252, 255
peer mentoring 240–1
peer-to-peer feedback 55
phoneme-grapheme
  correspondences 34
phonics
  activities 48–9
  curriculum 34–5
Pillette, Martine 47, 49, 146
Pinkham, Hannah 57
podcasts, professional
  development 236
Poésiæ 214–15
presentations 17–18
probing questions 99–100
professional development 227,
    241, 242–5, 258–9
  continuing professional
    development (CPD)
    235–8
  goal-setting and action
    planning 229–33
  mentorship and coaching
    238–41

  professional learning
    communities (PLCs)
    233–5
  reflective practice 227–9
professional learning
  communities (PLCs)
  233–5
professional learning groups
  (PLGs) 255
pronunciation and listening
  activity 45
pronunciation relay 45–6
Puissance 5 activity 141–2

Q and A 50, 79–80, 164–5
  exam-style questions 80–1
  hinge questions 164
  multiple-choice questions
    65, 99–100, 164–5
  probing questions 99–100
Quiz Quiz Trade activity 79
quizzes 64–5

reading activities 42–6
reading aloud 44–6, 177
reflective practices 19, 55,
    149, 227–8
  importance of 229
  lesson recording 228–9
  self-reflection diary 228
  student feedback 229
regular language practice 18
retrieval grid 65
retrieval practice 63–4, 83–6, 190
  fast translations/questions
    66–7
  free recall 66
  quizzes 64–5
  using flashcards 66
retrieval roulette 65

retrieval run 67
role-plays 18, 101, 117–18, 172
Rosenshine, B. 68
routines 12
   'describe your partner' (activity) 11
   greetings 10, 140
running dictation 53
Ryan, R. M. 15

Salgado, Esmeralda 83
scaffolding 8, 17, 68, 74, 120, 137, 149
school events 207–9
science of learning 3
   attention 6
   memory 4–5
   motivation 6–7
second language acquisition (SLA) 7, 24–6
   guiding principles 19–20
   language fluency 14
   language form 12–14
   language practice 18–19
   meaningful input 8–9, 16–17
   meaningful output 9–12, 17–18
   student needs 15
   supportive learning environment 19
secret mission cards 144
selective dictation 53
self-assessment checklist 81
self-determination theory (SDT) 15
self-determined motivation 15
self-directed tasks 78
self-reflection 19, 81, 149, 228
self-reflection diary 228
sensory memory 4

sentence extension activity 145
sentence starters 74–5
shared resource library 252
Sherrington, Tom 94, 136
short recap activities 55
'show me boards' technique 166
simulation 21
SLA *see* second language acquisition (SLA)
smaller group teaching 119
SMART framework 230–1
Smith, Steve 24
social media post (activity) 52–3
spaced repetition 4, 66
speaking activities 49–51
speech recognition tools 22
speed dating activity 14
spelling bee club 212
Stillman, Liz 147
story reconstruction activity 43
student autonomy 15, 20, 149
student needs 15
students with SEND and struggling learners 114
   adaptive teaching 119–20
   challenges and supporting strategies 115–17
   classroom adaptations 118–19
   confidence and motivation, building 124–5
   inclusive classroom for 125–7
   language learning of, enhancing 128–30

one-to-one support 119–20
positive reinforcement 125
role-plays 117–18
scaffolding 120–3
small achievements, recognising and celebrating 124
smaller group teaching 119
targeted intervention and support 118–23
subject associations 234–5
summative assessment 159, 173
 criteria for 173–4
 cumulative reading test 177–8
 end-of-unit listening exam 174–5
 integrated writing task 178–9
 oral proficiency interview 176–7
synopsis, activity using 143–4
systematic grammar instruction 36–7

task-based learning 18
teaching team *see* language teaching team development
'teaching to the top' approach 137, 138, 139
TeachMeets 238
technology and language learning 20, 155, 186
 and adaptive teaching 91–2
 for collaboration 253
 digital tools 22
 in goal-setting 232–3
 immersive virtual environments 21
 integration into teaching 22–3
 online collaborative tools 104–5
 online courses for professional development 236
 online platforms 20–1
thinking aloud 69
think-pair-share technique 171–3
Thompson, Marnie 168
Torture Tenses activity 147–8
transfer-appropriate processing (TAF) effect 25
translation tasks 214
 bubble translation 52
 fast translations/questions 66–7
 independent 79
 Quiz Quiz Trade 79
travel and cultural club 212
trips 18, 216–21

vague feedback 182
virtual reality (VR) 21
virtual tours 54
virtual worlds 21
visual aids 8, 119
visualisers 102–3, 184
vocabulary curriculum 35
vocabulary learning apps 22
Vygotsky, Lev 94

Wajnryb, Ruth 77
Warren, Dannielle 103
webinars, professional development 236

Wiliam, Dylan 95, 162, 168, 173, 185, 279
Williams, Tracy 106
working memory 4
workshops, professional development 237
World Book Day 209
writing activities 17, 51–3
written feedback 170, 181

zone of proximal development 94